The Phenomenal Woman

The Phenomenal Woman

Feminist Metaphysics and the Patterns of Identity

CHRISTINE BATTERSBY

Polity Press

First published in 1998 by Polity Press in association with Blackwell Publishers Ltd.

Editorial office:
Polity Press
65 Bridge Street
Cambridge CB2 1UR, UK

Marketing and production:
Blackwell Publishers Ltd
108 Cowley Road
Oxford OX4 1JF, UK

ISBN 0-7456-1554-6
ISBN 0-7456-1555-4 (pbk)

A catalogue record for this book is available from the British Library.

Typeset in 10 on 12 pt Plantin
by Graphicraft Typesetters Ltd., Hong Kong
Printed in Great Britain by TJ International, Padstow, Cornwall

This book is printed on acid-free paper.

What is your substance, whereof are you made,
That millions of strange shadows on you tend?
(Shakespeare, *Sonnets* 53)

But what if the 'object' started to speak?
(Luce Irigaray, *Speculum of the Other Woman*, p. 135)

I'm a woman
Phenomenally.
Phenomenal woman,
That's me.
(Maya Angelou, chorus from 'Phenomenal Woman',
And Still I Rise, p. 8)

Contents

Acknowledgements

It is, of course, conventional to claim that a book written over several years has incurred debts to others' thought, arguments and contributions. But nowhere is this more true than in the field of feminist philosophy – which exists as a collective (but much contested) enterprise, and in relation to networks of women (and now also men) working on adjacent themes. The writings generated by these debates – still only too frequently not recognized as philosophy – are part of what makes the late 1990s a time for hope, despite the often fierce philosophical and political disagreements. I hope the critique offered in this book of such theorists as Luce Irigaray and Judith Butler will be read as motivated by a respect for their work.

This book owes its origins – in an indirect way – to Margaret Whitford. It was she who first pointed out to me the analogies between the position that I argue for in my *Gender and Genius* (1989) and that developed in Luce Irigaray's early writings. Her comments led me to further explore the complexities of Irigaray's philosophy in a series of graduate seminars at the University of Warwick, and these helped me to become clearer about which aspects of Irigaray's philosophy I wish to endorse.

I am thus grateful to the large number of students who have contributed so much to my courses on Feminist Philosophy and Feminist Theory, and to colleagues and students (past and present) who have attended the Warwick Feminist Philosophy Society meetings over the years. I am particularly indebted to my PhD students in Philosophy and Women's Studies, especially those who have worked with me on feminist concerns: Catherine Constable, Irene Gedalof, Rachel Jones, Ewan Porter, Judy Purdom, Margrit Shildrick and Saul Walker. I am doubly grateful to Ewan Porter for agreeing to help with the indexing of this book, and to Catherine Constable and Rachel Jones who were always happy to answer my questions about a book-cover, the title and related concerns – and who also willingly provided me with a forum to try out philosophical ideas. The many philosophical visitors to Warwick have also helped with the impetus for this book: especially Adriana Cavarero, Ros Diprose, Moira Gatens and John Protevi. Other non-philosophical friends have also contributed enthusiasms and prevented me from becoming too lost in theory, especially Richard Dyer, Anthea Callen, Barbara Caine, Pat Moyer, Dick Smith and my Cornish friend who appears in chapter 1.

I have tried out versions of individual chapters at workshops and conferences in a variety of places outside Warwick. As such, the book has benefited enormously from feedback from more people than I can mention here. I owe debts to some of the long-standing members of a seminar group attached to the Society of Women in Philosophy (UK), including Alison Assiter, Morwenna Griffiths, Jean Grimshaw, Kimberly Hutchings, Kathleen Lennon, Anne Seller and Alessandra Tanesini, as well as to Margaret Whitford (again), who generously gave up time to comment on the manuscript in final draft form. I am also grateful to Justin Dyer who acted as copy-editor and to Joanna Hodge who acted as reader for Polity Press.

I would like to thank the University of Warwick for providing generous periods of leave from teaching. I would also like to thank Barbara Caine for arranging – and the British Council for funding – a trip to Australia in 1994. This enabled me to test some of the early chapters in an unfamiliar context. Finally, I would like to thank Rebecca Harkin at Polity Press for her patience, for her encouragement and her editorial care.

1
Introduction: Fleshy Metaphysics

PHENOMENAL: *extraordinary, exceptional, prodigious, unnatural, marvellous, amazing; often used hyperbolically in reference to some object or person of extraordinary power, gifts or other quality which excites wonder.*

PHENOMENAL: *in philosophy, that which has the nature of a 'phenomenon' (pl. 'phenomena') and is the object of sense experience; applied to that which only seems to exist but which is a mere illusion of the senses; often opposed to that which is 'real', 'objective' or 'noumenal'.*

In the history of western metaphysics 'woman' is phenomenal in a double sense. She's something wonderful, amazing, astonishing, peculiar. But she's also just a surface deviation; mere 'appearance'; unrepresentative of that distinctive, underlying 'essence' of humanity that philosophers have associated with 'truth'. She falls outside 'essence' – or the defining characteristics of a species or thing – in ways that have been supposed to make it a mistake to look for an essence of female nature or experience.

I write from within a post-Kantian tradition of philosophy, analysing the philosophical concepts of the transcendental ego, 'personhood' and related notions of spatial and temporal self-identity. However, since the subject of woman has always only ever been at the margins of philosophical discourse, I move between two conceptual and experiential registers. On the one hand, there are the language and traditions of philosophy in which the 'real' world has been constituted as the merely 'phenomenal' world. On the other hand, there is also the language of women's singularity and the need to talk of that 'real' or 'phenomenal' female body which has fallen outside the universals of philosophy.

In my current project I am seeking to use the antinomies of the female subject-position to think identity anew. I am not positing an 'other' form of subjectivity which is that of the 'feminine' or 'female' subject. Instead, I am asking what happens if we model personal and individual identity in terms of the female. Rather than treating women as somehow exceptional, I start from the question of what would have to change were we to take seriously the notion that a 'person' could normally, at least always potentially, become two. What would happen if we thought identity in terms that did not make it always spatially and temporally oppositional to other entities? Could we retain a notion of self-identity if we did not privilege that which is self-contained and self-directed?

Immanuel Kant's 'Copernican revolution' sought to rewrite philosophical tradition by placing man – instead of God or the object – at the centre of the reality which we inhabit. My own feminist philosophical turn displaces the apparently gender-neutral Kantian self at the centre of the knowable world. However, instead of dispensing with the self in ways now fashionable in the postmodern tradition, I am attempting to construct a new subject-position that makes *women* typical. In effect, this means dispensing with the (Kantian) notion that the 'I' gives form to reality by imposing a grid of spatio-temporal relationships upon otherwise unformed 'matter'. Focusing on the female subject involves treating humans as non-autonomous, and instead thinking relationships of dependence (childhood/weaning/rearing) through which one attains selfhood. It also involves thinking the process of birthing as neither monstrous nor abnormal. Mothering, parenting and the fact of being born need to become fully integrated into what is entailed in being a human 'person' or 'self'.

In 1994, as I started to write the opening chapters of this book, I sat looking at the sunset over the sea, and chatting with one of the villagers from the obscure Cornish village which I had decided to make my base. He was in his mid-forties, had not been to college, and had instead worked on boats, as well as at a variety of clerical jobs. Now on long-term sick-leave, he was embarked on a programme of distance learning, and this included some Philosophy courses. As I started to talk about my project for a feminist metaphysics, and the need to think through a philosophy that deals seriously with birth, the man became excited and uneasy. He then suddenly offered the following unexpected remark:

'It's odd. Philosophers say that it is not really possible to understand and accept the idea of one's own death. However, that is not what I find hard; it's rather to believe that I was born. Indeed, when I try to think of my own birth, my brain goes all red and I feel sick and dizzy. I once tried to tell my mother that I could not accept that I had been born. But she told me I was just being silly.'

Of course, as the man knew well, it is absurd not to accept that one has been born. But this man's remark is also acute, in that it reveals a central failure in our culture. Philosophers have notably failed to address the ontological significance of the fact that selves are born. Furthermore, there is also a more general inability to imaginatively grasp that the self/other relationship needs to be reworked from the perspective of birth – and thus in ways that never abstract from power inequalities, or from issues relating to embodied differences. We carry on idealizing autonomous 'individuals' who have equal rights and duties, and look away from the fact that 'persons' only become such by first moving out of a state of foetal and childhood dependency on others. Just thinking about being born made this (fiercely independent) man's 'brain go all red'. And yet this man's illness made his continued existence as an embodied self intimately dependent on the care of others: doctors, home-helps, social-workers, family, friends, neighbours.

In so far as we focus on these issues, we do it primarily in terms of ethical and political dilemmas. We see the failures in modern western philosophy and in our modes of imagining most clearly in current debates about abortion and about medical technology, for example, or in the current row over the 'identity' of a Europe that is made up out of individual states. However, this book does not deal with the question of identity on such overtly ethical or macro-political levels. Instead, it works more abstractly – and explores an ontology in which 'self' and 'other' intertwine in ways that allow us to think identity alongside radical novelty, power-dependencies, singularity and birth. In so doing, I will offer a critique of the metaphysical pessimism implicit in much poststructuralist and postmodernist feminist theory. But my conclusions are not just relevant for those immersed in the complexities of contemporary feminist discourse.

The response of my friend from Cornwall shows that even though this book starts from a feminist perspective – and asks how we need to rework notions of identity if we are to take the female human as norm – the conclusions that I reach are also relevant to males. Indeed, I would suggest that the model of identity that I put forward is more adequate for men (as well as women) than the classical philosophical understanding of the subject, substance and identity. There are imaginative and conceptual gaps – places where the 'brain goes red' – even for males who attempt to think the continuity of their lives in apparently more 'commonsensical' terms.

'Common' sense is pretty strange if it leaves this man from Cornwall unable to think his own birth. Although some of the arguments in this book might seem counter to 'common' sense and at odds with some of our most 'intuitive' certainties about the nature of 'subjects' and also of 'objects', the arguments are no more strange than some of the models adopted in recent science. And, indeed, some of the underlying metaphysical schemas of the 'new' physics will be used in chapter 3 in support of the metaphysics of sexual difference argued for in this book. I write about embodied selves that are paradigmatically female; but I would nevertheless hope that the male reader can overcome this barrier (which, after all, a female reader has to negotiate most of the time) and follow the development of the argument. There are important consequences for *him* – as well as for *her* – as I explore the theoretical grounding for a self which is born, and which is gradually shaped as it negotiates and renegotiates otherness, registering the resonances and echoes that the repeated movements produce.

As far as my female readers are concerned, I am only too aware that many of them will be distinctly uneasy with a feminist metaphysics that includes an emphasis on birth. Women have very good reasons to feel uncomfortable with any attempt to link female identity to reproductive capacities. I will need to return to this point later, in order to emphasize that 'sex' (one's identity as a 'female') is no more a brute 'given' than is one's 'gender': the 'femininity' – or 'masculinity' – that a woman's behaviour might reveal. But perhaps it is enough to point out here that the hypothetical link between 'woman' and 'birth' that matters is 'If it is a male human, it cannot give birth', not 'If it is a female human, it can give birth'. I will be suggesting that the dominant metaphysics of the West have been developed from the point of view of an identity that cannot give birth, so that birthing is treated as a deviation of the 'normal' models of identity – not integral to thinking identity itself.

Metaphysics Defined

Many feminist theorists would also object to my starting point on the grounds that any feminist metaphysics involves a contradiction in terms. In subsequent chapters I will argue that some of the most powerful critiques of metaphysics emanating from within feminism are only effective because these feminists keep Aristotelian parameters for metaphysics in place. In fact, the term 'metaphysics' came from the way that Aristotle's writings were ordered by his followers. Thus, Aristotle's analysis of being (*ousia*) and substance came after or beyond (*meta*) his writings on natural sciences (*physica*). As a consequence, the word came to stand for the branch of study (ontology or the science of existence) that was treated in these writings and that was supposed linked with, but ulterior to, the sciences proper. 'Metaphysics' became synonymous with that which transcends the physical, and with the study of 'being', 'substance', 'time', 'space', 'cause', 'essence' and 'identity'. Furthermore, ontology was regarded as necessarily bound up with the study of a 'primary' and separable substance or 'being' that is fundamental, nonrelational and that remains constant through change.

What will be argued in this book is that other approaches to being, substance, time, space, cause, identity, and so on, are possible, and those who refuse to accept this are clinging to an Aristotelian tradition of 'metaphysics' that philosophers before me have also rejected. Thus, with Immanuel Kant in the eighteenth century it became possible to distinguish two kinds of metaphysical enterprise. There was, on the one hand, 'speculative' metaphysics that dealt with an 'unknowable' and immaterial substrate of things-as-they-really-are. This 'noumenal' realm is Kant's equivalent of Aristotelian 'being', but any speculation about it is rendered illegitimate – at least as far as knowledge is concerned. For Kant there was, on the other hand, 'descriptive metaphysics', which analyses what it is to 'exist' within the parameters of this space-time world: a world that was for Kant collectively structured via the underlying framework of human understanding, senses, imagination and reason. Descriptive metaphysics was, therefore, implicitly relational – and the 'substance' that was posited in respect of the space-time world reflected the relationality between 'self' and 'not-self'.

This book develops a kind of 'descriptive' metaphysics, and thus operates within a post-Kantian tradition of metaphysics. But it departs radically from Kant in that it seeks to add sexual difference to the Kantian frame by querying the space-time structures and subject–object relationships that Kant viewed as both universal and necessary for any subject that could think itself as a persisting self. In particular, it is argued that considering the question of sexual difference – and taking the embodied female as norm – makes it possible to focus on other possible modes of 'descriptive' metaphysics apart from the one necessary and 'transcendental' structure laid down by Kant as necessary to 'all' human understanding whatsoever. Thus, my own feminist metaphysics rejects those parts of Kant which retain – and rework

– Aristotelian 'substance'. I argue that to think a persisting self it is not necessary to posit a permanent, underlying substrate that persists beneath matter and that remains always the 'same'.

In effect, those who argue against any feminist metaphysics are blocking the imagination of an ontological alternative to those substances that the Aristotelian tradition posits as the bearers of qualities and attributes. In subsequent chapters I will be developing a relational model of identity that can deal with the specificities and paradoxes of the female subject-position. However, since within feminist theory metaphysics is an underdeveloped field, a relational model of identity is more strongly associated with various forms of 'feminine' ethics than with a concern with an ontology that can take the female human as norm. In particular, Carol Gilligan's *In a Different Voice* (1982) is often positioned as fitting with a model of the self as always in-relation. Given that I have strong objections to Gilligan's 'ethics of care' – and given that I also need to discuss relationships of 'care', community and dependence in discussing the ontological constitution of selves – it is important to insist that a model of identity that works with relationality does not entail an ethics of care. Some further comments on this will be found in the conclusion to this book.

Indeed, this is a book of feminist metaphysics, not a feminist ethics. Although I do not give up on notions of 'female identity', I will argue throughout this book that there is not *one* dominant 'feminine' response to the paradoxes and predicaments of the female subject-position in western modernity. Women's predicaments are infinitely variable – and so are women's experiences. The identities of individual women are scored by a variety of forces and disciplinary structures. Not all of these scorings relate to issues of sexual difference. Race, nation, religion, education, family-background, neighbourhood, class, wealth – all contribute to configuring and patterning the individualized self that persists through time. My analysis does not, therefore, start with the 'inner' experience of feminine modes of consciousness or of 'feminine' subjectivity. It is not another contribution to the ongoing debates about feminist epistemology, 'ways of knowing' or problems about epistemological (or ethical) 'objectivity'. Indeed, Adorno's attack on epistemology considered in chapter 7 is, in part, endorsed.

Instead, I am interested in models of identity for 'the object' – and, in particular, for a body that is capable of generating a new body from within its 'own' flesh and from within the horizons of its 'own' space-time. In other words I treat 'woman' as 'object', in order to find new models of the self/other relationship and new ways of thinking 'identity' – and, in particular, persistence of an embodied self through mutation, birth and change. The argument of this book will focus on the 'female', rather than on the 'feminine': on 'sexual difference' rather than on 'gender difference', but the analysis of 'essence' offered in chapter 2 of this book allows for individual difference – and, indeed, shifts in meaning in what a term denotes – whilst also emphasizing that for us (in our culture) to be a female human is tied to a body that could birth.

Recognizing natality – the *conceptual* link between the paradigm 'woman' and the body that births – does not imply that all women either can or 'should' give birth. Instead, an emphasis on natality as an abstract category of embodied (female) selves means that we need to rethink identity. The 'self' is not a fixed, permanent or pre-given 'thing' or 'substance' that undergoes metamorphosis, but that nevertheless remains always unaltered through change. Instead, we need to think of identity as emerging out of a play of relationships and force-fields that together constitute the horizons of a (shared) space-time. We need a metaphysics of fluidity and mobile relationships; not a metaphysics of fixity, or even of flexibility. However, that metaphysics must also be able to explain how a subject might be scored by relationality into uniqueness.

There will be appeals to my own specificity and to others' reports of their experiences at stages throughout the analysis. However, for the most part the argument proceeds by raiding the philosophical past for models of mobile identities that work without underlying permanent 'objects', 'substances' or unchanging and universal 'forms'. Although the position I am arguing does not fit with the dominant discourses of classical, modern or postmodern philosophies, it is important also to register that philosophical ages are not homogeneous, and that there always have been a variety of metaphysical traditions. Thus, both before and after Aristotle there were ways of thinking identity that privileged 'becoming', rather than 'being'.

The position that I am adopting does not lack philosophical precursors – and various philosophical voices will gradually be put in dialogue in these pages. Theodor Adorno, Judith Butler, Gilles Deleuze, Luce Irigaray, are amongst those who play an important role – although if the book has a 'hero' that hero is (perhaps surprisingly) Søren Kierkegaard, since it is the latter who develops furthest the model of a relational self using 'woman' as key. Simone de Beauvoir, Henri Bergson, Michel Foucault, Donna Haraway and Friedrich Nietzsche also play key (though largely mute) parts. I am also aware that other philosophers could have been given a supporting role: amongst them, Denis Diderot (for mobile identities), Alfred North Whitehead (for 'process metaphysics'), Maurice Merleau-Ponty (for embodiment) and Hannah Arendt (for 'natality' and also for her attempt to rework Kant).

The Five Features

These raids on previous theorists are always conducted with the problem of sexual difference to the fore. This involves taking natality seriously, but also four further characteristics of the female subject-position that make the position of the 'female' paradoxical (both excessive and lacking) if the male subject is taken as norm. The first of these additional characteristics relates again to the ontological dependence of the foetus on the mother, and to the fact that (in our culture at least) the woman is socialized as the primary carer for any children. This means that the 'female' subject-position is normalized as linked to a set of relationships in which power-dependencies and inequalities are basic. For the human female, inequalities in power relations cannot simply be treated as atypical, abstracted or put to one side. The idealized equal, individualized and autonomous subjects of Enlightenment thought do not fit the position of a subject who is normatively female, even though much contemporary ethics and metaphysics carries on using models of identity that treat power differences and relationality as philosophically irrelevant. For the (normalized) 'woman', society is not ever – not even ideally – a collection of equals.

The next (third) characteristic of the female subject-position that is relevant here is also linked with the ontological dependence of the foetus on the mother during the process of birth. For the (normalized) 'female' there is no sharp division between 'self' and 'other'. Instead, the 'other' emerges out of the embodied self, but in ways that mean that two selves emerge and one self does not simply dissolve into the other. The consequences of this are extreme in terms of the models of 'self' and 'other' that typify western modernity. This 'self' does not emerge out of the exclusion or abjection of the 'other' (as is too often suggested in poststructuralist philosophy). Instead, it is from intersecting force-fields that 'self' and 'other' emerge.

This 'self' is not a 'thing' – a 'substance' that remains permanent through change – it is more like an 'event' that is 'born' in the space and time of interactive forces. This does not mean that 'selves' no longer exist; nor that there is no way of talking about persistence of the self over time. On the contrary, I will argue that thinking about the female subject-position allows us to retain a notion of self, but construe identity in terms of living forces and birth, not as a 'state' of matter that is dead or as a characteristic of a 'soul' or a 'mind' that remains fixed and constant, no matter which of its qualities or attributes might change. This self is scored by relationality, and attains its uniqueness in 'experience' as potentiality is patterned through directional movements over time. For this self the 'other' is within, as well as without. Rhythmic repetitions provide the 'labour' that allows identity to emerge from conflictual multiplicities. In chapter 9 I will turn to thinking identity in a world of sound and music, in order to make it easier to grasp how identity can establish itself via a pattern of relations, and an intertwining with otherness.

Models of the self/other relationship based on sound will be remarkably helpful. However, in our culture, at least, female identities are fleshy identities, and this is the fourth characteristic of the female subject-position that I need to mention here. In this regard I need to talk briefly about the English language, which is unlike the other main European languages in that it is has two terms – 'female' and 'feminine' – with related, but different, meanings. 'Femininity' denotes a set of psychic or behavioural dispositions that are more commonly associated with women than men; but there is no contradiction in talking about a 'feminine male'. By contrast, a 'female male' involves a category-mistake – or, more precisely, a medical or biological 'problem' that it is currently deemed necessary to 'normalize' either hormonally or surgically. To be 'female' involves a reference to embodiment, in a way that to be 'feminine' does not.

Foucault (1980) has argued that it is only in the nineteenth century that western Europe insisted on 'normalizing' the bodies of hermaphrodites to fix identities to a sexual binary so as to rule out sexual indeterminacy. However, what matters to the argument of this book is not whether there might not be other (better) modes of dealing with sexually ambiguous bodies, but that the metaphysics developed is one that tries to think what happens if we develop a metaphysics based on the subject-position that in English is linked with the 'female', not with that linked to the 'feminine'. I will return to these issues in chapter 2. But this distinction is important if it is to be grasped how my position departs from more standard accounts of the 'feminine' in postmodern and poststructuralist theory. What matters to the argument of this book is that I am concerned with embodied subjects, not with 'souls', 'spirits' or an immaterial 'I' that is only lodged in the flesh.

This is particularly important, since not only is the subject-position of the 'female' more integrally linked with embodiment than that of the 'feminine', it is also more tied to fleshiness than that of the 'male'. As my historical analysis of the category of 'genius' in my *Gender and Genius* (1989) showed, males were allowed transcendence of their biological subject-position via the tasks of spiritual production. The paradigm genius was both 'feminine' and male. By contrast, women were deemed 'unsexed' by their 'genius'. They were seen as tied to a body that was designed for biologically reproductive – not culturally productive – work. In so far as there were women of genius they were not simply masculine women, they were 'made male'. Indeed, it became a kind of cliché to say: 'there are no women of genius; the women of genius are men' (Lombroso, 1863, p. 138).

The 'female' subject-position is linked to fleshy continuity, rather than to an autonomous and individualized 'soul' or 'mind' that merely inhabits the flesh. However, the dominant model of the human in western modernity is disembodied: a 'spirit', 'soul', 'consciousness' or '*cogito*' whose 'personhood' is bound up with rationality and soul, rather than with flesh. As Susan Bordo puts it,

> Not all historical conceptions view the body as equally 'inescapable'. . . . But what remains the constant element throughout historical variation is the *construction* of body as something apart from true self (whether conceived as soul, mind, will, creativity, freedom . . .) and as undermining the best efforts of that self. That which is not-body is the highest, the best, the noblest, the closest to God; that which is body is the albatross, the heavy drag on self-realization. (1995, pp. 4–5, second ellipses Bordo's own)

Susan Bordo is careful in her phrasing. She does not claim that there have been no changes in the history of western attitudes towards the body. Indeed, she recognizes that for the ancient Greeks body and soul were regarded as inseparable, except in death. She asserts only that over this history the body has been devalued (in a variety of ways), and that throughout women have been linked with the 'unbearable weight' of the body:

> 'weighed down,' in Beauvoir's words, 'by everything peculiar to it'. In contrast, man casts himself as the 'inevitable, like a pure idea, the One, the All, the Absolute Spirit.' (1995, p. 5, quoting Beauvoir, 1949)

Even Bordo's careful phrasing does not quite capture the complexities of our philosophical past, however. Whilst not denying that 'the body' is generally a negative term in the history of western philosophy, there are nevertheless writers in that tradition (Nietzsche, Deleuze, Foucault, Sloterdijk, for example) who valorize the body. The question then becomes are (mature) female bodies also valorized by these thinkers? Or do the very real possibilities opened up by their writings still continue to take as norm a (male) body that is incapable of birthing new selves from within the embodied self? Sloterdijk's sexy – but also sexually neuter (male) – bodies are subject to critique in chapter 7 below. We will also explore Deleuze's use of 'woman' in chapter 9. Here

I will argue that 'becoming woman' need not be conceptualized as no more than a 'flight' from all 'molar identities' – as Deleuze, and so many post-Deleuzian feminists and postmodernists, now suggest.

And that brings me to the fifth and final characteristic of the female subject-position that I need to mention here. This also derives from this historical link between the female and an embodied, fleshy self, and relates to the conflictual expectations bound up with the female subject-position. The 'experience' of the female human in our culture has direct links with the anomalous, the monstrous, the inconsistent and the paradoxical. Whatever the (very great) differences between women, all female (not 'feminine') subjects in western culture have to negotiate the paradoxicality of a mode of selfhood that is positioned somewhere between freedom and rationality, on the one hand, and passive and thing-like embodiment, on the other. This fifth feature is that woman is 'monstrous', but in a way that allows us to think identity otherwise.

'Here There Be Monsters'

I will be using this monstrosity – this 'phenomenality' – productively. Thus, I will argue that 'woman' is not simply all that has to be excluded in order for the (masculinized) self to establish its (fragile) autonomy and identity – as the psychoanalyst Jacques Lacan, and so many post-Lacanian feminists and deconstructionists, would insist. Instead, I will be developing what might be termed a 'metaphysics of immanence' (in Kantian language), or also a 'metaphysics of becoming'. In particular, I will be interested in a metaphysics of morphological transformations and identities that emerge through repeated patternings, intersecting force-fields, and flow. In chapter 6 this is related to Irigaray's account of the 'red blood' that metaphorically links the mother to the daughter. There I develop further Irigaray's notion of the 'other of the Other', which in Lacanian and Derridean frameworks cannot possibly exist. I also offer a critique of Judith Butler's position on Irigaray's 'monstrous' rethinking of identity, since Butler remains closer to Lacan and Derrida than to Irigaray herself. The quarrel with Butler is taken further in chapter 7, where her deployment of Nietzschean weapons for epistemological ends is contrasted with that of Adorno in the context of developing an 'anti-metaphysical metaphysics'. However, I am also indebted to Butler's 'queer' philosophy, which directs attention to power inequalities between women that have been underplayed by Irigaray herself.

Butler opposes any kind of metaphysics of identity and uses temporality to disrupt the categories of 'woman' and 'women' by parodic interventions. By contrast, I will explore what happens to the notion of 'subjects' and 'objects' if we start from a consideration of the paradoxes that characterize the human female. In chapter 3 I will appropriate the concept of 'dissipative systems' from contemporary physics, and employ this model of structuring to help us think the female subject-position – as well as related concepts, such as 'patriarchy' or 'post-colonial' or 'diasporic' identities. Then in subsequent chapters, via an engagement with the ontological positions of Kierkegaard, I will move on to explain how habit, repetition and the temporary equilibrium of force-fields can be used to explain how stability can emerge in a world of 'events' and 'becoming', and how we can think 'essence' without positing underlying 'substances' that remain unaltered through change.

I am not concerned to argue the only metaphysics possible is this 'metaphysics of becoming'. Instead, my concern is to show that it is not necessary to think in terms of fixed 'essences', permanent 'substances' or unchanging 'being' to secure stable patternings. Persistence of a 'subject' or 'object' over time can also emerge from within intersecting force-fields, dependence and flow. The subject that I will posit is neither completely free nor autonomous, but is also not simply passive. It is both marked – 'scored' – into specificity by its relationships with 'otherness', and yet is itself also capable of agency and of resisting modes of domination. This self is not only shaped by 'the other', it is also self-shaping as potentiality is transformed into actuality via echo and the feedback-loops of memory.

In developing the notion of such a self, this book will, of necessity, open a dialogue with those postmodern feminists who have regarded any account of 'feminist metaphysics' with deep suspicion – or, worse still, with hostility. I will be claiming that the accounts of 'metaphysics', 'modernity' and 'postmodernity' offered in many postmodern feminist texts are generally too simplistic – even where it is allowed (with Jean-François Lyotard) that postmodernity does not come after modernity, but is implicit within modernity. (See Lyotard, 1982.) Here, however, it is necessary to offer a caution. As is well known, 'postmodernism' is a notoriously slippery term and has developed in markedly different – indeed conflicting – ways across a variety of disciplines (and countries). (See Bertens, 1995.) What I have termed 'feminist postmodernism' is not typical of all forms of postmodernism. Furthermore, many of the most influential theorists on 'postmodern' feminisms would (or did) explicitly distance themselves from such a labelling: including Judith

Butler, Gilles Deleuze, Jacques Derrida, Michel Foucault, Luce Irigaray and Gayatri Chakravorty Spivak. Although my own preference is for making a sharp distinction between 'poststructuralism' (which involves a thesis about language 'after' structuralism) and 'postmodernism' (which involves a variety of theses about modernity and temporality), in feminist theory these strands are not clearly distinguished.

What matters to the argument of this book is that within many feminist texts that recycle these theorists as 'postmodern', a kind of orthodoxy about the undesirability of 'metaphysics', 'ontology', 'identity' and 'essence' has become a kind of mantra. Furthermore, 'Otherness' is generally positioned as antithetical to the ego, such that identity can only be established by the refusal of 'Otherness'. Indeed, in much film, literary and art theory it also seems to have become an orthodoxy to insist that the 'feminine' cannot be represented and can only be mobilized as a site of disruption. It is this epistemological 'take' on postmodernism that I will argue against – not 'postmodernism' *per se*.

For me what is most exciting about postmodernism is the radicalizing of ontology that a number of the key theorists produce: including Deleuze, Foucault, Irigaray and Haraway. But this ontological radicalism is lost when these same theorists are viewed through an epistemological frame. Thus, for example, in chapter 3 I will discuss Haraway's 'A Cyborg Manifesto' (1984) in ontological terms. However, Haraway's figuration of the 'cyborg' – a machine/human hybrid – has been generally read as 'anti-metaphysical' or 'postmetaphysical', as we will see in the discussion of Rosi Braidotti's *Nomadic Subjects* (1994) in chapter 9 below. To a large extent, such an epistemological bias is due to the influence on feminist theory of 'the two Jacques' – Lacan and Derrida – who both place the '*féminin*' outside the bounds of the knowable, instead of emphasizing woman's potential to transform the actual.

In this book I argue against those who would demonize metaphysics – and who see no ontological alternative to the 'metaphysics of presence' or the 'metaphysics of substance' that have been deemed a necessary feature of 'phallogocentric' thought. Instead, I explore models for conceptualizing ontology that would allow us to retain a notion of sexual difference whilst also theorizing difference *amongst* women. Such a radicalized ontology does not deal with individualized substances, nor with a form which shapes matter in a top-down kind of way – by the imposition of spatio-temporal or categorial structures, for example. The identities I describe emerge out of patterns of movement and relationality, including 'resonance' and 'echo' in which the past is taken up into the present in ways that do not simply 'copy' a neutral 'real'. Although this ontology has been developed primarily with the problems of female specificity in mind, it should be clear that it is also useful for men and also for a variety of 'minoritarian' groups.

I am not pretending that Irigaray, Deleuze, Haraway and Foucault have not offered their own versions of an ontology in which 'otherness' is not always oppositional to the self. However, because these theorists have been so frequently read (and misread) through an epistemological frame both within feminist theory and also by other commentators on the 'postmodern' scene, I have found it useful to look back at the philosophy of Søren Kierkegaard. For me, at least, this has provided a useful way of separating the ontological and epistemological confusions that seem frequently to mire contemporary debate. Leaving aside Kierkegaard's 'religious' and 'ethical' writings, which have attracted most attention from the philosophical commentators – and concentrating instead on the aesthetic writings in which he explores the 'phenomenal' – will allow me to open up some of the potential of 'a metaphysics of fluidity' to deal with sexual similarities and fleshy singularities.

The metaphysics of flesh and fluidity that is developed in this book is far from being a new 'common' sense. However, in chapters 3 and 10 I will also suggest it is not all that strange, and that it is one of a number of ontological frames that are already operational. I would even go so far as to suggest that in the twenty-first century it is the metaphysical despair of the postmodern feminists that will come to seem odd, and that the currently fashionable dream of a fleshless cyborg will also seem naïve. If there is to be a human/machine hybrid, we need to think one that does not just rework traditional models of identity in which 'real' identity is not fleshy. The 'cyborg' needs to incorporate a matter that can 'morph' new identities from within itself. In addressing these gaps in past and current philosophical theories – gaps in which selves are born and the 'brain goes all red' – it will be necessary to think female specificity. We will thus need to start by examining the problem of 'essence' in terms of a body that bleeds with other potential 'realities', and that generates new selves from within the embodied (fleshy) self.

2
Essentialisms, Feminisms and Metaphysics

I define 'patriarchy' as that form of social organization which takes male bodies and life-patternings as both norm and ideal in the exercise of power. In the patriarchal tradition of metaphysics, birth, growth and differential modes of embodied selfhood remain remarkably untheorized subjects. I am, of course, by no means the first feminist theorist to focus on these issues. But what is distinctive about my own approach is the emphasis on finding a new *metaphysics* that would allow us to take the female as norm. This is at odds with much recent writing in feminist theory where the issues under debate have focused much more centrally around feminist epistemology and the validity of ascribing distinctively female ways of knowing, experiencing, gazing, writing or speaking. Indeed, metaphysics itself has got a bad name, with many theorists maintaining that there has only been one metaphysics in the history of the west and that all metaphysics is necessarily complicit with patriarchy.

From such a viewpoint, feminist metaphysics would be a contradiction in terms. The only way forward would be to move 'beyond' metaphysics, 'beyond' firm identities – often, beyond sexual difference itself. But this is, I would argue, to adopt a too partial view of the history of philosophy and, indeed, of contemporary science. It is not necessary to be so defeatist. There are metaphysical alternatives that model identity in ways that would help us topple the patriarchal view that thinks human, sub-human and superhuman essence in androcentric terms. However, no such move would be possible if – as some theorists have claimed – any talk of essence or ontology is anti-feminist in operation or intent.

For some time feminist theory has seemed caught on the horns of a dilemma. On the one hand, there are those who – recognizing differences amongst women – end by denying any form of female identity. On the other hand, there are those who – supposing male/female difference overrides other differences – look for a female 'sameness' or 'essence' based either on nature or on shared work or life practices. Although since 1984 a number of the most important feminist theorists have argued that it is worth adopting an essentialist 'strategy', essentialism has continued to be presented in most Anglo-American feminist contexts as a theoretical vice.[1] For those theorists who advocate taking the 'risk' of essentialism, it is just that we cannot avoid working *as if* there were female sameness if feminism is to work for political change. A few feminist theorists have adopted a slightly less unsatisfactory form of Lockian nominalism to find a way out of the predicament.

Lockianism will be considered later in this chapter, along with a more 'risky' essentialism. However, to preview my own solution to current dilemmas, I will be concerned with developing a theoretical model that allows us to deal with difference-in-sameness and sameness-in-difference, without reifying a given female 'nature', and also without supposing that there is such a thing as a shared female consciousness – or even styles of life. I will defend the notion of a female essence; and yet I will also insist that women's experiences are diverse – so diverse as to be untheorizable in terms of empirical generalization. Our identities are shaped by a conglomerate of forces and regulative practices, not just by the single matter of sexual difference. In so far as there is 'sameness' between women, this is not a matter of shared experiences or life-histories. It is, rather, a question of a shared positioning *vis-à-vis* the founding metaphysical categories that inform our notions of individuality, self and 'personhood'. Thus, whether or not a woman is lesbian, infertile, post-menopausal or childless, in modern western cultures she will be assigned a subject-position linked to a body that has perceived potentialities for birth.

This point comes out in a recent interview with Judith Butler, who is amongst the most extreme of those who would deny any form of female sameness, insisting in her book *Bodies that Matter* that 'women' is a term that 'marks a dense intersection of social relations that cannot be summarized through the terms of identity' (1993, p. 218). However, questioned by *Radical Philosophy* about the omission of issues relating to impregnation and birthing from her account of what is involved in being ascribed a body that is 'female', Butler responds by suggesting that she is unsure that the question of reproduction 'is, or ought to be, what is absolutely salient or primary in the sexing of the body. If it is, I think it's the imposition of a norm, not a neutral description of biological constraints' (1994, p. 33).

What interests me here is Butler's argumentative slide from what 'is' to what 'ought' to be the case about the body marked as female. We can agree that there is nothing 'neutral' about any such description, but Butler implicitly recognizes the normative connection of the link between female identity and the capacity for pregnancy. Thus, Butler first of all points to the variety of women who cannot be impregnated or choose not to be impregnated. But she then goes on to explore the practical consequences of the way discourse works to establish sex-differential markers:

> It's a practical problem. If you are in your late twenties or your early thirties and you can't get pregnant for biological reasons, or maybe you don't want to, for social reasons – whatever it is – you are struggling with a norm that is regulating your sex. It takes a pretty vigorous (and politically informed) community around you to alleviate the possible sense of failure, or loss, or impoverishment, or inadequacy – a collective struggle to rethink a dominant norm. (1994, p. 34)

Butler seems to be implicitly accepting that the potential for pregnancy acts as regulative norm for women in modern western culture. However, whereas her concern is to find a supportive community and a philosophy of gender that can be used to counter the link between the female sex and the potential for reproduction, my own philosophical concern is to ask what happens if we treat the potential for pregnancy, and the other four features of the 'fleshy' female subject-position, as central to the notion of personhood and self.

Butler would seem to think that there is nothing fruitful about my question – that the interesting work on the connection between being assigned to the female sex and the potentials for birthing has all already been done. However, although I have political sympathy for her oppositional politics, in philosophical terms a major question remains unaddressed in ways that also have consequences in terms of what is involved in living life as a female. What potential for opposition is open to those who cannot – or would not – reject the connection between being female and birthing? Indeed, philosophically speaking, what is it to think identity, personhood, essence, from the position of one who is normalized by the discourse of patriarchy as abnormal – with a body that bleeds with the potentiality of new selves?

Philosophers have endlessly written about death, about living towards death, about life after death and about finitude and fortitude as experienced in the face of death. However, there were very few philosophers prior to the feminist philosophers who took birth into account in the analyses that they offered of freedom, self-identity, virtue or the good life. Reading many philosophers we might, indeed, suppose that man experienced himself always first in isolation from others; that he never had to learn where the boundaries of his own self, his will and his freedom lie; and that he (or rather she) does not carry within himself (or rather herself) the gradual capacity to become two selves. We are lacking models that explain how identity might be retained whilst impregnated with otherness, and whilst other selves are generated from within the embodied self.

This lack of theorization of birth – as if birth was just 'natural', something that simply happened before man 'is' – might be most evident in some continental philosophers (in Heidegger, for example, whose theorization starts with an existent who is simply 'thrown' into the world); but it also evident in the way that the debates abut abortion are conducted in analytic philosophy. The debates about the 'rights' of the foetus feed on a tradition of locating rights in individuals, as if individuality was something that was established with maturity and was retained until death, unless there was some 'fault' or 'illness' or 'failure' in the individual. Similar assumptions can be seen in play in theories of freedom and justice which do not recognize power-dependencies, and treat individuals as if they were all equally rational, equally autonomous, equally self-legislating, equal partners in an implicit social contract – as if, in other words, children and babies did not exist and we were all equally (simultaneously) mature.

Feminine/Female

In the early years of second-wave feminism, there was an attempt to substitute the term 'person' for 'woman'; to get rid of linguistic examples and expressions in which women were treated simply as objects, instead of fully human subjects. These reforms are by no means complete, and I am not arguing against them. But what is now recognized is that it is no good simply demanding that women are treated as, and referred to as, 'persons' if it turns out that our very concept of a person is itself gendered; if it turns out that we understand what it is to be a person or a self only by normalizing the mind/body relationship that marks males in our culture; and if it, also, turns out that this model of the mind/body relationship generates an inadequate ideal – even for men.

To exhort a boy to 'become a man' is, in our culture, to exhort him to take charge of his own life: to adopt codes of behaviour and conduct that involve, at the very least, a control of – and often an outright denial of – his emotions and his appetites. The anthropologist Alfonso Ortiz

(1969) has recorded that in the culture of the Tewa Indians men who undertake demanding tasks are encouraged with the words 'Be a woman, be a man', whilst women are simply exhorted to 'Be a woman' (Hastrup, 1993, p. 38). For us, by contrast, it makes sense to enjoin a woman to stand up to danger 'like a man'; but we hardly ever use 'Be a woman' – even to women themselves. Indeed, if we ever used such a phrase, we would probably be enjoining a teenage girl to accept her developing body. And that is because becoming a woman involves a privileged relationship to a bodily morphology – to breasts, body hair, menstruation, and the like.

A young woman is trained to fashion herself as a body and, often, to employ her mind solely in order to make herself more pleasing as a body. This is not (of course) identical with being judged as a body with a potential for pregnancy. However, these two characteristics of the female predicament are not unconnected, in that it is in terms of a relationship with her body that female identity is secured. By contrast, as I insisted also in the last chapter, males are permitted a form of identity that is less self-evidently bodily and that can more easily be located in terms of a disembodied mind or spirit. In so far as the body comes into account, the (white) male body is frequently represented as a thing that is capable of being transcended – or as ennobled by forms of agency ('manliness') in which full humanity is expressed. Women's flesh is, by contrast, monstrous – with a materiality which is more fully immanent, and yet with the capacity to birth new selves from within the embodied self. As such, 'woman's' identity falls into an unrepresentable zone: somewhere between less-than-one and a becoming more-than-one.

For many poststructuralist feminists it has become conventional to link the monstrous 'otherness' of woman to the claim that there can be no essence of the feminine. The appeal to the 'feminine' in these theories draws on the gender/sex divide that played such a key role in the early years of second-wave feminism, but is also a consequence of the fact that the English language is being used to translate French philosophical theories and that in French the word '*féminin*' means both 'female' and 'feminine'. The word '*femelle*' does exist, but is generally employed only for plants and animals. '*Féminin*' is thus used for all the varieties of sexual difference that relate to 'woman'. By contrast, the 1970s socialist feminists in English-language cultures saw a way of improving women's lot by making a sharp distinction between being 'female' (a matter of 'sex' and biological 'givens' which cannot be changed) and being 'feminine' (a matter of 'gender', cultural conditioning and hence open to change).

In the poststructuralist tradition in English-language cultures, it is the monstrous (and dispersed) 'feminine' that moves to the centre of attention. The 'feminine' fluctuates and cannot be defined. Indeed, under the influence of Lacanian psychoanalysis and deconstructionist discourse, the 'feminine' is treated as the signifier of that which is excluded and at the margins of 'phallogocentric' language. As we will see in chapter 5, for Jacques Lacan the 'I' is only ever established as a unity, by pushing away all that threatens its fragile and fictional identity. That unity is the prerogative of a masculinized self. Thus, for theorists in this tradition, talking about the essence of the feminine is regarded as self-contradictory. But so also is any talk about the essence of the 'female'.

Any attempt to reconstitute a female subject-position as linked to a body that could birth is viewed as being guilty of a triple category-mistake: firstly, of essentializing the 'female'; secondly, of privileging 'birth' and assuming the 'naturalness' of heterosexual orientation; and, thirdly, of consolidating female selves into autonomous, closed unities. Thus, for many postmodernists it is also problematic to talk of a female 'subject' who preserves her identity from birth to death. Instead, the self is fragmented into a fleeting array of desires and impulses, driven by symbolic and cultural propulsions that come from beyond the self – with the 'feminine' that which represents this dissolution of self.

In recent years this 'feminine'/'female' divide has been subject to critique, as a consequence of the fact that the 1970s sex/gender distinction has itself been re-examined. As Moira Gatens put it in an essay written in 1983 (before the so-called 'new French feminisms' had had much impact): it is a mistake to regard the body (= sex) as 'neutral and passive' and consciousness (= gender) as socially determined. On this, I think Gatens is right, and I would also accept her blunt claim:

> Concerning the neutrality of the body, let me be explicit, there is no neutral body, there are at least two kinds of bodies: the male body and the female body. . . . If one accepts the notion of the sexually specific subject, that is, the male or female subject, then one must dismiss the notion that patriarchy can be characterized as a system of social organization that valorizes the masculine *gender* over the feminine gender. Gender is not the issue; sexual difference is. The very same behaviours (whether they be masculine or feminine) have quite different personal and social significances when acted out by the male subject on the one hand and the female subject on the other. (1996a, pp. 8–9)[2]

I would also go along with Gatens in emphasizing that 'biological' male and female bodies are themselves historically and culturally shaped. Being 'female' is not just a matter of biological 'fact' that somehow precedes the cultural markers that constitute 'gender'. Biology itself is a mode of discourse, and cannot be separated out from other symbolic codes and practices that assign privilege in the social networks of power. Biological 'facts' – and bodies – are themselves socially and historically constructed. Unmediated 'givens' play a relatively small role in the way in which we live out our sexual identities as 'female' or 'male'.

Although I accept Gatens' argument that 'biological' bodies are as socially marked as are the characteristics of 'gender', I would also wish to insist on a separation of the categories of the 'feminine' and the 'female' along the lines developed in *Gender and Genius* and also emphasized in the preceding chapter. As previously explained, there are two differing, but related, sets of terms in the English language which provide a set of distinctions that operate differently in French, German and also in Italian feminist theory and philosophy. In English, 'femininity' (gender) is not necessarily linked with the female body, and instead involves differences in behaviour or (socialized) disposition that have come to be associated with females rather than with males. There is nothing paradoxical about being a 'feminine' man. Being 'female' (a matter of 'sex'), by contrast, involves a necessary reference to bodily morphology and results in a specific positioning in terms of the social networks of power and the conceptual networks by which identity is determined. Even given that the bodily/sexual categories of male and female are not simply given to us by 'nature' and are historically and culturally variable, it remains the case that being assigned to the category of 'female' is not simply the same as being assigned to the category of the 'feminine'.

Gatens claims in this 1983 paper that 'It is not masculinity *per se* that is valorized in our culture but the *masculine male*' (1996a, p. 15). However, I would insist that this is too simple. The argument of my *Gender and Genius* (1989) shows that for privileged classes and races of males 'femininity' is also valued in modes of productive activity. 'Geniuses' (the super-males) are regarded as transcending ego and as possessing characteristics – intuition, emotion, imagination, illogicality – which in our culture are more often associated with the female sex. *Normal* selves are attached to male bodies; *supra-normal* selves are also attached to male bodies; women, by contrast, are credited with *abnormal* selves. In matters of cultural transcendence, the high evaluation of male 'femininity' effects a radical split between the 'female' and the 'feminine' – and in ways that mean the sex/gender dichotomy cannot simply be renounced.

As such, I would adopt a rather different solution to the sex/gender puzzles from that outlined by Gatens. Whereas in this paper Gatens preserves a link between sex and gender via the culturally mediated 'experience' of an 'imaginary' body, I am more concerned to stress the diversity of female experiences – but retain the underlying sameness of the female predicament. Other feminist theorists have used Moira Gatens' paper to argue for a more 'fluid' understanding of the sex/gender relationship in ways that I also find unsatisfactory. (See, for example, Chanter, 1993, pp. 186, 194 fn. 23.) This also seems to be suggested by the remarks on embodiment by Gatens herself in her subsequent book, *Feminism and Philosophy* (1991, pp. 114–15). Here Gatens suggests that it is a theoretical advantage to leave the concepts of the 'female' and the 'feminine' blurred in the manner of the French theorists Hélène Cixous and Luce Irigaray.

By contrast, it seems to me important to retain the sex/gender distinction – whilst *also* stressing that 'sex' is a non-primitive given. Cixous's and Irigaray's categorial blurring I interpret as a disadvantage, and as a consequence of the fact that the French language limits the use of '*femelle*' in everyday speech. I should stress, however, that Gatens' most recent 'Spinozist' position offers a stronger and more complex account of the links (and differences) between sex and gender, but it does not entail an abandonment of all talk of a female essence, as she seems to suppose. Indeed, Gatens herself notes that she is going beyond Spinoza in making this move (1996a, pp. 78, 134–6).[3]

For Spinoza 'matter' and 'mind' emerge from the one underlying process – or substance – which is materially grounded. Using Spinoza, Gatens argues against a body that is passive matter, and that which is then imposed on by an active mind. Sexual difference does not 'cause' gender difference; but neither does gender difference overlay bodily difference in a constructivist way. Instead, sexual difference (bodily and thus 'extensive') and gender difference (behavioural and 'affective') are different patterns of relationality in a nature that is transformative, and constituted by modes of power relations that connect all 'things' at all places and times.

This is a useful and productive way of rethinking the bogged debates about 'sex' ('female') and 'gender' ('feminine'). Since there are analogies between Gatens' position and that of Deleuze – considered in chapter 9 below – Gatens comes in some ways close to the 'process metaphysics' developed later in this book. (See especially Gatens, 1996b.) However, although Gatens sometimes writes as if a Spinozist ontology implied getting rid of any notion of essence relating to a class of things, I do not think this follows from her position. What does follow, however, is the need to think 'essence' in a fluid way, so that it is not thought of as a fixed and static 'real' that is located in the body and merely subject to historical and cultural variation. It also follows that belonging to a particular category or class of subjects or objects is not to be conceptualized as imposed by the mind 'from above', on a set of particulars that are not in relationship until so grouped by the individual mind – or by 'language'. Both 'real' essences and an entirely 'artificial' mental constructivism are undermined by Gatens' Spinozist critique.

Against Gatens, I am arguing that the 'female' subject-position is one that points to embodiment – and to what women share with animals – in ways that differentiate it from the 'feminine', and also from the 'male'. However, I would agree with Gatens that to talk about embodiment – or what women and female animals have in common – does not imply that there is some single 'real' property that is instantiated in women's bodies or that there have not been evolving (indeed conflicting) definitions of the female. Indeed, what interests me from the point of view of a feminist metaphysics is the specificity of the *female* – not *feminine* – subject-position in western modernity. This subject-position is, however, not immediately and biologically given, but a historically and socially emergent norm that changes over time. Furthermore this norm does not *describe*, but *prescribes* categorial 'fit' based on the perception of bodies. The body is emphasized, but in ways that allow for differences between individual women or between groups of women. I would also want to insist that these sexually differentiating 'norms' can themselves change over time – and that such an account is reconcilable with essentialism.

Philosophical Essentialisms: Fighting Back

My concern with asking what happens in philosophy if we try to think identity in terms that take as norm female embodiment obviously leaves me vulnerable to the by now time-honoured charge of being a feminist essentialist. Thus, for the remainder of this chapter I wish to examine the extent to which such a charge should leave me feeling guilty. It will be convenient to introduce this discussion via an engagement with a conversation between Ellen Rooney and Gayatri Chakravorty Spivak (Spivak, 1989) in which Rooney notes that within feminist theory the label 'essentialist' is used to discredit certain kinds of discourses; but that this term has not been 'historicized or related to the history of high philosophical essentialisms' (1989, p. 7). Rooney insistently questions Spivak about why there has been no 'philosophical essentialism that fights back' – and whether it might not be possible to develop a notion of a 'nonessential essence' which could counter the ahistorical (and vague) feminist critiques (pp. 7, 20). Rooney, thus, flirts with the position developed in this chapter, but only in an interrogative mode.

Spivak is in conversation with her earlier self as she responds to Rooney. As the translator of Derrida's *Grammatology* and a formidable theorist of Indian feminisms, Spivak had gone through an early phase of repudiating an essence of 'woman' – especially since western cultural models obscured racial, ethnic and cultural differences. Then from 1984 Spivak defended a form of 'strategic' essentialism, which privileged feminist practice over theory (1984, p. 11). Now, however, in this 1989 interview Spivak is having third thoughts. She has 'reconsidered' her 'cry for a strategic use of essentialism' (1989, p. 5). Instead, she is now advocating vigilance with respect to differences, but also claiming that essentialism is unimportant – and that what is important is deconstructive philosophy. The latter, she claims, opposes essences, but is also against anti-essentialism. Deconstruction is linked with philosophical nominalism (discussed below), but defended as a form of epistemological scepticism that remains neutral about 'the real' (p. 16). Deconstruction concerns itself not with ontology, but with knowledge and belief: it 'invites us to think through the counterintuitive position that there might be essences and there might not be essences' (p. 10).

Spivak's third thoughts indicate part of what is the matter with the 'wrong in theory, but right in practice' answer to the dilemmas of feminist essentialism. If strategically we need to talk about the female subject-position in order to change it, then we need a mode of conceptualizing essences which offers the imagination new models of thinking identity at an ontological level. The 'strategic' reversals – and Spivak's epistemological balancing act – are only enough if there is no alternative to thinking identity except in terms of a metaphysics of substance. In that case we would be forced to treat each category – 'women', 'Indians', 'Asians', et cetera – as a unified 'thing' that remains constant through change, whilst also asserting that each category is an epistemological fiction. However, as an excursus into the history of philosophy will show, there are alternatives for conceptualizing essence that do not make change extraneous to the real, and all difference merely accidental. There are other modes of imagining the 'real' apart from those both asserted – and also simultaneously denied – by the deconstructionist strategy of moving 'beyond the binary'. I will return to these issues in chapter 5, and also below.

Spivak's own way of moving forward in this 1989 interview does not address this history. Pressed by Rooney as to why there can be no *philosophical* answer to the feminist problems relating to essentialism,

Spivak makes it seem that essentialism is not a philosophical problem at all. Thus, she remarks: 'The question of antiessentialism and essentialism is not a philosophical question as such', and 'essentialism is a loose-tongued phrase, not a philosophical school' (1989, p. 7). Here Spivak registers the contemporary debate in analytic philosophy about essences, but suggests that this has nothing much to do with the issues raised by poststructuralist feminists. However, this is only partially correct. On the one hand, Spivak is correct to say that within feminist theory 'essentialism' is a term that is used loosely and without reference to its philosophical past. On the other hand, the debates within analytic philosophy are also being used by philosophers – albeit sporadically – to draw (too rapid) conclusions about a (lack of) female essence. (See, for example, Dupré, 1986.)

I thus do not think that it would be a waste of time to take Ellen Rooney's questions more seriously than Spivak herself does, and make an excursus into the history of western metaphysics in order to situate current dilemmas. In exploring this history, I will argue that it is an Aristotelian notion of essence that has been privileged in the debate as it is currently formulated in both feminist theory and analytic philosophy. We will also see that other notions of essence are available in the history of philosophy that would help us think the specificities of being female without reifying feminine experience or female lifestyles into a monolithic unity.

Aristotelian Histories

Histories of the concept of essence always start with Aristotle, even though Plato had previously defined the dialectical method of philosophy in terms of finding what it is that all members of the same class have in common, and can thus be read as having laid the foundations for essence. 'Essence' is the normal translation of the Aristotelian phrase '*to ti ēn einai*': 'the what it is to be'. However, the Greek term *ousia* – much used by Aristotle – is also frequently translated as 'essence'. For Aristotle, the essence of a thing is linked to its 'substance' or 'being' (*ousia*), and to the timeless and necessary element in the species or genus which persists across change. Essence is bound up with the minimal necessary and sufficient conditions that enable us to identify and reidentify entities as belonging to the 'same' kind. This essence is grasped by a particular act of the mind, the *nous*, and involves abstracting that which makes a species distinctively itself (its form) from the composite of form and matter that presents itself to the senses.

Aristotle's logic was buttressed by a kind of metaphysical biology that employed a notion of essence to classify and grade organic kinds into genus and species. The connection between Aristotle's metaphysical biology and his logic is a matter of considerable dispute, as also is the connection between his doctrines of essence, substance and being. However, in the traditional reading of Aristotle, essences can be thought of as *species-forms*: the forms or essences that are common to all members of a natural kind or species.[4] Thus, what makes somebody human is a universal essence: what all members of the species have in common, and in virtue of which they are classed as 'human'. However, not all members of the species instantiate the essence in similarly adequate ways.

For Aristotle, in particular, females are failed and botched males who, through lack of heat during conception and the subsequent period of foetal growth, failed to develop their full potential as members of that species. Thus, although women are human (and thus have the minimal characteristics, or essence, of the human), they are also lacking: they are not its end or 'final cause'. It is not that women have any distinctive essence of their own; it is rather that to be a woman is to partake in the essence of being human, but to fail to instantiate that essence in its most perfect form. It is ironic to note that many feminists who assert that there can be no essence of the female are (often unwittingly) repeating this Aristotelian doctrine that links 'essence' to some one defining property of a species that is common to all members of that species, but that cannot be found in females. This feminist opposition to essence turns a philosophical history that bonds femaleness to a deformation of a (supposedly gender-neutral) species (that just happens to be best instantiated in males) into a conceptual necessity. On this view, it becomes impossible to develop a notion of a specifically female essence.

Aristotle provides a model for thinking sameness-in-difference; but on the traditional reading of Aristotle, this model works straightforwardly only for 'natural species' or kinds. However, Aristotelianism has also been interpreted as locating essence within individual substances or things, as well as within species. Thus the notion of 'essential properties' that re-emerges in modern analytic philosophy is sometimes made on the basis of non-traditional readings of Aristotle (see, for example, Copi, 1954); sometimes on the basis of an engagement with the notion of 'essential properties' first introduced into analytic philosophy by Saul Kripke (1970). Kripke develops a notion of 'basic' properties very different from that of Aristotle; but what remains constant is the notion of an 'essence' as an underlying 'real' that secures identity and that persists through a variety of changed circumstances.

For Kripke, naming is basic to the functioning of language, and here he means the ascription of proper names, such as the name of a person, a city or a country (1970, p. 24). Furthermore, the act of naming involves 'rigid designators' that pick out things that have 'essential properties'. These properties are non-accidental, and true in that they would pick out the same object in every possible world (p. 48). As such, these essential properties are integral to what makes that individual thing or substance itself, and not something else. Kripkean essence depends on three types of property: properties of origin (what caused it); sortal properties (such as 'being a human' or 'being a female'); and properties of substance (to do with the type of matter from which it is made). For Kripke, the essence of a thing is not primarily a matter of falling under universals of species or genus (as it was for Aristotle); but neither is it simply a question of abstracting from experience or describing all the properties an individual might possess. For Kripke things are more than mere bundles of properties, in that some properties are more necessary than others in securing identity.

Accidental properties are those properties that could be otherwise without identity being affected. Essential properties are those that could not be changed without identity being sacrificed. Kripke's claim is modal; it is not a claim about temporality. He does not ask: 'If Queen Elizabeth suddenly becomes a male, is she still the same entity?' Rather, he asks: 'If it is Queen Elizabeth, could it be a male and also Queen Elizabeth?' Basically, Kripke's claim is that it would not be possible for Queen Elizabeth to be herself if she had a different causal origin (was born of different parents); if there were different sortal properties (being human, being female); and if she had different material properties (was made of plastic, instead of flesh and blood).

There are clear continuities between Kripke's account of essence and the Aristotelian tradition. (See, for example, Witt, 1989, pp. 1–3, 180–97.) In particular, Kripke's three necessary or essential properties of (i) origin, (ii) kind and (iii) matter correspond very closely to three out of four of Aristotle's determining causes: (i) efficient, (ii) formal and (iii) material. Aristotle lists a fourth kind of causality – the final cause that tends to an end – and it is this that is altogether missing from Kripke's account. Nor is this surprising in that it was final causality that, for Aristotle, was most bound up with the metaphysical biology that underlay his theory of species, and Kripke has replaced the notion of the essence of species with that of the essence of individuals. Kripke does extend the notion of essential properties to that of 'natural kinds'. However, this is done by noting that these 'have a greater kinship with proper names than is generally realised' (1970, p. 134). As such, for Kripke, as opposed to Aristotle, it is individualized substances – and not species – that provide the paradigm case for the ascription of essence.

In Aristotle, it was final causality which involved teleological development towards perfection of species; and this was also the factor that women (as monsters) lacked. However, the omission of final causes in the Kripkean account of essences does not straightforwardly mean that his notion of an essence can be applied to the class of female humans. Whereas for Aristotle what was odd about females was a failure to live up to the universal of species identity, on the Kripkean model what is odd about speaking about the essence of women is the departure from a model that thinks essence in terms of individualized substances. It is only with difficulty that we could extend Kripkean 'properties of origin' or 'properties of substance' so as to account for the essence of the human female. But some feminist theorists have nevertheless employed Kripkean considerations as a part of their attack on sex and/or gender 'essentialism'. Thus, for example, Judith Butler employs Kripke in her *Bodies that Matter*, and it is via Kripke that she concludes there that it is a mistake even to look for a homogenized female identity (1993, pp. 210ff).

Nominalism and Feminist Anti-essentialism

It is not part of the argument that I will be making here to decide on the adequacy of Kripkean essentialism. But it is important to note that those less concerned with deconstructing, and more concerned with reconstructing, an account of a specifically female subject-position could very easily turn to philosophical accounts of essence that worked more comfortably at a level between species and individual. The notion of a nominal essence is the oldest (and most established) way of rethinking the issue of essence. This position is associated with the seventeenth-century philosophers Hobbes and Locke, and is half-way between the Aristotelian doctrine of essences and the extreme nominalism of some of the medieval schoolmen and of Berkeley and Hume.

Nominalists insist that only names (or more generally words) are universal. As such, nominalism involves a complete denial of essences. Hobbes' and Locke's opposition to Aristotle was more muted, by contrast. With the nominalists Hobbes insisted that definitions are of names, not of things. The essence of a thing is its verbal definition: it is no more than 'that accident for which we give a certain name to any body, or the accident which denominates its subject' (Hobbes, 1655, Pt 2, ch. 8, § 23, p. 117). Locke builds on this move to distinguish the real essence of a thing from its nominal essence. The latter is the idea of the property or properties which justify the application of a particular name. Thus, the universal attaches to the idea of the thing – and to language – rather than to natural kinds or some real underlying cause hidden in the object that causes it to be as it is. Locke opposed 'real essences' – which he associated with Aristotle – but claimed that there are, nevertheless, general ideas ('nominal essences') which are gradually reached via a process of abstraction 'whereby *Ideas* taken from particular Beings, become general Representatives of all of the same kind' (1690, Bk 2, ch. 11, § 9, p. 159).

Locke had an unsatisfactory account of language. In this chapter 'Of the Names of Substances' he imagines Adam naming the world in good empiricist fashion, simply combining simple ideas into complexes 'without any regard to any Archetype, without respect to any thing as a Pattern' (Bk 3, ch. 6, § 44, p. 467). Words 'copy' simple ideas. Complex ideas are themselves made out of simples; meaning is caused by individualized qualities and things. As such, Locke is famously incapable of explaining the origins of language, or the individual child's linguistic development. Indeed, in this chapter he imagines Adam as mature and as 'naming' a new country to Eve. However, although there are serious weaknesses in Locke's account in terms of the way that the ideas of abstract universals are formed, it should be clear that this model of nominal essences is more useful than Aristotle's 'real essences' or Kripke's 'basic' particulars for thinking the specificity of woman. This is because the Lockian account of essence can fully recognize the vicissitudes of language, without being tied to a model whereby only individual entities have full identity. Thus, a feminist advocacy of 'nominal essences' could deal comfortably with linguistic, historical and cultural variations in the way that the female is defined. Indeed, it is intriguing to note that it is Locke's notion of a nominal essence that Teresa de Lauretis employs in 'The Essence of the Triangle' (1989), her celebrated defence of the kind of 'essentialism' prevalent within the Italian tradition of feminist theorizing. Fuss (1989a, 1989b) makes a similar move, but combines it with a more 'strategic' essentialism.

There are problems with Locke's own account of nominal essence; but there are even more severe problems with the most extreme kinds of nominalism that would assert that there is nothing common to a class of particulars called by the same name other than the fact that they *are* called by that name. Take, for example, the current scientific paradigm for sexual difference in mammals which involves both genes and hormones. Currently, it is claimed that the normal 'male' needs not only XY chromosomes, but also exposure to androgens *in utero*. Without this hormonal 'bath', there will be reversion to the female – the 'default' – sex. Currently, some aspects of this causal account of the formation of sex differences are unclear and subject to investigation. In particular, it is currently uncertain whether a single gene on the Y chromosome determines the outcome. Thus, it might so happen that to be 'male' in our culture comes to be redefined.

For the supporter of extreme nominalism, the question is only which characteristics in our culture act as linguistic definers. However, for paradigms of human sexual difference to evolve there have to be perceived similarities – and discrepancies – between the class of entities compared. To maintain this is 'just' linguistic and social plays down the capacity of data to disturb the definition in a 'bottom-up' way. To allow that empirical 'evidence' might play a role in dislocating and redrawing current paradigms of sexual difference does not entail that linguistic and social practices do not also enter into current definitions. Nor does it entail that there might not also be social reasons why the markers for sexually differentiated bodies should change. Opposing extreme nominalism does not entail positing underlying, unchanging, 'real truths' about female bodies or forms.

To strengthen Lockianism, it is not necessary to become a more extreme nominalist. Instead, Lockianism can be strengthened by a Kantian move. Thus, Kant denied that abstract ideas are obtained simply in a bottom-up way, by simply generalizing from particulars. Instead, he posited an intermediate level of *rules* that mediate between the categories of the mind and experience itself. These rules – which Kant termed 'schemata' – act as a kind of template or grid for the operations of vision and of the imagination. These schemata are not derived from experience, but are devices for grouping images under concepts and within linguistic categories. Although apparently applied in a 'top-down' way, schemata latch on to experience in ways that mean that concepts (and also language) are capable of revision when the diversity or recalcitrance of experience cannot be easily reconciled with the categorial frame that is being applied. Since some of these schemata are more contingent than others (in the sense that they could be changed without identity being affected), within a post-Kantian understanding of schemata there is no necessary need to shy away from cultural variability.

In the *Radical Philosophy* interview, Judith Butler made much of the fact that if the issue of reproduction is a primary consideration in the sexing of the body, it ought not to be since 'it's the imposition of a norm, not a neutral description of biological constraints' (1994, p. 33). However, from the position of the post-Kantian nominal essentialist, there *are no neutral descriptions*: everything is a regulative practice that has its origin in discursive practices. However, some of those practices play a more privileged role in securing the identity of classes or particulars than do others, since within a particular culture at a particular time, some of these norms are more central than others. These privileged 'norms' are what determines essence, but since they are only 'norms' there is no insistence that all members of the class share the same property or single set of properties.

A feminist essentialist of this post-Kantian persuasion can allow essences and also register differences between standards adopted across different cultures and historical epochs in securing sexually differentiated bodies. In the case of sexual indeterminacy or categorial conflict, is it visible female genitalia, the absence of a penis, the presence of a womb, or other 'secondary' sexual characteristics that is the factor privileged in ascribing an infant to the category of 'girl'? Or is sexual definiteness only accorded later, after puberty and/or after specific cultural rites of passage? Whatever acts as the dominant regulatory norm in different cultures and historical periods would count as the 'schematic essence' of the human female – with the possibility of employing a Foucauldian model of the relationship between discourse and regulatory practices to then explain the centrality of the dominant norm within a particular society.

I hope it is clear from the above comments how much Aristotelianism still marks contemporary feminist thought in English-language cultures. This is true of those feminists who would get rid of the notion of a female essence on the grounds that there are no essences of anything – and who, in effect, refuse Locke's notion of a nominal essence. These feminists retain an Aristotelian notion of essence as something 'real', and not merely a linguistic way of grouping classes and kinds. A second group of feminists also remain within Aristotelianism when they insist that it is contradictory to look for an essence of the female not because there are no essences of anything, but because the 'female' is not the sort of 'natural kind' that is capable of having an 'essence'. Like Aristotle, these feminists are assuming that essences must relate to 'natural' and 'real' groupings of things that can embrace species-identity, but not identity-as-females.

A third group of feminists also remain within Aristotelianism when they assert that it is not contradictory, but simply a mistake, to look for the essence of the human female. The grounds for dismissing the essence of 'woman' is, on this model, apparently merely empirical – namely the great variations between individual women. This objection looks non-metaphysical, but does, in fact, continue to employ Aristotelianism in so far as it supposed that what essence involves is an unvarying character-istic that is shared uniformly by all members of the class. In the history of philosophy all three of these facets of Aristotelianism have been questioned in ways that would allow us to think the specificity of woman.

In particular, the fact of difference amongst women is not, as such, grounds for denying essence, since what 'essence' provides is a model of thinking sameness through difference. Talking about a female 'essence' does not necessarily entail hypostatizing a 'true' female 'nature' which reflects an underlying (real) heterosexuality or a bodily 'design' that will consign a woman to the fate of becoming a mother. Instead, my own defence of the notion of a female 'essence' involves registering the norms and regulative practices that at one particular time and in one type of culture act as sexual definers. The capacity to birth is one factor used in deciding that a person is 'female', rather than 'male'. However, as I argued in the last chapter, there are four other (not unrelated) fea-tures of the female subject-position in western modernity. These are also contingent, and thus also subject to change.

Beyond Nominalism

I want now to consider Wittgenstein's and Derrida's very different responses to this issue, since both are currently influential and both could also be read as providing a more radical attack on the notion of essence than any of the alternatives to Aristotle considered above. Wittgenstein is sometimes referred to as a 'resemblance theorist'. Whereas nominal-ists claimed that only words are universal and that things themselves are singular and individual, Wittgenstein got rid of the notion that words and names function as universals – at least in the majority of cases. Instead of supposing that there is some single feature that unites all usages of a word, Wittgenstein suggested that language itself works in terms of a series of vague and overlapping likenesses analogous to those observable within a family grouping. It is not, for example, that there is some one defining property that makes us characterize board-games, card-games, ball-games and Olympic games as 'games'. Rather, there is *nothing* common to all, only 'family resemblances': 'similarities, rela-tionships, and a whole series of them at that' (Wittgenstein, 1953, Pt 1, § 66, p. 31). As such, Wittgenstein provides a useful preliminary move for a feminist theorist, although it is a move that surprisingly few feminists have opted to take.

The question that feminists must ask on the basis of the Wittgen-steinian move is: what is the ground for the 'family' similarity in uses

of the term 'female'? What are the discursive practices that regulate its
use and serve to distinguish the 'female' from such related, and oppositional, terms as 'feminine', 'masculine', 'male'? Wittgenstein himself
employs two higher-level notions – 'language games' and 'forms of life'
– as grounds for his 'family resemblances'. Essence disappears into a
set of interrelated resemblances, bound together in terms of rule-based
activities that are intersubjective ('language games') or that constitute
a unity over time ('forms of life'). However, Wittgenstein is also notoriously vague as to what counts as a 'language game' or a 'form of life'.
As such, the Wittgensteinian move displaces the nominalist refusal to
explain the identification and reidentification of classes and things to a
deeper level.

For Derrida also essence disappears into a play of relationships. A
word attains its meaning not in virtue of corresponding to or matching
a 'real' world, nor in terms of fixed essences and properties. Rather,
using Saussure's theories of language, Derrida indicates that a word
attains its meaning in terms of its position in a signifying system and
in terms of the way it combines with, differs from and is in tension
with other members of that set. In particular, the meaning of a term is
dependent upon negation – and exclusion – in ways that mean that the
contrary is always in play. Thus, for example, a man (= male human)
is defined in terms of his not being a woman. It looks as if 'man' is the
privileged term (with 'woman' merely that which is excluded and at the
margins of discourse); but since it is only ever possible to define man
in terms of its exclusions, it turns out that 'woman' plays a key role
whenever the discourse of 'man' is in play. On both the Derridean and
Wittgensteinian accounts of language we would seem to be able to
account for meaning without bringing in an appeal to 'essence'.

I will return to Derrida's account of meaning, and my unease with
his treatment of essence, metaphysics and the feminine, in chapter 5 of
this book. Here I need only to explain that although Wittgenstein and
Derrida provide a critique that would seem to counter a traditional idea
of essence, neither of them provides a model that would necessitate
getting rid of essence as understood in Bergsonian terms.

> Now, life is an evolution. We concentrate a period of this evolution in
> a stable view which we call a form, and, when the change has become
> considerable enough to overcome the fortunate inertia of our perception,
> we say that the body has changed its form. But in reality the body is
> changing form at every moment; or rather, there is no form, since form
> is immobile, and the reality is movement. What is real is the continual
> *change of* form: *form is only a snapshot view of a transition*. . . . When the
> successive images do not differ from each other too much, we consider

them all as the waxing and waning of a single *mean* image, or as the deformation of this image in different directions. And to this mean we really allude when we speak of the *essence* of a thing, or of the thing itself. (Bergson, 1907, p. 302)

Putting this together with the Kantian account of the schemata, an essence would become a rule or norm that can itself fluctuate, but which functions as a paradigm – a kind of idealized image or snapshot – that is used to arrest the fluid and the manifold into a temporary stability of form.

So why am I interested in retaining such a notion of essence? At first sight, there might seem little difference between this Bergsonian model of essence as a 'snapshot' used to control an underlying fluidity and the Derridean emphasis on meaning as a shifting set of signs. But from the point of view of feminist theory there are distinct advantages in trying to keep hold of a notion of essence – however radically that notion might seem to depart from standard Aristotelianism. For one thing, we have seen that the notion that there can be no essence of the female has a long and time-honoured pedigree in the history of patriarchal thought and has been implicit in western metaphysics at least since the time of Aristotle. We need to explore what happens if we retain the notion of essence, but allow within it the kind of fluidity that can encompass female difference – and also the type of female embodiment in which self can be impregnated with otherness.

By retaining a notion of a (fluid) 'real' and an overlaying structure of language that would seek to contain fluidity, the Bergsonian notion of essence also gives feminists a frame within which to think the conflicts between the 'real' (the object of their experience) and the discursive (through which all their experience is mediated). Too much work in the deconstructionist feminist tradition ends by suggesting that there *is* no real beyond the linguistic domain. Bergsonianism keeps the 'real' as a regulatory ideal: a flowing, unstable reality behind the horizons of discourse. Retaining a notion of (fluid) essence also allows a conceptual clarity that is necessary to thinking the non-equivalence of similar concepts when applied to persons of different sexes (and races). This fluid notion of essence is also, I would argue, particularly useful to thinking a female form of embodiment in which identity is established without an oppositional relationship between self and otherness, but in which self is (from time to time) permeated by otherness – in pregnancy, for example.

Such an account of the 'real' that is fluid, and that remains beyond language, does, however, retain an implicit idealism – particularly because Bergson suggests that it is by acts of non-rational intuition that it imposes on the mind. Such a view will be subject to modification in chapter 7 of this book where Adorno's criticism of Bergson is used to open up a more materialist explanation of how 'difference' might suddenly emerge from within the linguistic and conceptual structuring that secures essence and 'sameness'. With changes in life patterns and work practices, singularities emerge that had been 'forgotten' as particulars were folded together under concepts. These 'forgotten' differences gradually transform the real so that 'schematic essence' does not have to be conceptualized as a 'rule' that is simply imposed by the mind on an entirely plastic and neutral set of 'givens'.

In his use – and critique – of Bergson, Adorno provides us with a model that allows us to register that material and historical changes can effect a transformation in what is perceived and, indeed, in what counts as an 'object' or a 'subject'. It is, however, perhaps worth pointing out that Adorno's emphasis on historical change is more easily reconcilable with the Wittgensteinian move into 'family resemblances' than with the Derridean emphasis on allowing the subordinate term in a pair of binary oppositions to destabilize the very notion of self and identity. Furthermore, Adorno's critique of the mechanisms of Bergsonian recollection does not entail dispensing with Bergson's account of essence as a kind of 'snapshot' or 'mean' that provides a (temporary) arrestation to an always-changing evolution of 'forms'.

Essence and Existence

Given the influence that Simone de Beauvoir has exerted on second-wave feminism, I will end this chapter by comparing my account of a 'fluid essence' with her existentialist account of a mode of 'being' that emerges from 'becoming'. Thus, via the slogan 'existence precedes essence', the existentialism of Jean-Paul Sartre and Beauvoir also made it possible to think the essence of the human more fluidly: in terms of the sum of human acts, instead of in terms of a prior (Aristotelian) understanding of species biology. There are, however, important differences between Beauvoir's analysis of the female and the one that I am offering here.

Interestingly, despite the restricted use of the term '*femelle*' in the French language, it is with an analysis of the '*femelle*' – or what women and animals have in common – that *The Second Sex* opens (1949, pp. 35–69). Beauvoir's describes the *femelle* in terms of a kind of passive embodiment: a materiality that the female human is able to negate in virtue of the fact that she is more than 'thing-like' (more than a mere 'in-itself') and also more than an animal. For Beauvoir (as for Sartre), embodiment, biology – and, in particular, female biology – is negated by the authentic, 'free' self that transforms the past and the present by projecting itself towards the future.

Beauvoir describes female biology in terms that render it horrid: a kind of 'facticity' that pulls against the transforming consciousness in ways that involve the resistance of otherness – the clinging, slimy, flabby, sticky, fleshy 'in-itself'. What interests me about the female subject-position is thinking this necessary relationship to embodiment and the ambiguous boundaries between self and other more positively. I am interested in using this apparent (but none the less resistant) passivity – using 'flab' – to mark out a subject-position that is characteristic of those who are ascribed identity first and foremost through becoming bodies. Like Luce Irigaray, I am also interested in a more positive thinking of that sticky boundary between self and other. Indeed, I regard Beauvoir's obsessive desire for a freedom that is only exercised through the negation of flesh as itself a form of bad faith that comes from taking the male subject as norm.

Furthermore, although the notion of essence that I am adopting is as anti-Aristotelian as that of the existentialists, it is not equivalent to the existentialist notion that you are what you do – or that the essence of something can simply be characterized in terms of a bundle of performative parts. What is specific to the female subject-position (its essence) is not simply a product of the sum of all female subject-positions. Nor can there be the kind of appeal to 'authenticity' that the existentialists mounted. All our experience is mediated through language; 'authenticity' is historically and socially constructed. There are no 'true' female experiences, although there are – as in the case of Beauvoir herself – forms of self-deception that result when freedom, autonomy and selfhood are thought through a model that takes the male as typical and perfect, and woman as always excessive or lacking.

Female lives and female experience are immensely variable and immensely complex, with Bergsonian fluidity of form. However, that very fluidity does not mean that it is not possible for there to emerge a series of 'snapshots' that will provide the notion of a (shifting) 'essence' – an essence that (at least in western modernity) has only been established by the positioning of the female relationship to her body as 'abnormal' and as an inappropriate starting point for thinking self and personhood. It is not necessary to agree that we need to retain the term 'essence' for what it is that characterizes the female subject in modern western culture. But what it is necessary to see is that the kinds of reasons adduced by philosophers and feminists against employing a notion of a female essence are far from knockdown arguments – unless, of course, what is retained is an Aristotelian notion of essence that links essence with 'natural kinds', 'invariant properties' or an underlying sameness of substance.

It is also necessary to see that this Aristotelian notion of an essence is not the only one available in the history of western metaphysics. Locke, Bergson, Spinoza and the existentialists are amongst those who provide us with very different resources for thinking the specificity of the female subject-position. The history of metaphysics is not a monolithic unity. There are resources within it that mean that a feminist metaphysics need not simply involve a negation of the philosophical past. And neither need feminist metaphysics simplistically proceed by homogenizing woman, or by looking inside female consciousness for a 'true', 'authentic' female experience. Feminist metaphysics may start by deconstructing – but can also move on to reconstruct – such notions as 'self', 'person' and identity itself, taking female (not feminine) embodiment as its point of departure.

3
Her Body/Her Boundaries

My concern in this book as a whole is to ask what happens to the notion of identity if we treat the embodied female as the norm for models of the self. In the opening chapter I argued that there are five features of the female subject-position that are discrepant if we take the dominant models of identity from the metaphysics of the west. There is first of all natality, and the need to think the normality of the body that can birth. Without ever implying that every woman either could or should give birth, I stressed the way that natality troubles the notion of identity as a fixed, permanent or pre-given 'thing' or 'substance'. Natality considered as an abstract category allows us to think identities as emerging from a play of bodily relationships: an emergence that is not sudden, but that occurs over time.

The second feature of the female subject-position that I emphasized derives not only from natality, but from the fact that modern western cultures have regarded the female as the primary carer of children and as the most suitable 'nurse' for other dependants within the so-called 'private' sphere. For the (normalized) woman, selves are never just 'equals'; not even on an ideal level. Instead, there are both ontological and power-dependencies which work to constitute self.

The third feature of the female subject-position that I discussed was that for a woman 'self' and 'not-self' are sub-contraries, not contradictories, when considered in logical terms. In other words, it might be possible (when pregnant) to be both self and not-self. 'Self' is capable of interpenetration by 'otherness'. However, even if there is no sharp 'cut' between 'self' and 'other', this does not imply that 'self' dissolves into 'not-self'. Gradually, over a period of time, an 'other' emerges from within the body of the normalized female and from the work of child-rearing. This 'other' has its own genetic and immunological patternings; its own spatio-temporal boundaries; its own goals and modes of directionality.

My fourth factor emphasized the profound links between 'being a woman' and fleshiness. I suggested that in our culture 'femaleness' is linked to modes of embodiment in ways that make it not simply the converse of maleness. As such, it is hard to think of a female self in terms of the dominant models of selfhood and personhood that have come down to us from history. The category 'female' troubles the notion of a free or autonomous and individualized 'soul' or 'mind' that merely inhabits the flesh, as well as the notion of a 'synthesis' of temporal moments that is imposed by the thinking 'I'. To talk of a woman remaining the same self from birth to death involves an emphasis on fleshy continuity, rather than structures maintained by – or provided by – the *cogito*. As such, female identity is non-hylomorphic: it erupts from flesh, and is not a form (*morphe*) imposed on matter (*hyle*) by the mind in a top-down way.

The fifth feature of the female subject-position that I mentioned was the only one which was based on the experiential. I indicated that the historical link between the female and an embodied, fleshy self brings with it conflictual expectations that are necessarily bound to the paradoxicality of the female subject-position. Given the aberrant nature of the 'female' with respect to the 'normal' (male) modes of selfhood and personhood in western modernity (and postmodernity), the female subject has to negotiate the monstrous, the inconsistent and the anomalous. Positioned somewhere between freedom and autonomy, on the one hand, and embodied and thing-like passivity, on the other hand, the female subject either registers, or conceals from herself, the 'peculiarity' and 'singularity' of her own 'difference' from the norm (which is male) and from other modes of 'deviation' (which are both female and male).

In this chapter I intend to use my own experience of discrepancy when considered against an androcentric norm of selfhood and embodiment.[1] I will start with a critique of the account of the body/ mind relationship provided by one of the key theorists in the new field of 'cognitive semantics', and then gradually move on to build an alternative model of identity that seems better to fit the five discrepant features of female identities as set out at the start of this chapter. As such, this chapter starts out with a critique of one current model of selfhood: a model that sets itself up as providing a universal 'truth' about the structures of the human psyche and about the 'logical' structures necessarily based on 'our' experience of embodiment. However, this chapter then moves on to reconstruct – not deconstruct – notions of 'subject' and 'object', 'self' and 'not-self'. In so doing, I register experiential differences amongst women, but argue that these divergences do not rule out a reconceptualization of identity in ways that take the female as norm.

I should emphasize, however, that the argument that follows is not intended to suggest an alternative absolute 'truth' – that of a forgotten 'female' reality – that those working in cognitive semantics have forgotten or repressed. Instead, I will be concerned to disturb various 'common sense' beliefs about what embodiment and selfhood involve. I will offer a revisionary metaphysics, but also go on to indicate that this revisionary descriptive ontology does not reflect a newly emergent 'common sense'. However, I also do not mean to imply that there are not those in our culture who already think in these ways. Nor do I intend to suggest that such an ontology is only suitable for women. Although I have developed the alternative ontology in order to think more productively about the lived modes of embodiment that characterize female selves, this model for conceptualizing identity also meshes with the experience of many males in the late twentieth century. It is not only women – but also some men – who now experience themselves as 'monsters' in relation to the descriptions of the self on offer in cognitive semantics: descriptions that, as we will see in the next chapter, in effect rework one of the dominant models of selfhood in western modernity – that of Immanuel Kant.

The Body in the Mind

In one of the key texts in cognitive semantics, *The Body in the Mind* (1987), Mark Johnson seeks to base strong metaphysical, epistemological and logical claims on a experience of embodiment that is described as universal. He tells us:

> Our encounter with containment and boundedness is one of the most pervasive features of our bodily experience. We are intimately aware of our bodies as three-dimensional containers into which we put certain things (food, water, air) and out of which other things emerge (food and water wastes, air, blood, etc.). (p. 21)

Johnson then goes on to spell out five characteristics of the containment relationship from which I infer that, for him, the self is inside the body in much the same way that a body is inside a room or a house. Bodies are containers that protect against and resist external forces, whilst also holding back internal forces from expansion or extrusion. All that is other is on the outside, and the inner self is shielded from the direct gaze of others by skin and other non-transparent features of the body-container (p. 22).

Mark Johnson develops large claims on the basis of this analysis. Containment is made one of a number of underlying structures of embodiment which shape and constrain the imagination via gestalt-type patterns or 'schemata' which operate at a preconceptual level. Johnson adds bodies to an essentially Kantian account of the functioning of the understanding. Difference between humans is registered, but only at a superficial level. 'Meaning' is a product of the way an experience, a theory, a word or a sentence is understood by an individual who is 'embedded in a (linguistic) community, a culture, and a historical context' (p. 190). However, at the most basic level, this understanding rests on schemata of the imagination which arise out of the (universal) experience of embodiment. Cultural differences act merely as an overlay which affects the way meanings are encoded and transformed; underneath there is human sameness. We all inhabit bodies in similar ways. We all experience the body as a container for the inner self.

These claims are elaborated in another book of cognitive semantics: George Lakoff's *Women, Fire, and Dangerous Things* (1987). Because we live in bodies and move between containing spaces via our bodies, we recognize that 'Everything is either inside a container or out of it' (p. 272). Our grasp of the law of Boolean logic which determines the relationship of classes – of 'P or not P' – is grounded on our experience of being embodied selves. Lakoff refers to Johnson's 'proof' to establish the links between the law of the excluded middle and the intimate experience of bodily containment. 'On our account, the CONTAINER schema is inherently meaningful to people by virtue of their bodily experience' (p. 273). Lakoff addresses the problem of whether there might be cultures that fail to fit the cognitivists' model of meaning, but secures the 'universal' status by arguing that even the Australian aboriginal language of Dyirbal – which puts together in a single category human females, water, fire and fighting – obeys the logic of containment, despite the strangeness of its classificatory system (pp. 1, 92ff). Just fitting things into categories relies on the fundamentally human experience of embodiment.

For feminist theorists who have long complained of the neglect of the body by western philosophers, the development of cognitive semantics might seem a promising move. However, as I read Johnson's and Lakoff's accounts of embodiment, I register a shock of strangeness: of wondering what it would be like to inhabit a body *like that*. And that is because

I do not experience my body as three-dimensional container into which I 'put various things' – such as 'food, water, air' – and out of which 'other things emerge (food and water wastes, air, blood, etc.)'.

The shock intensifies as I note that the description purports to be of a preconceptual experience that is so immediate and obvious that it would command intuitive assent. I live/have always lived in the west, and am a full – and I hope sophisticated – user of the English language. So why do I feel so alienated as I read these descriptions of what it is like to inhabit a body? How is it that the cultural imperialism of the cognitivists' model can manage to position aboriginal Australians within the 'universal', whilst managing to make me feel singular: odd; a freak; outside the norm?

My reaction raises a dilemma that constantly confronts feminist philosophers. By the double use of the definite article in the title of his book – *'The' Body in 'the' Mind* – Mark Johnson gestures at a level of the universal which must be registered by all linguists and philosophers interested in the cognitive aspects of language and metaphor. However, feminist philosophers know that in terms of actual practice philosophers throughout the history of the discipline have taken (and continue to take) male life-patterns, personalities and life-experiences as ideals and/or norms. Thus, writing and reading self-consciously as both a philosopher and a woman, a feminist philosopher always confronts a methodological dilemma. She cannot easily know whether her failure to recognize herself as fitting the philosophical paradigms is due to simple idiosyncrasy; to issues of sexual difference; to historical and cultural factors; or to the fact that the theories were false even for males at the time they were propounded.

In order to think which of these explanations is right in this instance, I will explore five competing hypotheses for my 'failure' to recognize myself in the cognitivists' description of what it is like to inhabit a body. In so doing, I will gradually displace the focus of my analysis away from an experientially based semantics and confront current debates within feminist theory regarding the nature of boundaries. I will end not by demanding their deconstruction in the manner of many postmodern and poststructuralist feminist theorists, but by using the perspective of sexual difference in order to reconstitute the inside/outside, self/other, body/mind divides. In so doing, I will turn to the sciences for new models for thinking identity in ways that will, in effect, undermine the semantic and epistemological approaches to the questions of philosophy that have dominated Anglo-American philosophy this century. I will also be countering those who would seek to model woman's 'otherness' in terms of a Lacanian or Derridean understanding of language.

This latter issue will be considered in more detail in chapter 5. However, here it can be noted that looking to the sciences allows us to theorize a 'real' that is not 'unspeakable' or 'ungraspable', but that nevertheless falls outside the framework of the Lacanian symbolic that looks to the (masculinized) self for its model of identity.

These are the five hypotheses that I will examine for my 'failure' to think of my body as a container:

1 That I am idiosyncratic or peculiar: that there is something the matter with my image schematism, perhaps in the manner of Oliver Sacks's freakish case studies in *The Man Who Mistook His Wife for a Hat* (1985). Sacks's subjects are neurologically peculiar in the way they match bodily and mental imaging to concepts, and thus in terms of the way that they use language.
2 That I do think in the bodily containment schemata that Johnson outlines; but that something (too much philosophical introspection? some crisis or trauma?) has made me repress this awareness.
3 That I, as a woman, have a different relationship with my body than does a man, and that the containment model for bodily boundaries and selves might be more typical of male experience.
4 That I as a westerner living in the last decades of the twentieth century no longer think in terms of the outmoded science that this container model presupposes; that something (exposure to media, science fiction, fiction, philosophy) prevented me ever developing (at least in a way that I can recall) the containment model.
5 That there have in the west always been alternative models for thinking the relationship between self and body and self and not-self; and that for contingent reasons (reading? social environment?) exposure to these alternative models prevented the container model from ever really taking hold in my case.

Hypothesis One: Idiosyncrasy

Taking these hypotheses in order, I wish first to reject the claim that my response might simply be idiosyncratic. I do not (I think!) manifest the bizarre disturbances of correlation of spatial co-ordination and behaviour and word-usage which characterize Oliver Sacks's neurological case studies. I am not like Sacks's 'Disembodied Lady' who has lost proprioception and with it the ability to feel her body. It is not that I – like Sacks's Christina – am unable to remember or even imagine what embodiment is like (1985, pp. 49–50). As support for my claim that I am not merely a freak, I would appeal to Emily Martin's analysis of the way women talk about themselves as bodies in *The Woman in the Body* (1987).

This book is particularly relevant in this context, since Martin is an anthropologist who applies to western female subjects some of the techniques of metaphor analysis which Lakoff and Johnson adopted in their earlier, co-authored, *Metaphors We Live By* (1980). Emily Martin uses the imagery employed by women to describe their reproductive processes (menstruation, pregnancy, childbirth, menopause) to determine the woman-as-body-image of the subjects she interviews. Arguing that different models are prevalent in the language of middle-class and working-class women, her work demonstrates that women of all classes quite frequently talk about their bodies in ways that suggest extreme fragmentation, with the self located 'outside' the body. Working-class women tend to resist altogether the spatialized model of the body as 'container' of eggs, blood, womb, and so on. Although many of the middle-class women do use the language of bodily containment and inner functioning to describe their reproductive processes, a number of them also go on to note that 'this internal model was not relevant to them' (1987, p. 106). Martin thus interprets the containment imagery as the educated subjects' (unsuccessful) attempts to make body-image coincide with the 'medical' or 'scientific' renditions of female reproductive processes. Her research thus implicitly undermines any simplistic understanding of bodily containment as a universal schema, as well as any attempt to restrict the containment schema to a homogenized 'western' self.

Hypothesis Two: Repression

The second hypothesis for explaining my cognitive failure to image my body as a container posits that I do (unconsciously/subconsciously) think in this way; but the sense of my body as a container is subject to repression. Now this might be true. But it would be hard to know how to test this. I have very clear memories of my childhood relationship with my body: of the way the 'I' was 'zoned' into body regions that were at war with other body regions; but I have no memory at all of thinking of my body of some form of containing, safe space that encloses an 'I'. It is true that I use such linguistic expressions as 'pain in the foot'; but are those who infer from this some reference to spatial or territorial containment right so to do? Not all prepositions referring to bodily happenings are ones of containment. We might now think of the preposition 'in' primarily in terms of the mapping of a location, but cartography was only developed as a science with the invention of compasses, globes and other 'objective' means of recording place towards the end of the fifteenth century. In Latin and old English the term 'in' did not necessarily imply spatial containment or territorial inclusion. And nor does it now, as the *Oxford English Dictionary* shows via some quite bewildering examples of diversity of usage: 'in a blaze', 'in tears', 'in all weather', 'in confidence', 'in crayons', 'in the Lord'.

Anorexics carry on referring to things happening 'in' their bodies, even though a number of researchers have shown that typically they 'grow up confused in their concepts about the body and its functions and deficient in their sense of identity, autonomy, and control'. It seems that in many ways anorexics feel and behave as if 'neither their body nor their actions are self-directed', and as if their bodies are 'not even their own' (Bruch, 1978, p. 39). Anorexics typically describe their 'stomach' as rejecting the food – a process based on horror at food or disgust. Helmut Thomä quotes from one treatment session with a female anorexic:

> Bottle – child – disgust, if I think of it – injections – the idea that there is something flowing into me, into my mouth or into the vagina, is maddening – integer, integra, integrum occurs to me – untouchable – he does not have to bear a child – a man is what he is – he need not receive and he need not give. (Thomä, 1977; quoted Bell, 1985, p. 16)

This anorexic woman uses disgust to try to produce body boundaries; but the way that she talks about herself makes it simultaneously clear that she does not view herself as a spatial container closed off from the outside.

In *Powers of Horror* (1980b) Julia Kristeva ascribes to the mechanism of disgust a constitutive role in the formation of identity during the process of weaning:

> *nausea* makes me balk at that milk cream, separates me from the mother and father who proffer it. 'I' want none of that element, sign of their desire; 'I' do not want to listen, 'I' do not assimilate it, 'I' expel it. But since food is not an 'other' for 'me', who am only in their desire, I expel *myself*, I spit *myself* out, I abject *myself* within the same motion through which 'I' claim to establish *myself*. (p. 3)

According to Kristeva, the boundary of the body and the distinction between self and not-self is established through the processes of repulsion which occur at a preconceptual stage and before the infant has clearly demarcated the boundaries between self and 'other', self and mother. Inner space is thus not known intuitively or immediately, but is secured only via an expulsion of things that cannot be embraced within its borders.

In the Kristevan model identity is secured at the level of the imaginary; before the child is inducted into language (and hence in Lacanian terms before entrance into the realm of the father). Disgust operates at the level of the pre-oedipal *féminin*. What is entailed by this claim will become clearer in chapter 5, as I explore the Lacanian system that provides the grounding for Kristeva's thought. We will see there that for Lacan there is no necessary connection between femininity and women. And the same is true for Kristeva also. The words of the anorexic filled with disgust at drinking from a bottle might lead us to question this, however. The female anorexic in the above example – and ninety per cent of all anorexics are female – knows that the normalized female body is permeable; penetrable; with the potential of becoming more-than-one body through a gradual process of growth and the labour of separation. The boundaries of the female anorexic's body – in so far as they are establishable at all – are insecure and thus require careful policing. And this observation thus leads on to a consideration of the third hypothesis for my failure to register my body as a container with a self safe 'within' and the dangerous other on the outside: the claim that this is typical of women.

Hypothesis Three: Female

There is a good deal of work by psychologists, artists and theorists of opposing political persuasions that shows that females in our society employ space differently – even whilst young – and that this can be detected by observing their games, their bodily movements and the projects that they devise for themselves. The problem, however, is in deciding what this difference means, particularly if what we are asking is whether this shows that women typically lack an awareness of their bodies as containing spaces. Thus, on the basis of research conducted on boys' and girls' games in the 1940s and 1950s, Erik Erikson concluded that girls' bodies destine them towards a preoccupation with inner space that fits them for child-bearing. Supposing that all females must experience their bodies as empty containers until filled by pregnancy, Erikson asserts that 'in female experience an "inner space" is at the centre of despair even as it is the very centre of potential fulfilment. Emptiness is the female form of perdition . . .' (1964, p. 121).

This 'inner space' or 'void' is presented as a 'clinical observation' of what determines women's personalities, potentialities and development. As such it becomes a biological 'fact' that each menstruation is experienced – presumably subconsciously – as a form of 'mourning' over lost potentialities, and that menopause effects a permanent 'scar' on women's psyches (p. 121). With such false (and implausible) universals in the public domain, it is not surprising that many feminist theorists should have gone to the opposite extreme. Like Marianne Wex (1979), they frequently write as if female space-manipulation is entirely a function of socialization, and can thus be modified, in ways that allow public – and hence also private – body-space to be reclaimed.[2]

Via anorexia, slimming, cosmetic surgery, the fashion industry and simply the way they stand, move or play, women discipline their body boundaries intensively (Bartky, 1990, pp. 63–82). In her classic *Throwing Like a Girl* (1990), Iris Marion Young has ascribed the constricted posture adopted by middle-class, white women in western societies when stretching, reaching, catching, throwing and moving generally to the construction of a spatial field surrounding the female body which is experienced as an enclosure, instead of as a field in which her intentionality can be made manifest. But why this occurs and what it shows about the phenomenological body-experience of women is a matter of dispute. Not only is there the obvious difficulty that women exist in a patriarchal reality and hence use the same language as men to describe the body/mind relationship, but there is also a surprising lack of work on masculine embodiment.

Some recent theorists, such as Elizabeth Grosz (1994, pp. 198ff) and Paul Smith (1988), suggest that the 'repressed' of masculine consciousness might be the sense of the flowing out and away of ejaculated bodily substances. On this model, the boundaries of normal male selves are secured against flowing out, in ways that would make sense of Mark Johnson's account of (male) selves as 'three-dimensional containers' for food, water, air and the like: 'out of which other things emerge (food and water wastes, air, blood, etc.)'. Since the same logic would not apply to the construction of female identity, we could indeed have a hypothesis here that would explain why I as a woman would fail to recognize this as a description of what it is like to inhabit a body. My identity is secure precisely because I do not envisage my body-space as a container in which the self is inside: protected from the other by boundaries which protect against and resist external forces, whilst also holding back internal forces from expansion. I construct a containing space around me, precisely because my body itself is not constructed *as* the container. Adopting the container body-ideal and inhabiting a female body would be likely to pathologize me, as the anorexic's commentary on herself as a container lacking integrity would tend to show. The anorexic desires the completion that pertains to the ideal male body-image.

Fascinating though such speculations are, it makes little sense to treat these claims about the phenomenological relevance of male and female body-spaces as testable psychological hypotheses. It is more useful to consider these psychoanalytic claims in terms of the metaphysical boundaries of the self and the not-self as constructed in the history of western philosophy. This is the move that Luce Irigaray makes – most notably in 'Volume without Contours',[3] 'The "Mechanics" of Fluids' (in Irigaray, 1977) and 'Is the Subject of Science Sexed?' (1985). According to her, identities based on spatial containment, substances and atoms belong to the *masculin* imaginary, and what is missing from our culture is an alternative tradition of thinking identity that is based on fluidity or flow. It is important to note that Irigaray is not making an experiential claim: she is not asserting that women's 'true' identity would be expressed in metaphors and images of flow. What she is claiming, by contrast, is that identity as understood in the history of western philosophy since Plato has been constructed on a model that privileges optics, straight lines, self-contained unity and solids. According to Irigaray, the western tradition has left unsymbolized a self that exists as self not by repulsion/exclusion of the not-self, but via interpenetration of self with otherness.

Irigaray's analysis of the history of philosophy can be read as a discourse on boundaries. She explores the way that woman/the mother serves as the protective screen, barrier and the (unobtainable) obscure object of desire that remains always just out of reach. Woman is both the boundary/the Other against which identity is constructed, and that which confuses all boundaries. In the tradition of philosophy that reaches from Plato and Aristotle to Freud and Lacan, woman falls both inside and outside the boundaries of the human, the genus, the self itself. Although I will later argue against Irigaray's tendency to close down the history of philosophy to a trajectory in which sameness is always privileged over difference, viewed as a commentary on woman as boundary *Speculum of the Other Woman* (1974) makes a powerful case.

For Plato woman was – despite the apparent moves towards egality in *Republic* Book V – the state of existing transitional between animal and man. Thus, he tell us in *Timaeus* that a male who failed to live the good life would be reborn as a woman; a second failure would mean that the next rebirth would be as an animal (*c.*350 BC, 42b–c, 90e–91a). Furthermore, as we have also seen in the last chapter, for Aristotle woman was literally a monster: a failed and botched male who is only born female due to an excess of moisture and of coldness during the process of conception. A female lacks essence: that which makes an entity distinctively itself and not something else. She is both of the species and not of the species: she is neither the goal of the processes of reproduction, nor is she able to pass on to her offspring characteristics which represent the species.

In Aristotle the female is instead allied with matter – an undifferentiated mass of unshaped material – which can only be formed into an entity by the *logos* or generative power of the male. Change is hylomorphic: an active form (male) imposed on homogeneous matter (female). As such, the female cannot even be said to have an identity of her own. She represents the indefinite: neither one nor two. The female sex is, literally, 'this sex which is not one': the title of Irigaray's book of 1977. Woman is indefinite; she exists at the margins – an enigma – but in ways that problematize the human subject placed at the centre of the traditions of philosophy and psychoanalysis.

Irigaray uses the techniques of philosophical terrorism to mount raids on past philosophers and psychoanalysts. And via these skirmishes an intriguing conjecture emerges: that the privilege given to form, solidity, optics and fixity in the history of the west has, in effect, delayed us from developing alternative models of identity which would treat flow or the indefinite in its own terms, and not simply as a stage en route to a new developmental fixity. In Irigaray's texts the Lacanian account of the 'fixing' of identity in the mirror of the (M)other's eyes becomes symptomatic of the west's refusal to think a self that is permeated by otherness. Psychoanalysis is presented as a repetition of the philosophical moves of Kant and Hegel, in which self is only established via opposition to, and spatial symmetry with, a not-self. Via insistent questioning and mimicry, Irigaray suggests that this model of identity is the oedipal one of the world of the boy: in which self-identity is established against an oppositional other.

What remains unsymbolized in the whole process according to Irigaray is mother/daughter relations: the formation of a self which can be permeated by otherness, and in which the boundary between the inside and the outside, between self and not-self, has to operate not antagonistically – according to a logic of containment – but in terms of patterns of flow. Irigaray is not claiming, of course, that western philosophy and psychoanalysis have not theorized female identity. Her claim is simply that it has been understood according to what she will term the '*hom(m)osexual* economy of the same' (1974, pp. 102–3). Irigaray puns on the French term '*homme*' – the (supposedly) gender-neutral 'man' – as she points to the fact that woman has been conceived as 'like' the male, only 'different': both lacking and excessive. To put it in my own language: the male has acted as both norm and ideal for what it is to count as an entity, a self or a person.

Hypothesis Four: *Fin de Millénium*

I will return to the problem of how identity might be constructed according to a different logic, but first I want to comment on a problem with Irigaray's position: one that bears on the fourth hypothesis that might be used to explain why I 'fail' to think of my body as a three-dimensional container. This was the hypothesis that my deviance from the container model was not to be ascribed to my sex, but to the fact that I am a westerner living in the last decades of the twentieth century. For although it is surely true that in the history of western science there has indeed been a privilege given to solidity, space as a container and the mechanics of solids, there have been alternatives developed since around the time of the 1914–18 war. Indeed, during the last twenty-five years the mathematics of fluidity and the indefinite have become central to the scientific tradition. If Irigaray wants to characterize an emphasiz on the indefinite as 'feminine' science, then we now live – and also kill each other – with the techniques of femininity.

New scientific, mathematical and topographic models now stand alongside hylomorphism, with its attempt to explain change by reference to an active form imposed upon an inert, homogeneous and unshaped matter. Classical science is reductionistic. Although not strictly speaking limited to static models of form, it is limited to conceptualizing and measuring movement or change in linear terms (Kwinter, 1992). Modern topological theory became possible on the basis of work produced by the mathematician Henri Poincaré during the years 1889–1909. On the new model, matter is not in any sense homogeneous, but contains an infinity of singularities which may be understood as properties that emerge under certain, but very specific, conditions. What topology does is provide a way of mathematically explaining the emergence of those singularities. Thus, 'ice' and 'water' as well as 'magnetism' and 'diffusion' are forms on the new model, and these forms all depend on singularities for coming into existence. As Sanford Kwinter puts it: 'A singularity in a complex flow of materials is what makes a rainbow appear in a mist, magnetism arise in a slab of iron, or either ice crystals or convection currents emerge in a pan of water' (1992, p. 37).

Although the classic differential calculus could successfully plot the movements of a body within a system, it did so by regarding the system itself as closed and as incapable of change. By contrast, in the new theory it is possible to measure not only translational changes within the system, but also transformations that the system itself undergoes. Because of this shift of reference, modern topological theory is able to offer a dynamical theory of birth, manufacture and change, in which form is not something that is imposed on matter, but which instead irrupts in matter or is a state of matter. On the new model there is no fundamental difference between states and forms: forms simply are structurally stable moments within the evolution of a system (or space). Indeed, for a new form to emerge on this model the entire space or system is itself subject to transformation or distortion from exterior spaces or systems. We are dealing here with open dissipative systems and with leaks of energy into and out of the system. Spinoza's account of substance mentioned in the last chapter comes forcibly to mind. We can also think of Bergson, and my advocacy of his account of fluid 'essences' or 'forms' emerging from within the shifting patterns of flow.

To make the links with Irigaray more explicit, Irigaray claims that the west has been slow to develop a science that can measure and model patterns of the indefinite and of fluidity. However, even if that science was slow to come into existence, it does now exist. The new topologies see form as no more than an apparent and temporary stability in the patterns of potentiality or flow. To quote Kwinter:

> A potential is a simple concept: anything sitting on one's desk or bookshelf bears a potential (to fall to the floor) within a system (vector field) determined by gravity. The floor on the other hand is an attractor because it represents one of several 'minima' of the potential in the system. Any state of the system at which things are momentarily stable (the book on the floor) represents a form. States and forms then are exactly the same thing. If the flow of the book on the shelf has been apparently arrested it is because it has been captured by a point attractor at one place in the system. The book cannot move until this attractor vanishes with its corresponding basin, and another appears to absorb the newly released flows. (1992, p. 37)

Forms – apparent stabilities – are brought about only because dissipative systems tend to remain in equilibrium or at a state of rest up to a certain threshold of destabilization. However, because energy pervasively leaks to and from the system and is also transported between macro- and micro-levels within the system, such destabilization could occur at any moment and be triggered by an apparently minor deformation in a contiguous system. Catastrophe theory is one of the models for mapping this. Slow and gradual change within a system can suddenly flip over to produce different patterns of behaviour, of turbulence or of random patterning. To borrow a celebrated example from chaos theory (another of the new topologies), something as slight as the flapping of a butterfly's wings in the Pacific might act as the trigger that 'causes' a hurricane at the other side of the world.

For my purposes, what matters is not the details of the theories, but the metaphysics that underlies many of these new topological models. For on at least some of these models – and here it is necessary to register two different traditions in the complex multidisciplinary field that comprises 'chaos theory'[4] – forms are not fixed things, but temporary arrestations in continuous metastable flows, potentialities or evolutionary events. If we think about boundaries, then, from the point of view of the new sciences, the boundaries of our bodies need not be thought as the edges of 'three-dimensional containers into which we put certain things . . . and out of which other things emerge'. The boundary of my body can also be thought as an event-horizon, in which one form (myself) meets its potentiality for transforming itself into another form or forms (the not-self). Such a body-boundary entails neither containment of internal forces nor repulsion of/protection against external forces. Those who are aware of themselves as centred 'inside' an insulated container – free from contamination by the threatening other which is located on the 'outside' – are captured by an illusion generated by the mechanisms of ego-protection, as well as by spatial models inherited from a classical science which is now no longer compelling. To imaginatively construct the self as inhabiting a 3D 'container' is to treat the self as a system that is closed: a form of narcissism. It means blocking out other systems (including other selves) from which and to which energy might leak. It means to refuse to model the self as a dissipative system.

In terms of the way the new topological paradigms impinge on feminist theory, Donna Haraway can be read as seeking to align 'woman' with the new sciences. In 'A Manifesto for Cyborgs', Haraway takes the image of the cyborg – a machine/human hybrid – and evokes an imaginative schematism in which there is no nostalgia for the (illusory) oneness of the autonomous (male) self. What Haraway is doing here can be easily misunderstood and assimilated to just one more form of North American postmodernism in which the impossibility of defining what women have in common is supposed to entail the necessity of abandoning gender as a framework for political organization. But what Haraway is rejecting is not feminism as such, but merely the dialectics of self versus other as figured by those feminists who both recognize the one-ness of the self as illusion, and identify with the 'other' rather than the self. This is Haraway characterizing the type of feminism that she will reject: caught between excess and lack, impaled on a model in which the male provides the standards for self-unity:

> The self is the One who is not dominated. . . . To be One is to be auto-nomous, to be powerful, to be God; but to be One is to be an illusion, and so to be involved in a dialectic of apocalypse with the other. Yet to be other is to be multiple, without clear boundary, frayed, insubstantial. One is too few, but two are too many. (1984, p. 177)

Haraway is, in effect, rejecting the predominant forms of deconstruct-ive, cultural and psychoanalytic feminist theory. She envisages another form of feminism which charts the self – and disruptions to the 'system' of patriarchal control – by cybernetic schemata made possible by the new topologies.

> Our bodies, ourselves; bodies are maps of power and identity. Cyborgs are no exceptions. A cyborg body is not innocent; it was not born in a garden; it does not seek unitary identity and so generate antagonistic dualisms without end (or until the world ends); it takes irony for granted. One is too few, and two is only one possibility. . . . The machine is us, our processes, an aspect of our embodiment. We can be responsible for machines; *they* do not dominate or threaten us. We are responsible for boundaries; we are they. (p. 180)

Thus, read carefully and in terms of the new scientific paradigms of form and identity, it can be seen that Haraway is embarked on much the same project as Irigaray: of asking that female identity be concep-tualized in terms of a different understanding of boundaries. This emerges perhaps best in her 'The Biopolitics of Postmodern Bodies' (1988), in which she analyses discourse relating to the immune system. Haraway uses a biological vocabulary; but interpreting her points back into the language of the new physics, we can understand her bodies as dissipat-ive systems. It is not that all identity disappears on this model; but rather that identity has to be understood not in terms of an inner mind or self controlling a body, but as emerging out of patterns of potential-ities and flow.

Coming back to the hypotheses as to why I might not have picked up the 'container' view of my body (with the self safe inside it), I would like to suggest that hypotheses three and four are not mutually exclus-ive, and perhaps even reinforce one another. Hypothesis three ascribes my 'failure' to schematize my body as a container to sexual difference. I have offered limited support for this thesis by indicating how women in western culture are precariously placed by reference to boundaries. This is both because the primary model of the self is based on that of an individual who does not have to think of himself each month as potentially evolving into two individuals; and also because women are accustomed to seeing 'humanity' and 'persons' described in ways that both include and exclude women. Hypothesis four ascribed my 'failure' to historical factors. The fact that new models for self/other, mind/body relationships are now prevalent in science – and hence, whether we are aware of it or not, in fiction, computer-games, advertising and in the media generally – can provide a resource with which women are able to resist the schemata that would render bodies containers and selves autonomous. Although the new models provided by the sciences by no means constitute a new 'common sense', they do involve alternative models for the phenomenology of the self to those provided by 3D spatiality. However, it is also notable that the richest accounts of phenomenological experience (Sartre, Merleau-Ponty, Beauvoir) also stressed potentiality, force, flow, over stasis and containment. There always has been more than one way of thinking the mind/body, self/other relationship in the history of the west.

Hypothesis Five: Alternative Histories

This brings me to the fifth and final hypothesis that I wish to consider: that my 'failure' to think of myself in terms of a container might be ascribed to currents in the history of western thought that preceded the new sciences. Again, I want to say that I see this hypothesis not as a contrast to the two preceding explanations, but as an additional factor. Kwinter describes catastrophe theory as a 'fundamentally Heraclitean "science"' (1992, p. 39). We can also find in Nietzsche a model for individuation that conceptualizes the ego as an (unstable) balance between different, overflowing sources of energy. Thus, Nietzsche claims throughout his mature writings that 'life simply *is* will to power', and that, as such, a 'self' is a collective that 'will strive to grow, spread, seize, become predominant – not from any morality or immorality but because it is *living*' (1886, § 259, p. 203). The self is 'living' whilst it is expansive, but it expands only until it finds some energy field that it cannot appropriate.

For Nietzsche, health or individuality is not a given, but something that is only maintained via a war of energies. Whatever does not kill a living entity makes it stronger, and resistance is what forms the boundaries of the ego. Thus, the Nietzschean body does not involve a containment which entails protection against external forces or which holds back internal forces from expansion. On Nietzsche's model the boundaries of the self are potentially fuzzy, and hardened only by the processes of appropriation and expansion. The dangers come from within as well as without: decadence and disease simply are the tendency for the parts to exert energies in an anarchic way and act independently of the whole. Death is merely an intensification of this process, and entails dissolution into the micro-organisms that constitute any apparent unity.

Although this antagonistic account of self/other differentiation is not identical to modelling individuality in terms of leakages of energy between levels of system or contiguous systems, it certainly provides a model for thinking the self that involves an acceptance of flux. Furthermore, although antagonism and conflict mark the Nietzschean world into an infinity of sub-systems, in discussing the overman Nietzsche also suggests a less conflictual form of energetic relationships: via the economy of the gift. Thus, the potential overman, Zarathustra, finds a productive 'chaos' within the 'selves' of his followers, and seeks to exploit it: 'one must still have chaos in oneself to be able to give birth to a dancing star' (1883/5, Pt 1, p. 129). Indeed, Zarathustra's own 'virtues' involve an 'overflowing' of the energies that constitute 'self' and 'other' via the 'will-to-power'.

The move 'back' to a Heraclitean science has not simply occurred in the new physics, but was already present in the writings of Friedrich Nietzsche at the end of the nineteenth century. Henri Bergson can also be read as developing a Heraclitean model in which 'becoming' is privileged over 'being', as we saw in chapter 2. Furthermore, both of these writers were important influences on modernist and avant-garde art. Thus, Bergson's emphasis on 'flux' and 'flow' influenced the Cubists, the *Fauves*, and also the Futurists. (See Antliff, 1993.) And in this respect it is significant that Sanford Kwinter developed his account of the new topological models of form in the context of an analysis of a futurist triptych by Umberto Boccioni which he also links with Bergson's description of movement as more basic than matter. (See Kwinter, 1992, p. 36; and Bergson, 1896, pp. 201ff.)

I am not then disagreeing with Irigaray's suggestion that patterns of meaning and inference have in the west been shaped by containment metaphors and relationships. However, I am denying that this sense of the self as housed by a container is common to all socialized western subjects. Indeed, the homogenizing of the west in this fashion is a dangerous political move. The potentiality of thinking beyond the predominant models of the self/other, mind/body schemata has been severely limited by the tendency in poststructuralist and postmodernist feminist theory to look back at that history and find only an 'economy of the same'. It is on this point that I depart most radically from Irigaray, who, despite criticizing Lacan for his synchronic treatment of language and the imaginary (and despite being profoundly influenced by Nietzsche), views the history of western philosophy since Plato as a unitary symbolic system.

As we will see in more detail in chapters 5 and 6, Irigaray finds only one oedipalized – and masculinized – model of the self in the history of the west. This model becomes more sophisticated as it evolves, but remains caught within a logic that privileges form, solidity and optics over the indefinite, fluidity and touch. For Irigaray, the history of western philosophy remains the expression of a seamless masculine imaginary. For her, therefore, change can only come from attempting to symbolize that which exists but which has remained unsymbolized in historical times: mother/daughter relations. It is this relationship that forms the 'other of the Other': a position of speaking/viewing from beyond the masculine symbolic that orthodox Lacanians would fiercely deny. Although I agree with Irigaray as to the prevalence of the masculine model for the self, I do not see the history of the west as homogeneous. There have been singularities within it. Openings come from the writings of some familiar philosophers, such as Nietzsche, Diderot, Kierkegaard, Bergson or Foucault. But we need also to look in some unfamiliar places: in texts by past women writers who register that they must count as abnormal, peculiar or singular in terms of the dominant models of the self – and then go on to make imaginative or theoretical adjustments. (See Battersby, 1994, 1996; also B. Martin, 1991.)

If the emphasis is on generalities (about philosophy, science or 'the west'), singularities (and hence women) can be overlooked: they are merely exceptions to the rule. By contrast, the new topologies work with singularities. Indeed, singularities embody radical transformative potential. By adopting the paradigm of patriarchy as a dissipative system, feminists can register the centrality of masculine models of identity to all existing symbolic codes, without becoming trapped in an impossible dualism: of having to choose between the (over-pessimistic) strategy of deconstruction or the (over-optimistic) strategy of searching for a place to speak from that is beyond the symbolic. Dissipative systems are not closed: there are other systems both without and within. Without a model of the system of patriarchy as itself a dissipative system, speaking from the position of 'Otherness' – even from the position of 'the other of the Other' which in chapters 5 and 6 we will see Irigaray positing – has limited political point. Applying insights from the new topologies allows us to see how patriarchy might itself be inherently unstable as a system, and hence how the slight flapping of the wings of a feminist butterfly might – metaphorically – provide the trigger that would enable it to flip over into a state of radical change.

Revolutionary Spaces

At this point I need also to emphasize again the difference between my own position and more standard treatments of the 'feminine' (or *féminin*). Having registered thát it is the male self that is privileged as unitary and contained in the history of the west, postmodernists, deconstructionists and poststructuralists have frequently proceeded to argue for an abandonment, transgression or deconstruction of boundaries. I hope it is clear from the argument that I have mounted here that I would sharply disagree. Without talk of identity (and hence also of boundaries), I do not see that there can be a basis for responsibility or action, including political action. What I have been wanting to stress throughout this chapter is that not all talk of identity involves thinking of the self as unitary or contained; nor need boundaries be conceived in ways that make the identity closed, autonomous or impermeable. We need to think individuality differently, allowing the potentiality for otherness to exist within it, as well as alongside it. We need to theorize agency in terms of patterns of potentiality and flow. Our body-boundaries do not *contain* the self; they *are* the embodied self. And the new sciences give us topological models for imaging the self in these terms.

Some recent uptake of these new topologies has, however, been fundamentally misleading. Thus in a recent book, *Flexible Bodies* (1994), Emily Martin has taken further the model of metaphor analysis that characterized her earlier work, *The Woman in the Body*. Once again she explores the use of metaphors by contemporary American subjects in describing their bodies. This time she explores the language used by both sexes; and this time also her analysis is less satisfactory. Thus, Martin looks to the discourse of disease and health – particularly AIDS and the immune system generally – and argues that there has been a breakdown in the metaphors which are currently employed to understand the relationship between self and not-self. Martin suggests that the metaphors used by present-day Americans show that they are 'coming to think of their bodies as complex systems embedded in other complex systems' (p. 115). However, the key to the new metaphorics for being an embodied self is represented as 'flexibility'.

Puzzlingly, Martin uses an analysis of the notion of a 'complex system' found within chaos theory to help make her case, whilst then moving speedily from the metaphorics of the new physics to the very different metaphorics of the body as a 'loosely coupled system' taken from manufacturing or service organizations. It is within discussion of the latter framework that the human body is represented as: 'a flexible organization [that] can respond quickly to changes in its environment and can initiate changes in innovative ways' (p. 144). The argumentative slide shows that Martin has failed to register the power of the new physics to disrupt that which gets characterized as an identity or a 'form'. Thus, she seeks to combine an ontology of flux with an ontology of flexibility, as she charts 'the delicate outlines of an emerging new common sense, entailing changes in notions of identity, groups, wholes or parts' (p. 13). But despite the paragraph (p. 144) which juxtaposes these two conflicting conceptual networks, there could not be anything more at odds with an ontology based on flux than one that is based on flexibility.

Flexibility involves an adaptation of 'the same'; by contrast, an identity based on flux entails a far more profound morphological irruption. Thus, on the one hand, the new metaphorics that Martin detects in contemporary American culture generally privileges a self that has a pre-existent identity (and then flexibly 'responds' or 'reacts' to changes acting within and without). On the other hand, the Heraclitean model of identity suggested by the order-out-of-disorder stand of chaos theory, by Nietzsche, Irigaray and also by Bergson, entails not flexibility, but generation (and degeneration and regeneration) based on singularities.[5] Here, as Martin herself puts it, the complex system is generated, is subject to decomposition and recomposition 'in a continuous flow of its components' in a kind of Heraclitean 'dying and becoming' (1994, p. 118). Thus, in the case of fluidity (but not in the case of flexibility), new identities are born out of difference; self emerges from not-self; and identity emanates from heterogeneity via patterns of relationality.

What Martin's research shows is not a new 'consensus' which represents a new 'common sense', but traces of conflicting ontologies currently operational within everyday discourse. Furthermore, the notion that this is 'new' is also too simple. The strand of contemporary thinking about the relation between self and not-self that privileges flux has been prefigured by various (fairly isolated) voices in western modernity and pre-modernity. Thus, my own turn to the sciences is not intended to provide some new model of 'consensual' reality that reflects the needs of this 'postmodern' age. Nor am I claiming that all women *do*, as a matter of empirical fact, fail to think of themselves in terms of the containment schemata. It is rather that feminists *need* – for political ends – to exploit the difficulties of containing female identity within the schemata provided by classical science and metaphysics, and use the resources provided by contemporary science and the history of philosophy to think selves, bodies and boundaries in more revolutionary terms.

The rethinking of the female self that I am demanding does not entail a cognitivist claim: it is not necessary to essentialize a specifically female experience. Instead, looking towards the new sciences for a different understanding of the mind/body and form/matter relationships allows us to theorize a 'real' beyond the universals of an imagination or a language which takes the male body and mind as ideal and/or norm. Positing this 'real' in terms of a fluid force-field and a network of power relations gives us a way to move on beyond the deconstruction of boundaries, and towards the reconstruction of the subject/object and self/other divides. In this respect I agree with Donna Haraway in her alliance with the cyborg. It is time to turn our backs on those forms of feminist theory that castigate all science and all western philosophy as rationalist, masculinist and weapons of the enemy. It is time to investigate the imaginative schemata that old philosophies and new sciences offer us for re-visioning the female self.

However, my (temporary) alliance with cyborgs should not be read as aligning me with those postmodernists who look to machine/human hybrids – and clones and cell replications – for different understandings of the embodied self. For women are not clones; and neither do they reproduce like amoebae. The reproductive work of bearing and rearing children involves necessarily non-equal power relations, as well as a body that is messy, fleshy and gapes open to otherness – with otherness 'within', as well as 'without'. However, to explore the metaphysical underpinnings of the current debates about the self and sexual difference, I need first to move further back into the history of philosophy.

This historical analysis will position Kant as typical of modernity, and will claim that postmodern feminisms often fail to capture the specificity of the Kantian 'I' that is not self-present to itself (in the manner of Descartes's *cogito*) and is also only ever established indirectly – by the construction of spatio-temporal objects that act as oppositional to the self. As such, this historical account will begin to show why the question of developing a feminist metaphysics of both subject and *object* is now urgent – more urgent, I would claim, than the epistemological questions that are now dominating contemporary feminist debate. The consequences of positioning Kant (and not Descartes) as central to modernity for feminist strategies will be considered further in chapter 5. First, however, in chapter 4 it is necessary to outline the Kantian system: including his (inadequate) attempts to contain 'birth' and 'growth' within the horizons of a 'nature' that is constructed by the 'I', and what he himself described as a 'chasm' in his thought relating to sexual difference.

4
Kantian Metaphysics and the Sexed Self

To further the aim of developing a feminist metaphysics that takes as norm the female subject-position, this chapter will tease apart two notions that seem to be too easily conflated in contemporary feminist theory in both the postmodern and liberal traditions – the self and personhood. I will be arguing that both the concept of person and the account of the transcendental subject that Kant offers us are sexed, but in very different ways. Whereas personhood, as defined by Kant, is based on ideals of autonomy and closure that remain inimical to any form of embodiment, for Kant the transcendental self exists only in relation to bodies. The problem with the Kantian transcendental self is not its inability to bring mind and matter into relationship, but rather that the self is established via an oppositional relationship to matter – a matter, moreover, which is dead, and which is hence incapable of birth or of 'morphing' into new shapes or identities. It is only the notion of the 'person' as conceived by Kant that requires radical deconstruction. The transcendental ego, by contrast, requires relocating. It needs embodiment – and hence also matter – capable of radical metamorphosis and evolutionary change.

In order to explain the essentials of the Kantian position, it is useful to employ the analogy of spatio-temporal sunglasses. For Kant, neither space nor time is an absolute reality that is objectively 'out there'. However, space and time provide the necessary framework through which we read experience. Just as everything that we see through pink sunglasses looks pink, so the Kantian model suggests that we perceive what we call reality through spatio-temporal sunglasses which we are unable to remove from our noses. The world – the phenomenal world – that we perceive is represented in terms of 3D spatiality in which we construct objects, and a unitary temporal sequence by which these objects are related together into an ordered whole. What does the constructing is the transcendental imagination. This is what synthesizes the data supplied by the senses and brings those data (or 'intuitions') under rules ('categories') supplied by the understanding.

For Kant, the world that we encounter through our five senses is always and only the phenomenal world. As such, it is an illusion: a construction of the senses, the imagination and the understanding. However, the phenomenal world is not a merely arbitrary world; it is only via this act of imaginative synthesis that it becomes possible to say 'I' and to distinguish self from not-self. The ego could not know itself as self unless it simultaneously constructed a world – the phenomenal world – that is other than self. This what Kant means by describing his philosophical 'turn' as a revolution as fundamental as that of Copernicus (1781/7, Bxxiifn.).[1] It is man's transcendental ego – not matter or God – that constitutes the creative centre of the knowable (phenomenal) world.

Transcendental schemata of the imagination provide rules for bringing images under concepts and thus provide the primary 'glue' that enables us to attain the notion of a world 'out there' and to which the self belongs:

> However exaggerated and absurd it may sound, to say that the understanding is itself the source of the laws of nature, and so of its formal unity, such an assertion is none the less correct, and is in keeping with the object to which it refers, namely, experience. (1781/7, A127)

Not only nature, but also the self itself is constructed by the activities of the transcendental imagination. And this is where the sunglasses analogy breaks down. It is not that there is a pre-existent self onto whose nose the sunglasses fit. Rather the space/time sunglasses are really rules for attaching images to concepts and bringing them to consciousness. It is these rules that create the notion of a unitary ego, as well as the body that inhabits the merely phenomenal world.

Kant thus makes a threefold distinction, and this distinction applies to both objects and subjects. As well as phenomena (appearances) and noumena (things-in-themselves), there is also the transcendental self and its correlate, the transcendental object. To take each of these three aspects of the self in turn: the noumenal self is the self as it really is in itself, seen without the space-time filters and the categorial rules that impose order on the world. Although we cannot know that such a self exists, we also cannot know that it does not exist. Indeed, in moral action, Kant insists, it is necessary to act *as if* the self were a noumenal self. The second aspect of self is the phenomenal, and involves the self as an object of awareness, and hence as structured by the framework of intuitions and rules that impose spatio-temporal form. The third aspect of self, the transcendental, provides the grounding for the fleeting impressions of the phenomenal world – and also for the phenomenal self. This 'I' supplies the necessary framework of rules and imaginative schemata that we use to unify experience into a coherent (single) self and its correlate world. As such, the transcendental is relational: it links more firmly with the 'phenomenal' than with the 'noumenal' worlds.

Kant insists on a sharp divide between the transcendent and transcendental self (1781/7, A296). A *transcendent* self is altogether divorced from the spatio-temporal world; it is another name for the noumenal and, as such, would exist in an some absolute, objective realm, its ontological status in no way dependent on the beliefs, imaginings or experiences of human subjects. About the transcendent self we can *know* nothing: not even that it exists. Although Kant offers grounds for *hope* that it does exist and that it will persist beyond death, that it is a unity and capable of agency, he carefully delimits knowledge so that it stretches only to the spatio-temporal grid that is imposed by man upon the manifold of data. Speculative metaphysics about 'pure' being – the noumenal – is strictly debarred. On the level of knowledge, speculative metaphysics only re-emerges as part of reason's drive towards an infinity that must forever elude the understanding. However, this illegitimate (but nevertheless irresistible) drive leads curiosity onwards, and thus contributes indirectly towards the ordering of Kant's systematized, space-time world.

Sexing 'Persons'

Since the transcendent/noumenal self exists outside that space-time grid, the transcendent self cannot be an object of knowledge. A phrase that Kant uses in *The Metaphysics of Morals* as a synonym for '*homo noumenon*' is 'person' (1797, 6:418, p. 174).[2] As such, a 'person' is not an object of epistemology, but a matter of faith: the kind of faith, Kant argues, that is involved in moral action and in treating another *as if* he were an end in himself. 'Person' is a technical term within the Kantian system, and is restricted to some varieties of moral and legal selves. By 'person' Kant means a subject whose actions are impelled neither from forces outside the self nor from natural instincts and drives that stem from the body. A 'person' is rational, autonomous and free. His actions are engendered by his own autonomous will. Kant's substantive moral claim is that although we cannot prove that humans are 'persons', we have a duty to treat ourselves and others as if they were persons – as autonomous, self-directed agents who could appropriately be held responsible for their actions. Legal personhood builds on this notion of responsibility. Via personhood, rights are conferred on the citizen. Personhood is associated with freedom of choice, and this is something that the state needs to respect if the law is itself to be moral.

In *Religion Within the Limits of Reason Alone*, Kant divides the determining forces of human behaviour into three main types: animality; humanity or '*Menschheit*'; and personality or '*Persönlichkeit*' (1793, 6:26, pp. 21ff). 'Animality' involves a merely machinic mode of agency, based on instinctual drives or passions. Humanity is a step up, and involves the ability to judge, reason and posit ends for action based on a comparison between the self and others. However, humanity does not imply personhood since the latter entails free-will and pure rationality; a 'person' has the capacity to act in accordance with the dictates of reason and the will. Reading Kant's remarks about women in the *Anthropology* (1798) and elsewhere in the light of this division it becomes clear that for Kant women are fully animal and also human; but he is much more ambivalent about their status as persons. Sometimes women are granted personhood, as in the discussion of marriage in *The Metaphysics of Morals* (1797, 6:278, pp. 62–3). However, more frequently, women are refused personhood, as when Kant groups women with domestic servants, minors, apprentices, hairdressers and other so-called 'passive' citizens who are described as lacking 'civil personality' (1797, 6:314, p. 92).

This tendency to treat women as non-persons is also evident elsewhere in Kant's writings. Thus, whereas Kant's essay 'What is Enlightenment?' (1784) defines enlightenment in terms of the independence of opinion and speech appropriate to autonomous and rational persons, in the *Anthropology* Kant carries on insisting that within the public sphere husbands (or other males) should act as the guardians of women, and speak for women (1798, 7:209, pp. 79–80). Perhaps most strikingly, in his early *Observations on the Feeling of the Beautiful and Sublime*, Kant went so far as to deny women the capacity for duty-based action and autonomous choice that he would later make the foundation for personhood:

> The virtue of a woman is a *beautiful virtue*. That of the male sex should be a *noble virtue*. Women will avoid the wicked not because it is unright, but because it is ugly; and virtuous actions mean to them such as are

morally beautiful. Nothing of duty, nothing of compulsion, nothing of obligation! . . . I hardly believe that the fair sex is capable of principles, and I hope by that not to offend, for these are also extremely rare in the male. (1764, 2:231–2, p. 81)

As I have argued in more detail elsewhere (Battersby, 1995), Kant's account of the sublime in his later writings on aesthetics also reveals the intimate connection between issues of sexual difference and his notion of personhood. Kant's critical writings carry on linking the sublime with superior modes of moral action, and also carry on refusing women this kind of enjoyment that proves moral superiority. For Kant, the appreciation of the sublime is the negation of fear (1790, § 28, pp. 119–21). It involves a kind of pleasure-in-pain that originates when the mind runs up against its own limitations via contact with the boundless, the infinite and the indefinitely great (§ 26, pp. 107ff). In this, the 'sublime' contrasts with the 'beautiful', which is a form of aesthetic pleasure that arises when the mind creates a (phenomenal) reality that is in harmony with man's (limited) understanding and imagination (§ 9, pp. 62ff).

Since the sublime is linked with immensity or with objects of great power or force, to appreciate it requires both an appreciation of the terribleness of the object surveyed and a (simultaneous) transcendence of terror (§ 28, pp. 119–20). For Kant such terrible pleasures are closed off to all except the 'moral man' who has been educated into confidence in the power of his own ego over nature (§ 29, pp. 124–5, 128). Kant does not make it a logical impossibility for a woman to thrill to the sublime; but he regards this as undesirable. Thus, Kant claims in the *Anthropology* that it is important for women to be timorous in the face of physical danger. Since the future of the human race is in the hands – or rather the 'womb' – of women, to ensure the continuance of the species women should respond to fear (1798, 7:306, p. 169). But this necessary *female* concern with physical safety would block the transcendence that is necessary to the experience of the 'sublime'.

This is an important rider to the Kantian system, since his moral philosophy makes a strong distinction between acts performed out of mere 'feeling', and those performed out of 'respect' for the 'universal law'. Kant's aside links 'women' to the 'feelings' he downgrades in his critical system: love, fear, sympathy, and the like. 'Man' has a duty to act in accordance with the 'universal' moral law – but 'man' here means 'men'. It is *men* (males) who are obligated to respond to that state of 'respect' or heightened attention (*Achtung*) that Kant also associates with the experience of the sublime (1790, § 27, pp. 114ff). And here again it would seem that Kant's women are not strictly 'persons', since 'personhood' entails treating the self as purely rational, and transcending mere emotion (1793, 6:26ff, pp. 21ff). Neither fully rational ('persons'), nor fully instinctual ('animals'), women are 'humans' who can follow commands, but who are also denied the kind of self-generating, transcendent inner freedom that makes a 'person' a kind of junior God-the-father who *creates* himself and a new reality through his own actions.

In the *Anthropology* Kant goes on to require males to act as the protectors of women – not to demand that women's weakness should be corrected by women themselves (1798, 7:306, p. 169). Since Kant then proceeds immediately to make reference to a kind of 'cultivated propriety' that masquerades as true (duty-based) virtue, we can be sure that he had recognized the implications of this sexing of human excellence. Here, in the context of thinking about women and children, Kant cautiously approves of actions motivated by feeling. Like Carol Gilligan (1982), who will be discussed further in chapter 10, Kant implicitly genders morality. Males have to be motivated only by that 'respect' for the 'universal' law which is 'duty'. Women, by contrast, are rather creatures of empathy and care. Unlike Gilligan, however – and like Lawrence Kohlberg, Gilligan's teacher and eventual opponent – Kant gives an explicit grading of the duties of 'law' over the emotions of empathy, love or sympathy. Kant has devised a so-called 'universal duty' of controlling and transcending emotion; but it is a duty that gains its legitimacy only by taking the male body and mind as ideal and norm.

Sex and the Transcendental Self

I will now argue that just as Kant's women both do and do not count as 'persons', so also Kant's women both are, and are not, granted the status of having a 'transcendental' self. A more extended analysis is, however, required before this can become clear since, at least at first sight, the Kantian woman would seem to be denied noumenal transcendence, but secure in her fleshy immanence – and hence able to be intermeshed with the phenomenal world at the level of the transcendental. However, as we will see, the supposedly 'universal' structures of the Kantian space-time world also make the female body – and her transcendental 'I' – a transitional structure, somewhere between self and not-self. As we will see, his model of spatiality is inadequate to deal with the relation between self and other within the (pregnant) female body; and this is serious since this model of spatiality is what upholds the persistence and stability of the transcendental 'I' itself. Furthermore,

Kant represents matter as entirely passive and dead, in a way that is also essential to his system. He situates the self against a permanent and changeless 'substance', and acknowledges sexual difference as a monstrous 'chasm' in his thought.

Unlike personhood (which is transcendent for Kant), the *transcendental* self attaches to the phenomenal world. As such, it is centrally implicated in the network of space-time schemata by which we identify and reidentify entities. Although never an object of direct awareness or introspection, it is, according to Kant, that which has to be presupposed by the knowing or experiencing subject if the manifold data of experience is to be taken up by the mind and formed into one overarching, unified, coherent body of knowledge. The transcendental self is not itself within the space-time framework or grid that the Kantian subject imposes on the world. It is rather part of the *a priori* grounding which makes the space-time framework operative. It governs the conditions of experience. It is not embodied; but since it is established only in relation to space-time embodiment, it is not incompatible with embodiment.

For Kant, the transcendental self requires – and cannot exist without – imaginatively constructing a cut from its other: the transcendental object or not-self. This is an important point, and one that marks a clear contrast between the Kantian 'I' and the third feature of the female subject-position discussed in chapters 1 and 3 above. Kant's transcendental subject is not a Cartesian rational subject, self-centred and transparent to itself. The transcendental self requires its other. Indeed, the transcendental self requires a body. But *what* body each self requires brings back in issues of sexual difference. As we will see, despite making the transcendental ego no more than a (necessary) fiction, Kant treats space and time in ways that mean that the ego is located *inside* the bodily container, and all that is 'other' is outside – in space. Indeed, the container is described in ways that mean that inner bodily spaces cannot make a difference in terms of identity.

Within the Kantian system, it is only the noumenal self or 'person' that lacks any connection with material substance. The Kantian transcendental self does not say '*Cogito, ergo sum*', 'I think *therefore* I am', in the manner of Descartes. The Kantian self is known not through introspection, but by a complex process of synthesizing intuitions and experiential data and bringing them under spatio-temporal rules in ways that allow him to separate self from not-self. Implicitly in the first edition, and much more explicitly in the second edition of the *Critique of Pure Reason*, Kant establishes the existence of the transcendental self only by arguing for the illusory and unsatisfactory nature of Descartes's 'I think therefore I am'.

As Kant puts it in the *Opus Postumum* (*c*.1788–1801) in a way that is merely an extension of his critical position: 'I must have objects of my thinking and apprehend them; otherwise I am *unconscious* of myself (*cogito, sum*: it cannot read "*ergo*")'. He goes on: without objects of thought, the 'I' would remain unable to think its own self – 'thoughtless, even with a given intuition, like an animal, without knowing that I am' (21:82, p. 248). Although Descartes envisaged animals as made out of dead matter (with merely the appearance of animation), for Kant, animals are alive and have representations, but are not-fully-conscious. Because animals fail to bring their representations under concepts, they have also failed to construct a unified self in ways which would enable them to mark self from not-self. Thus, if there were a subject who failed to make the self/not-self divide, s/he would remain *unconscious*, like an animal. The Kantian self is not inherently solipsistic, as was the Cartesian soul. It always exists in relation to objects, and these objects constitute the 'transcendental object' or 'not-self'.

Furthermore, as we are about to see, this transcendental object that acts as the counterpart to the transcendental self belongs with (and, indeed, serves to ground) the spatialized, phenomenal world. Thus, the transcendental 'I' is also kept in potential – but also problematic – contact with matter through a kind of 'cut' from its 'other', or 'not-self', which is marked off from the 'I' and designated not 'subject', but 'object'. Put in simple terms, Kant's argument is that the transcendental self can never be directly observed, but that the notion of a single self is a necessary presupposition if I am to impose order onto the multifarious chaos of intuitions that I receive via my senses. If the world appears as an ordered whole to me (as it does), then Kant's argument is that this can only occur if I refer these experiences to a single consciousness (the transcendental self) that persists through time and that lasts from birth to death. Also, as an analogue to this transcendental ego I need to refer the synthesized space-time data onto an external reality that would anchor it in bodies. This reference point is 'the transcendental object, that is, the completely indeterminate thought of *something* in general. This cannot be entitled the *noumenon*' (1781/7, A253).

Jacques Lacan's reworking of this Kantian account within a psychoanalytic frame will be subject to critique in chapters 5 and 6, and alternatives to Kant will also emerge in subsequent chapters. Kant himself argues most forcefully for the necessary relationship between the transcendental self and spatial embodiment in the 'Refutation of Idealism' (1781/7, B274–9) and the subsequent amendment in the footnote to the second 'Preface' (Bxl–xli). In both these passages Kant argues against

Descartes's claim that it is possible to prove the existence of the self simply through introspection. To say 'I am' involves saying more than 'I think', since 'I am' entails persistence through time. To know that 'I am' it is necessary to grant a stable time-frame with changes happening within it. Without positing bodies in space as permanent reference points against which change would be measured, the persistence of the self through time could not be secured. If I locate this permanence simply within myself and my own representations, then I have no standard by which to secure my identity through time.

Identity – at least in the realm of phenomenal reality – entails constructing self against an inert matter and rigidly excluding real novelty or change. This is necessary to Kant's system, since he has argued that the unitary self can only be established by reference to *permanent* bodies in space. Thus even introspection – 'inner' experience which is temporal – 'depends upon something permanent which is not in me, and consequently can be only in something outside me'. Temporal self-awareness is made dependent on a spatial construction of permanent bodies in space:

> The reality of outer sense is thus necessarily bound up with inner sense, if experience in general is to be possible at all; that is, I am just as certainly conscious that there are things outside me, which are in relation to my sense, as I am conscious that I myself exist as determined in time. (1781/7, Bxlifn.)

Without supposing an underlying sameness in the not-self ('matter' and the underlying 'transcendental object'), there will be no permanent reference point which enables me to discriminate between real and imagined stability and establish an 'I am' that persists through time.

The insistence on permanent substance is often taken to be an over-statement of the argument that Kant requires at this point. Why must Kant insist on permanent (unchanging) bodies and not simply refer to bodies that are relatively long-lasting, in order to establish the unity of the self through time? Whether or not substance is sempiternal, it is, however, crucial to Kant's argument that matter should be conceptualized as inertial and as incapable of 'morphing' into new shapes and identities. On the Kantian system, a caterpillar that could turn into a chrysalis and then, subsequently, turn into a butterfly can count as the 'same' creature only after criteria for sameness have been established by reference to an ontologically more primitive matter – 'substance' – that persists through change and is itself, therefore, incapable of such evolutionary change.

Kant and Bodies

According to Kant, it is, then, permanent matter that grounds the self, and makes it possible for us to posit the transcendental self as a unity that persists through time. But although this matter is 'out there', it is only constructed as such by the self. Permanent, inert matter is the self's necessary other. Kant uses the phrase 'outer sense' to indicate the process of awareness of things other than the self. And it is at this point that we see Kant's difficulties in regard to his own body. Kant consistently refers to knowledge of things in space as involving 'outer sense' and also insistently links knowledge gained through outer sense as knowledge of that which is 'other' than the 'I'. Thus, for example, in order to establish that space is not a concept based on experience, Kant first argues that via outer sense 'we represent to ourselves objects as outside us' and then equates 'something outside me' with 'something in another region of space from that in which I find myself' (1781/7, A22–3). 'Inner sense', by contrast, is described as temporal and as having an essential bond to my own experience of myself. It is through inner sense that I introspect, but also all knowledge that comes through outer sense is then mediated via inner sense.

Here we see how Kant's own body slips between inside and outside. Thus, on the one hand, he insists that *all* appearances come to us ordered by inner sense into temporal sequences, whereas only some appearances are spatialized via outer sense. On the other hand, he also wants to make a sharp distinction between the 'inner' and that which is in space. Time, he says, 'is nothing but the form of inner sense, that is, of the intuition of ourselves and of our inner state. . . . [I]t has to do with neither shape nor position, but with the relation of representations in our inner state' (1781/7, A33). Introspection has no spatial co-ordinates: nothing 'inner' is spatializable; everything 'outer' is in space and is also other than me.

Kant needs a body in order to be a self; but the body he needs is neither self nor not-self. Thus, in the *Metaphysical Foundations of Natural Science* which Kant writes in the interim between the two editions of the first *Critique*, we find Kant illustrating the curious status of the embodied self via some comments which show his difficulties in dealing with inner bodily space:

> In things themselves (e.g., in the case of those rare human beings in whom, upon dissection, all their parts agree according to the physiological rule

with those of other human beings, but all the viscera are found displaced
to the right or to the left, contrary to the usual order) there can be no
conceivable difference in the internal consequences. (1786, 4:484, p. 23)

Kant goes on to argue from this observation that we can represent to
ourselves the difference between these mirror-selves 'in intuition', but
that these inner differences cannot be 'intelligibly explicated'. And he
interprets this as an argument in favour of his position that space is
merely a framework that we impose on our representations and that it
does not pertain to things-in-themselves.

If we think of these comments in terms of the foetus within the
mother's womb, we see that Kant would be unable to 'intelligibly explicate' the fact that the foetus might be facing to the left or right, with
its head to the top or to the bottom. Inner bodily space falls outside
Kant's framework for spatiality and temporality. He cannot adequately
explicate the spatial status of his own inner organs – let alone the foetus
as a potential self within the womb. Kant has a model of selfhood that
means he is unable to think otherness within the self, the foetus in the
womb – or even the relation between the inside and outside of the body.

Kant's inability to 'intelligibly explicate' inner bodily spaces also links
with what he himself describes as a 'chasm' in his thought relating to
the issue of sexual difference. As he writes in a 1795 letter to Schiller:

> The organization of nature has always struck me as amazing and as a sort
> of chasm of thought; I mean, the idea that fertilization, in both organic
> realms [of nature], always needs two sexes for the species to be propag-
> ated. After all, we don't want to believe that providence has chosen this
> arrangement, almost playfully, for the sake of variety. On the contrary, we
> have reason to believe that propagation is not possible *in any other way*.
> This gives us a look-out point towards something visually elusive (*eine
> Aussicht ins Unabsehliche*), out of which, however, one can make noth-
> ing at all – as little as out of what Milton's angel told Adam about the
> creation: 'Male light of distant suns mixes itself with female, for purposes
> unknown.' (1902–83, vol. 12, p. 11)

Here, at a point in his life when the system was supposedly complete,
Kant looks out over and into a precipice, and contemplates the pro-
spect of something about sexual reproduction which necessarily eludes
the gaze, and for which his critical philosophy can provide no clue.
Using conventional eighteenth-century metaphors relating to an 'out-
look' over the sublime landscape, Kant positions sexual difference as a
terrifying chasm that his imagination cannot fathom.

One and a Half Sexes

And here a short historical digression is necessary to explain why Kant should have found himself contemplating this 'chasm' – despite the fact that he also claimed that his critical system could explain all of nature's laws. During the eighteenth century pre-modern models for the relations of the sexes in the reproductive process had broken down. As Thomas Laqueur puts it, 'Sometime in the eighteenth century, sex as we know it was invented' (1990, p. 149). A predominantly 'one-sex' model of human nature was being replaced by a predominantly two-sex model which conceptualized the two sexes as radically different in kind. On the earlier, one-sex, model women were simply inferior, outside-in males. A woman's vagina was a penis that was 'folded' inside her. The female foetus lacked sufficient bodily heat for full bodily development to take place, and to enable the penis to emerge from inside the bodily 'folds'. This is the rationale for the description of the female sexual organs provided by Galen (AD *c.*130–200): 'Turn outward the woman's, turn inward, so to speak, and fold double the man's [genital organs], and you will find the same in both in every respect' (quoted Laqueur, 1990, p. 25).

According to Galenic orthodoxy (which remained dominant in medicine until the eighteenth century), women contributed semen or 'seed' to the processes of reproduction, as did also the male. But the female seed was also regarded as ineffectual on account of woman's lack of heat and hence formative power. The female was lacking in intensity and degree, as well as being extensively and spatially deformed by coldness. Other theorists in this pre-modern period – influenced primarily by Aristotle's metaphysical biology – represented the female as simply a container for the male seed and as providing the matter (*hyle*) which is shaped hylomorphically into identities by the defining formula (or *logos*) in the active male formative principle (Battersby, 1989). In either case, individuals emerge as form (male and active) shapes matter (female and inert). Both of these hylomorphic hypotheses were, however, under threat in this late eighteenth-century period as the uterus was no longer being standardly represented simply as an imperfectly developed penis 'folded' double with the body space. From this time on, it became problematic to think of women as simply underdeveloped (cold) males, or as lacking any formative force of their own – although plenty of philosophers carried on using the pre-modern vocabulary to represent sexual difference.

Kant himself did not opt for this conservative position. He recognized 'femaleness' as something *other*: something that cannot simply be explained by reference to a failure in intensive magnitude. But then a new problem emerged. If females have formative force, of what use is maleness? Why might not family resemblance and identity of species be secured solely by the contribution of the female to the processes of reproduction? Even more disturbingly, if females continued to be represented as providing the 'matter' to the reproductive process, might not matter itself be self-forming? Why isn't identity secured solely at the level of bodies? The new 'two-sex' model of reproduction reopened old debates in the history of philosophy. Seen in this context, it is clear that Kant's inability to 'intelligibly explicate' inner bodily spaces means that he is also unable to think sexual difference on the classic, Galenic model that made females simply outside-in – inferior – males.

To think sexual difference Kant needs to represent to himself woman as something other than a failed or monstrous male. But Kant is unwilling to pursue the consequences of this hypothesis. He clings to a model in which the unitary self is only established by reference to embodiment, but the self closes over the inner bodily spaces in ways that mean that any possibility of inner, sexually differentiated organs must fall out of account. The self is constructed as a homogeneous unity through its differentiation from the 'object'. As such, it seals over fractures within the self and treats the body as closed in ways that prevent Kant from thinking determinate biological principles that could account for sexual difference – or for the growth of another self within the womb. Furthermore, in Kant's mind-constructed reality it is important that 'matter' is only shaped into determinate 'things' by the spatio-temporal 'forms' that are imposed by the mind. Important elements of hylomorphism are retained.

Kant is not a 'realist' in a Platonic or Aristotelian sense about 'forms', 'essences' or 'universals'. He bans knowledge of speculative metaphysics, and hence of the Platonic world of Ideas. Nevertheless, Kant's descriptive metaphysics of the phenomenal world remains hylomorphic, with 'form' so to speak impressed on matter in a top-down way. Until matter is shaped by the spatio-temporal 'forms' of the mind, it has no identity. And when matter is shaped it is also necessarily shaped, Kant would claim, in accordance with the laws of Newtonian physics in which matter is inertial, and in which all change of motion or in a state of rest involves forces that act on that matter from without. Thus, Kant makes 'substance' a mind-constructed 'permanent' (the grounding of the 'transcendental object'), and he describes all change as resulting from a transformation that acts on this underlying 'sameness' from without. Change does not irrupt in substance itself. Matter is not by itself capable of giving birth to new possibilities or new entities.

Kant, Biology and Evolution

For Kant, change is modelled in terms of transfer of energies between one closed and homogeneous body and another – and this works well enough when Kant is thinking about physics, and thus about change in terms of the transfer of motion between existing 'bodies' or 'things'. However, Kant's model of change leads him into difficulties when he moves on to consider biology in the second part of the *Critique of Judgment* (1790). Thus, when thinking about the birth of new species in the so-called 'Critique of Teleological Judgment', Kant finds himself dissatisfied with his model for thinking change as always only acting on 'dead' matter. In particular, it is his attempt to think the role of the female in reproduction – or why there are two sexes, and not just one – that opens up the 'chasm' in his thought.

Kant can provide no analogous 'solution' for thinking the problems of biology to that provided in the 'Antinomies' section of the first *Critique*. There Kant made it clear that Newtonian spatiality is not the underlying 'real', but simply a necessary framework for the mathematization of space. However, if Kant were also to insist that biological 'species' were no more than mind-imposed 'rules' that simply order matter, then 'man' would no longer be marked out as a special 'species' in the way that Kant wants. Indeed, the very notion of a natural 'species' as a 'real' or an 'essence' would itself be under threat. On the other hand, if matter were allowed to be self-forming, and fall into patterns that were not products of the spatio-temporal schemata, then the starting point of Kant's critical system would also be put into question. In other words, if matter can form itself, why must Kant treat all form as if imposed by the structures of the human mind?

From the late 1780s on (the time of the composition of the *Critique of Judgment*), Kant engaged with contemporary biological, archaeological and philosophical debates about the ability of nature to evolve new forms and species in a fluid, self-organizational way. (See Zammito, 1992.) Kant registers the hypothesis of nature as a primal mother of self-forming matter, but in his published writings he is brusquely dismissive of this 'monstrous' thought. Instead, he retains matter as the 'sublime' and unlimited 'manifold' which remains chaotic and unstructured unless formed into shapes and identities via the synthetic power of the imagination. Kant thinks an 'other' that is prior to the formation of the self, but folds this material difference within the bounds of a critical system that makes matter inert – in much the same way as Galen folded the specificities of the female body within a shape and a sameness that privileges the male.

Again and again in the 'Critique of Teleological Judgment' Kant returns (rather desperately) to his 'official' solution to the problems of biological growth: that nature involves 'organisms' that are homogeneous wholes that act so much as unities that we model them as machines that were designed. Even though we cannot *know* that there was an architect or God-like creator that created the whole, the regularity of Kant's mind-constructed nature everywhere presents us with the overwhelming experience of 'purposiveness without purpose'. And this leads us to treat nature and natural kinds *as if* they were designed. However, because Kant thinks change primarily in terms of Newtonian machines, he also finds himself presented with profound difficulties in accounting for radical novelty or birth. In the third *Critique* – and in the series of late essays in which Kant 'replied' to the Romantics and the radical materialists who allowed a feminine matter formative force – we see Kant's unease with the notion that nature might be construed self-forming according to a 'technic' in which organic forms develop in ways analogous to the formation of crystals from fluids which 'are more ancient than solids' (1790, § 58, p. 223).

Kant's unease is specific and centres on the notion that nature might give birth to different species and races in the manner of an 'original mother' or *'Urmutter'* (§ 80, p. 304). In prose that is unusually vivid for Kant, he outlines the argument of an imaginary opponent: an archaeologist who would make

> mother earth (like a large animal, as it were) emerge from her state of chaos, and make her lap promptly give birth initially to creatures of a less purposive form, with these then giving birth to others that become better adapted to their place of origin and to their relations to one another, until in the end this womb itself, rigidified, ossified, and confined itself to bearing definite species that would no longer degenerate, so that the diversity remained as it had turned out when the fertile formative force ceased to operate. (§ 80, p. 305)

Here within the complexities of the argument of the *Critique of Judgment* Kant contemplates the possibility of a self-morphing matter. But then Kant rudely dismisses the hypothesis, forcefully condemning those 'pantheists' who would see 'a single all-encompassing substance' manifesting itself in the activities of nature. He also condemns those who regard nature as a simple substance with a variety of attributes: 'this is Spinozism, which is only a more determinate version of pantheism' (§ 80, p. 307).

Kant needs to assign 'mother'-matter a role in reproduction; but it must be a role that doesn't interfere with the way that identity is secured by mind-imposed forms or essences. In Aristotle these 'essences' or 'natural kinds' were real; in Kant 'essences' belong to a nature whose very reality (and laws) are mind-constructed. Nature itself is created as the 'other' of the knowing subject; an infinite, but unchanging immensity that is no more than the counterpart to the transcendental self. As such, the boundaries of Kantian essences or 'natural kinds' need to be secured so that they become as certain and as 'real' as the data of Newtonian science. But here the 'facts' are less certain, and the orderliness of Kantian nature is fragile. Thus, in 1785 Kant even resorts to voicing moral imperatives relating to the purity of species and races.

In this essay on the concept of a 'human race', Kant declares it 'a fundamental principle' to recognize no power that would 'meddle with the reproductive work of Nature' in such a way as to cause hereditary change. If we were able to imagine a way of modifying 'the reproductive faculty itself, of transforming Nature's original model or of making additions to it', we would be threatened by a breakdown of natural kinds and species:

> we should no longer know from what original Nature had begun, nor how far the alteration of that original may proceed, nor . . . into what grotesqueries of form species might eventually be transmogrified. (1785a, 8:97)

Thus, despite Kant's complete failure to even imagine what role the mechanism of two sexes plays in the securing of identity across generations and time, he is incensed at the thought that man might meddle with those reproductive mechanisms in ways that would disturb the permanence of nature that his epistemological theory demands.

We can understand why Kant should have found such possibilities threatening if we look at his response to an essay by a former pupil, Johann Gottfried Herder, who used Kantian premises for non-Kantian ends. Herder contemplated the 'dissolutions and revolutions' in lineages that must have preceded 'the manifold species of earth, of minerals, of crystalizations, even of the organization of mollusks, plants, animals'. Man, Herder speculates, is merely the final product of an evolutionary process:

> He, the son of all the elements and beings, their choicest totalization and at the same time the flower of earthly creation, could be nothing but the ultimate child of nature's womb. . . . (Quoted Zammito, 1992, p. 203)

However, in his review of Herder's book Kant expresses his horror at this suggestion, as he claims that the notion of a 'family bonding' (*Verwandtschaft*) amongst species or races that emerge from 'one single generative mother-womb' is 'so monstrous that reason shrinks back' (Kant, 1785b, 8:54). The idea of such an originary mother (*Urmutter*) would suggest that all difference between natural kinds is merely accidental.

The threat that Kant is warding off in his published writings is the threat of miscegenation. His transcendental 'I' requires a realm of permanence – and a stability that stretches to racial (and sexual) types. If matter were able to form new shapes and identities via gradual evolutionary change, then there would be no clear divide between man and the animals: between consciousness and self-consciousness. Man (like the animals) might inhabit a realm of 'darkness' and 'unclear' representations, in which there is unconsciousness, not full consciousness of self. (See Naragon, 1990.) To separate self from others, representations have to be brought into the light of consciousness which operates by means of rules imposed by reason and by the transcendental structures of the imagination. These rules become otiose if matter can give birth to itself. That man might be intimately related to the animals threatens the stability of Kant's orderly nature. Against Herder, Kant explicitly maintains that 'Throughout organic nature, amid all the changes of individual creatures, the species maintain themselves unaltered' (1785a, 8:97).

The Sublime Chasm

In his critical system, Kant continued to rule out Herder's hypothesis, adopting a fundamentally hylomorphic view of nature and the material world. But in the never-completed – and frequently self-censored – collection of notebooks that constitute his *Opus Postumum* Kant plays restlessly with the radical idea that there might be a single fluid material which runs through nature and is gradually formed into identities – rigidified – not simply through the mind, but by the conflicts that resulted from the tendency of all matter to expand. At the end of his life, Kant ended up trying to rethink the role that unformed matter plays in the securing of identity at a bodily level. Here Kant – surprisingly – tries to solve his difficulties in accounting for the role played by matter in the organization of bodies by hypothesizing that: 'All matter was primordially fluid, and everything fluid was expansible, not attractive. At least, this idea is the fundamental idea' (*c*.1788–1801, 22:241, p. 56).

In these final notebooks, Kant contemplates the possibility of gradually evolving identities that can only with difficulty be reconciled with his notion of mind-formed matter. Even here, however, Kant is careful to place a stop on any real potentiality in matter to gradually evolve into new shapes and forms. Identities are formed only as matter becomes coagulated and fixed. Organic essence entails closure against change. The 'all-producing globe' is itself 'an organic body which has emerged from chaos'. Within its 'organic unity' we can see species functioning as if formed for another species in a purposive way. Using fossil evidence to suggest that man is himself a late-comer in terms of the evolution of the earth, Kant positions man as the summit of evolutionary achievement. Or rather, at this summit is man of certain privileged racial groups that exist 'either simultaneously (as, for instance, Americans and Europeans) or sequentially' (21:213–14, p. 66).

In these notebooks we can see that as Kant flirts with a theory that means humans evolve out of animals, he also becomes more and more insistent on a gradation of species and races – and on 'personhood' as that factor which marks man off from the animals. Thus, Kant develops the account of an organic body as a 'natural machine' in ways that involve thinking constancy across time and across generations: 'not, indeed, of the same individual but of a body which preserves the species, from similar materials, through intercourse of two sexes' (22:449, p. 145). This is an extension of the argument in the 'Critique of Teleological Judgment' which used the notion of certain natural (but originally undeveloped) 'predispositions' to explain the evolution of individuals within the 'organized genera' that constitute natural kinds (1790, § 80, pp. 305ff). Even in the *Opus Postumum* there is no move away from the fixity of species – or of individual essences.

In these final notebooks Kant tries to contemplate the 'chasm' about reproduction and birth that we have seen him acknowledging in the letter to Schiller. But his comments on sexual reproduction show his difficulties in allowing a metaphysics in which all empirical possibilities are not already given from the start. It is important to the Kantian system that nature be represented as constant and fixed. But it is also important to that system that nature remains no more than an infinity of possibilities created by the tension between imagination and reason – in principle explicable, if also always beyond the grasp of the mind that constructs it. Like Goethe's 'eternal feminine', Kant's 'nature' is an ever-elusive presence that draws man – males – onwards. She/it is both a receding horizon of open possibilities, yet also fixed: permanent, stable, incapable of novelty or of radical transformation. Even when Kant contemplates a less hylomorphic view of matter in his unpublished notebooks, 'nature' remains pinioned in a position of false infinity – fated to give birth again and again to races and species incapable of change.

'Nature' is described as a 'mother' in Kant's published work, and also as the 'sublime' goddess 'Isis' who is hidden behind veils (1790, § 49, p. 185fn.). Kant does not employ these conventional tropes unthinkingly. Instead, he puts them to philosophical work, and argues that the infinity of 'nature' is not penetrated by the mind. (See Kant, 1796, discussed further in the next chapter.) Instead, 'nature' acts as an indefinite and ever-receding horizon that entices the gaze. It is a feminized nature that is the elusive 'object' that acts as the counterpart to the 'I'. 'Mother' nature is magnificent and infinite. However, she is also presented by Kant as horrid, in so far as he registers the hypothesis of a 'primal mother' of self-forming matter that is not created by the 'I'. In Kant's mind-constructed reality, the 'I' keeps itself at a regulated – and respectful – distance from the 'object' and 'nature' which acts as a kind of unknowable 'excess'. Nature, matter and the 'transcendental object' are feminized; but the 'I' is masculinized in ways that position women as both 'inside' and 'outside' the 'universal' structures that govern the self.

Kantian system requires 'excess'; it requires an 'other'; it requires a 'matter' that must hover always just out of reach. But that 'other' – and matter – are ultimately constrained and pinioned in a position of fake infinity. The term that Kant employs for this receding (but fixed) infinity is the 'sublime' – a term that is used to keep 'nature', the 'object' and 'matter' at a distance and in stasis, even when that 'matter' itself seems to change. The transcendental 'I' constructs itself as persisting and stable as it confronts this 'sublime' otherness that threatens to overwhelm it. In this chapter I have suggested the 'I' that constructs this world with the 'other' at its horizon is masculinized by Kant – less obviously, but also just as thoroughly, as his notion of the 'person' who transcends all feeling, appreciates the sublime and is fully moral, ideally rational and also ideally male. Kant manipulates the transcendental ego – apparently no more than a 'necessary fiction' and 'logical construct' – in ways that mean that it fits male bodies and identities more securely than those of female selves.

Just as important is the fact that Kant feminizes the transcendental object or matter, at the same time that he masculinizes the transcendental 'I' that imposes form on the phenomenal world. This feminization of matter will be explored further in the next chapter, as I begin to show how this supposedly infinite (but nevertheless contained) feminized 'other' has seeped into recent feminist theory via Derrida and Lacan. I will be arguing with Irigaray, and against the Lacanians and deconstructionists, that to think the consequences of sexual difference for the rethinking of identity it is not enough to play with that 'nature', 'object' or 'other' that falls outside the horizons of the masculinized gaze. Deconstruction works by an attack on a 'metaphysics of presence' that is supposed to be a constant in the metaphysics of the west. However, what we have found in Kant is an account in which identity is linked with a metaphysics of absence. This absence is gendered; and in a way that will not be unduly disturbed by Derrida's playful 'veiling' and 'unveiling' of the feminized excess.

We need to inspect the Derridean starting points more critically if we are to understand how it might be possible to escape Derrida's refusal of a new ontology. Against this tradition my own concern will be to devise a metaphysics that can think identity differently, so that the self/other relationship is modelled less oppositionally than in Kant, and so that the body becomes fleshy – and no longer seems hollow. I will suggest that recent developments in psychoanalytic and poststructuralist theory remain too close to Kantianism. The body is made to seem no more than a (real) phantom with inner spaces that fall outside the bounds of the (male) imaginary. The next chapter will explore further my objections to the Lacanian and Derridean starting points, at least as they have impacted on feminist theory. It will help establish the need for a different metaphysics of identity, in which an underlying fluidity and patterns of potentiality are not contained or forced into inertness in ways prefigured by Kant.

5
Feminist Postmodernism and the Metaphysics of Absence

According to F. H. Bradley, 'Metaphysics is the finding of bad reasons for what we believe upon instinct but to find these reasons is no less an instinct' (1893, p. xiv). What I have suggested in previous chapters is that the instincts that have been privileged in the history of metaphysics have been those which attach to a male body. However, what I have also indicated is that metaphysics is not a monolithic tradition, and offers us resources for thinking self and identity otherwise. It is possible to develop a new descriptive metaphysics to describe orderings in space and persistence through time, in ways that would be more appropriate to thinking female identities. Since this last claim is at odds with much written in postmodern feminist theory, this chapter will start by exploring these divergences.

Many postmodern and poststructuralist feminists have turned to Jacques Derrida for theoretical techniques that could disturb Lacan's account of the self as an illusion that is both necessary and also masculine. In so doing, they have incorporated Derrida's attacks on the 'metaphysics of presence' alongside a privileging of 'woman' and the 'feminine'. And here the analysis of Kant provided in the last chapter serves as a useful grounding for understanding the issues at stake. I will suggest that the analysis of the self offered by Kant is much more typical of modernity than that provided by Descartes. Then I will read Lacan as reworking Kantianism, and argue that Derrida's dialogue with Heidegger about the failure of 'metaphysics of presence' leads him to offer a critique of metaphysics that misses the sexual specificities of Kant's (and Lacan's) 'metaphysics of absence'. Both of these moves have had a profound effect on postmodern feminist strategies for mobilizing the 'feminine', and for analysing gender and the self.

According to Jane Flax, within feminist theory the attack on a 'metaphysics of presence' is associated with five forms of postmodern scepticism (1990, pp. 34–7). These five modes are:

(a) the notion that the mind itself is not homogeneous, but is an effect of discursive structures;
(b) the idea that truth is not absolute or objective, but a product of contextual, partial, local and incommensurable discourses;
(c) the claim that language does not correspond to experience, but rather that experiences are shaped by language;
(d) the claim that western metaphysics covers over a different order of the 'real' – one that is unstable and in permanent flux and that slips away from binary structures, such as identity/difference or male/female;
(e) the claim that philosophy itself is a self-defeating activity if thought of as a purveyor of truth, instead of as another form of fictionalizing activity.

In *Thinking Fragments* (1990), Jane Flax goes on to develop her own doubts about such a version of postmodernism. Moreover, in *Disputed Subjects* (1993), she develops a more interesting version of postmodern feminism that has been influenced by Adorno and that looks to radicalize D. W. Winnicott's psychoanalytic object-relations theory, instead of starting with Lacan. (See chapter 7 below.) However, what concerns me here is not the (many) potentialities within postmodernism, but how a postmodernism that rejected a 'metaphysics of presence' would seem to be pushing further certain aspects of Kantianism. Thus, for Kant also the self is not homogeneous; access to absolute truths and to the metaphysically 'real' is blocked; and we are all trapped within a framework in which language (or at least our concepts) shapes experience. True, Kant positions philosophy as more than just a fiction, at the same time that he tells us that all that we can know is based on necessary fictions. True also, Kant would deny that the 'real' that is covered over by the structures of language can be said to be unstable and in permanent flux. However, the opposition to metaphysics within the traditions of deconstructionist theory has blocked exploration of an alternative ontology – and seems to be leading us further and further into an epistemological relativism that develops out of Kantianism, and away from the question of reconstructing models of identity in ways that could fit the apparent paradoxicality of the female subject-position.

Modernity and Self-certainty

In her *Gender and Knowledge* (1990), Susan Hekman moves towards feminist postmodernism by rejecting the account of the self offered in 'modernity'. Furthermore, modernity is described in epistemological terms, as a search for 'certainty' and, in particular, for 'self-certainty':

> As many critics of modernity have noted, the modern episteme is defined by the Cartesian dichotomy between subject and object. The driving force of the modern age is the search for certainty, the effort to use reason to establish absolute and universal truth. Since Descartes that certainty has been firmly grounded in the rationality of the knowing subject. Descartes' *ego cogita* [*sic*] *ergo sum* placed the certainty that is the goal of the modern episteme firmly within man himself.... For Descartes and, hence, for modernity, the subject is the self-conscious guarantor of all knowledge....
> The subject-centredness of the modern episteme has been one of the principal themes of the attack on modernism by postmodern philosophers. (p. 62)

On the basis of this analysis of modernity, Hekman argues for the need to abandon all notions of a universal, objective and absolute truth, discoverable on the basis of reason. She also rejects the 'subject/object dichotomy' (p. 103). Furthermore, since the 'rationality of the knowing subject' is presented as a fundamental part of selfhood, it is suggested that the appropriate response to Cartesian modernity is to deconstruct or overturn traditional assumptions about 'truth' and the 'subject' (pp. 47, 189). Since these are but the effects of discourse, any assertion of a 'real' comes to be linked with the twin vices of 'essentialism' and the 'metaphysical' (pp. 149, 174).

What is striking about Hekman's approach is the extent to which it foregrounds epistemological questions as central to modernity. Epistemo-logical relativism is presented as integral to the radical ('postmodern') move that will also benefit feminists. In this chapter I will question this epistemological bias (which is fairly typical of postmodernists who have also been influenced by Derrida). Instead, I will suggest that by looking at the way Kant's ontology of phenomenal existence excludes the female, new possibilities arise for thinking metaphysics in ways that can deal with the self/other relation and fleshy identities in ways that could help us think the female subject. These new possibilities for a descriptive metaphysics do not arise, however, if we follow Hekman (and Derrida), and fail to make a sharp distinction between the accounts of the self offered by Kant and Descartes. The most interesting 'postmodern' moves are not epistemological moves, and also not relativist moves. Neither are they moves that involve a denial of the kind of 'anti-metaphysical' metaphysics of becoming that were introduced in chapters 2 and 3 of this book.

Hekman does not see that what is characteristic of modernity is not Descartes's epistemological certainties, but Kant's very different account of 'subject' and 'object'. By contrast, in Foucault's essay 'What is Enlightenment?' (1984b), we see that for Foucault Kant represents the 'attitudes' of modernity in ways that do not privilege epistemology.[1] Here, the 'modern' self is constituted by its relationship to time, and through a relationship to itself that is neither 'given' nor 'certain'. Hekman claims to be influenced by Foucault, but presents his analysis through a deconstructive frame that subordinates ontological questions relating to bodies, forces and power to debates about the problem of meaning, the structures of discourse and of 'knowledge' itself (Hekman, 1990, pp. 18ff). Foucault turns into a deconstructive philosopher (p. 186), as Hekman treats the (atypical) structuralist phase of Foucault's *The Order of Things* (1966) as typical. Foucault's later rejection of discourse theory and epistemology seems not to be taken seriously; and this is not atypical of those who would assimilate Foucault's ontological concerns to deconstructive epistemology.[2]

Hekman's 'postmodern' relativism is premised on the claim that the philosophers of modernity were committed to a 'certainty' that is 'within man himself' and 'grounded in the rationality of the knowing subject'. But none of these descriptors is characteristic of the Kantian transcendental subject. As we have seen, for Kant the self is positioned as the centre of all knowable reality; but Kant explicitly attacks Descartes, and makes the self neither transparent to itself nor indubitable. In so far as the unity of the self is a necessary (*a priori*) supposition for Kant, it is only given in relation to the space-time world.

In the Kantian world, if the self dreams itself and is conscious of its dream, it has also to dream something other than self. And that something has to be spatial: it has to involve bodies. Furthermore, the self – the transcendental self – that constructs this body-filled reality can never be conscious of itself in any direct or immediate manner. The self constructs itself as self. But that self needs an object (the so-called 'transcendental object' or not-self), in order to establish itself as self. The transcendental self and the transcendental object stand in a relationship of mutual implication and interdependence.

Thus, Kant's account of subjectivity eludes the primary criticisms of those postmodern feminists who take as their target an epistemology of self-consciousness that is absent in Kant. But it nevertheless still operates in terms of a metaphysics that is gendered – and not only within the moral sphere. Kant explains identity in terms of an active, shaping form that works to constitute inert, dead matter into identities and essences; and he also locates the self within a body in ways that locate all that is 'other' (or not-self) on the outside. As we have also seen, these two features of the Kantian system are bound up with a 'chasm' that exists in his thought: a 'chasm' which makes him unable to imagine the 'purpose' of sexual difference. But this 'chasm' does not fit with the account of modernity that Hekman describes.

Hekman's analysis of modernity as characterized by self-certainty would mean that even Kant would need to be counted as postmodern. So also would the Romantics and Freud, who, during the nineteenth and early twentieth centuries, adapted Kant's account of the 'I' (Freud's '*ich*' or ego) and the 'object' (Freud's '*es*', 'it' or id), so as to make it more explicit that self-identity is fundamentally dependent on that which is unavailable to self-conscious thought. The simplicity and reality of the soul may indeed be a 'truth' of (western) modernity, as Hekman claims. However, what is in general evoked is not the overweeningly confident Cartesian 'mind' that thinks itself into existence. Rather more typical is the 'I' that is guided by the unconscious – or even the soul as experienced by this character in Julio Cortazar's novel *Hopscotch* (1963):

> The invention of the soul by man is hinted at every. time the feeling appears that the body is a parasite, something like a worm adhering to the ego. . . .
> I swallow my soup. Then in the midst of what I am reading, I think: 'The soup is *in me*, I have it in this pouch which I will never see, my stomach.' I feel with two fingers and I touch the mass, the motion of the food there inside. And I am this, a bag with food inside of it.
> Then the soul is born: 'No I am not that.' (ch. 83, p. 403)

Here Cortazar's fictional character, Horacio Oliveira, seems to start with simple Cartesianism (the sense of the body as a parasite), but establishes the 'I' only via an act of Kantian separation whereby self is known not immediately or intuitively, but only by refusing all that is *not* self – the 'bag' of the body. ' "No I am not that." ' This oppositional view of the self is recycled in much post-Kantian metaphysics, in the psychoanalytic theories of Jacques Lacan and (via Lacan) in much contemporary feminist thought. Against this tradition, I am concerned to open up a model of the self/other relationship that works less oppositionally. Chapter 3 began to suggest ways in which an underlying fluidity and patterns of potentiality might serve to constitute alternative models for the identity of the persisting self. We need to bear these fluid possibilities in mind as I now explore the Lacanian and Derridean background to the current rejection of a 'metaphysics of presence' within some varieties of postmodern feminisms.

Lacan and Kant

Feminist theory and cultural analysis in the poststructuralist and postmodern traditions have been profoundly influenced by Jacques Lacan. However, although it has become conventional in recent years to see the psychoanalytic system of Jacques Lacan as reworking the Hegelian dialectic of self/other relationships, in this chapter I will be positioning Lacan as much more firmly entrenched within a Kantian understanding of the formation of the self. Despite recent attempts to read a philosophy of history onto Lacan (Brennan, 1993), his account of the attainment of self-consciousness involves psychologizing the ahistorical moment whereby the Kantian transcendental subject establishes itself as self via a process of displacing the transcendental object. Within Lacanian psychoanalysis there is simply no room for the kind of historical detail that Hegel offers on the types of consciousness and self-consciousness that are possible in the particular temporal and logical 'stages' of the 'unfolding' of spirit.

But Lacan does resemble Hegel in so far as there is not just the individualized ego, constructing the infinity of possibilities that are 'the laws of nature' via an act of transcendental imagination. The self is no longer alone – even if it is now lonely. The self is born. Or, rather, it becomes an 'I' through a gradual process of differentiation from the mother during the early years of infancy, and via an alignment with the father which comes with the acquisition of language. However, despite the apparent presence of other consciousnesses, Lacan insistently repeats many of the Kantian moves, with a divide between a 'real' (analogous to Kant's 'noumenal') and the world that is presented via the optics of sensual desire. As also in Kant, the Lacanian self is only constructed via a 'cut' from its 'other' – the not-self that is in the Lacanian system signified as the infant's Mother.

In Lacanian psychoanalysis language is conceptualized on the structuralist model: as a network of signifiers whose meanings are determined not by reference to some external reality, nor by coherence within the system, nor simply by an appeal to empirical usage; but by the pattern of substitutions and combinations shaped by the system. It is not that Lacan denies a reality outside language, nor that he denies pre-linguistic desires, wants or needs. It is the latter that produce the underlying schematism of images that are subsequently shaped by language. However, once we are inducted into language, we cannot both access that which is 'beyond' language and also consciously speak (or write) that beyond. What is signified by the signifiers is not an external reality, but concepts – which are themselves capable of acting as signifiers at another structural level. Lacan offers us a form of transcendental idealism without the Kantian transcendental subject at its epistemological and ontological heart. Identity in the Lacanian system is only fixed through language; and self-identity is established within the system by a process of exclusions, or differences.

For Lacan any structured network can be read as a language, including the unconscious. The latter is not a psychic depth, nor a hidden place of the soul resonant with psychic energies or forces: it is rather all that has been excluded from the self-conscious 'I' in order for identity to be constructed. And since that construction has gone on through language, the unconscious itself is a kind of echo: of refused signifiers that seem to threaten the identity of that I. Some of these refusals are visual. For Lacan language determines images; but images provide the resource (the imaginary) which makes language possible. To see oneself as a unitary subject involves a form of visual repression (Lacan, 1964). What is blanked out is everything that would disturb the illusion of the 'I' as controlling and autonomous. Because we cannot bear to view our body as non-unique – as no more than a collection of limbs and organs – the gaze narrows.

To give us a sense of power, we construct an image of the body as owned by the seeing/conscious/speaking subject. This image is not chosen or constructed by the subject himself: it precedes subject formation and is, indeed, what makes it possible to say 'I' when we eventually enter the domain of language (the symbolic). The body-image is the result of a dialectical interplay between the subject and the Other/ the mother which occurs during early infancy. This 'Mirror Stage', as Lacan most famously terms it, involves a dialectics that is initiated by desire and by the infantile experience of absence or lack (Lacan, 1949/ 36). Thus, within vision there is always a kind of shadow – the optical unconscious – which threatens to destabilize the subject's sense of visual control and his optico-geometrical mastery of space (Krauss, 1993).

In this last paragraph I have used masculine pronouns to indicate the viewing position adopted by both men and women on the Lacanian model. This is because, for Lacan, there is no speaking or viewing position which is that of woman. Indeed, in so far as women speak or gaze – or, rather, can linguistically (and hence conceptually) register vision – they are positioned as masculinized. 'Woman' and the 'feminine' do not exist, except in so far as they act as the necessary limit to the oedipalized self. Women can speak; but they cannot speak (consciously) from the position of woman. This is because self-identity is first prefigured in relation to a 'cut' from the Other: that which eventually gets characterized as not-self, but which is only thrust into Otherness as the infant experiences non-completion or lack in the absence of the mother. Thus, the eyes of the mother serve as a kind of mirror against which identity is constructed and boundaries determined. What is prefigured in that mirror is established more firmly later as the child is inducted into language. At that stage it is the father who comes to symbolize the break between the child and the mother/the Other.

For Lacan images themselves function as a network of signifiers, with meaning determined by substitutions and differences. The child forms an image of the mother as incomplete – castrated – in reference to the father, and thus comes to symbolize completeness, autonomy and power (the phallus) in masculine terms. The transcendental signifier around which the whole symbolic axis turns is the transcendental phallus, and at an early stage the child comes to dissociate the phallus (power) from the mother and, instead, to associate it with the penis (as outward sign of sexual difference). The boy images the possibility of castration; the girl images herself as already lacking/mutilated/castrated. Via one of these two doors – possession, threatened with loss, or that which is already lacking – all selves have to enter into the symbolic.

In the Lacanian model of the mind, those images that do not fit with the construction of the ego persist at the fringes of vision. 'Sanity' involves visual and linguistic repression. 'Woman' and the 'feminine' are associated with what is repressed. Indeed, in a sense, 'woman' simply is man's unconscious. And Lacan flirts with the 'feminine'; he is not straightforwardly on the side of sanity. Indeed, Lacan shows his surrealist ancestry when he indicates that in psychosis, hysteria, ecstasy, orgasm (*jouissance*), the artificial boundaries constructed around the self to divide the self from Otherness break open. There are intrusions and protrusions into the symbolic from levels laid down before the infant was fully inducted into language.

Explicitly in Lacan (as implicitly also in Kant), 'woman' falls outside the horizons of the 'I', and instead stands alongside the object against which the (masculinized) self is constructed as self. The 'I' becomes a form of necessary illusion. Thus, to see our selves – and even our bodies – as complete, we block off 'Otherness' and the infinite that persists at the edges of vision. As we will see in more detail in the next chapter, Lacan also employs the Kantian aesthetic vocabulary to describe that Other/that mother that threatens the identity of the (masculinized) self. Indeed, Lacan refuses Hegel's account of Antigone (who is, for Hegel, 'woman' in her purest form), and instead explicitly substitutes Kant's very different account of the beautiful and the sublime to delineate the relationship of Antigone to the (masculinized) 'I'. (See Lacan, 1959–60, pp. 249ff, 286, 301.)

'Woman' is that which the 'I' desires (the 'beautiful'), and also that 'Other' which threatens the 'I' (the 'sublime'). However, this obscure object of desire is pinioned as a static infinity, despite her links to the Kantian sublime. She recalls a (pre-oedipal) time before the child had separated off from the mother and, as such, seems to offer an annihilation of the boundaries of the self. But this threat is illusory or, rather, contained. Thus, it turns out that within the Lacanian system this boundless 'Otherness' provides the groundwork for the network of exclusions (abjection) that brings the – masculinized/unified – 'I' into existence, with its delusion of autonomy, self-control and freedom. The 'I' is trapped within a network of delusive images, as the 'real' falls outside the horizons of the gaze. However, it is also important to the Lacanian system that this 'real' that is linked to the elusive 'Other' is not simply negated, but is positioned as an absence that pulls at the edges of vision, in much the same way as the Kantian sublime.

Derridean Complications

Like Lacan, Derrida starts with the basic premise of structuralism: that meaning is not established by mimetically representing a 'real' which is external to language and that is 'out there', independent of thought. Philosophy is criticized for seeking to 'mirror', register or 'make present' an outer reality, and for representing truth in terms of a correspondence between language and the external or universal object or substance. Instead, meaning is established as constituted via placement within a set of linguistic signs. Thus for Derrida, as also for Lacan, it is the system of language (*langue*) which works to produce the binary oppositions of philosophy and thought itself: subject/object; being/becoming; truth/error; mind/body; good/evil; purpose/accident; noumena/phenomena; man/woman; self/other, and the like. However, for Derrida the conceptual order that philosophy upholds ('being' over 'becoming', 'truth' over 'error') is in each case subject to disorder, rearrangement, deconstruction, as we are made to notice that the supposedly privileged term only obtains its meaning by its oppositional dependence on the (absent) other that works to support the hierarchy though a system of traces.

Derrida denies that there is a centre to the symbolic system – *langue* – that is used to establish meaning and identity itself. Whereas in Lacan the chain of signifiers always reaches back to the phallus (and the Other/the mother that functions as the border of the masculinized self), in Derrida there is apparently no centre to the network of meanings and binary oppositions through which identity is constructed. Meaning is established via a network of differences (as on the classic structuralist model), but the centre is dispersed through the system like a spinning spider that has dissolved itself into its web. But does that still mean that the centre is still there? As Derrida put it in his 1966 lecture, 'Structure, Sign, and Play in the Discourse of the Human Sciences':

> Successively, and in a regulated fashion, the center receives different forms or names. The history of metaphysics, like the history of the West, is the history of these metaphors and metonymies. Its matrix . . . is the determination of Being as *presence* in all senses of this word. It could be shown that all the names related to fundamentals, to principles, or to the center have always designated an invariable presence – *eidos, archē, telos, energeia, ousia* (essence, existence, substance, subject) *alētheia*, transcendentality, consciousness, God, man and so forth. (pp. 279–80)

'Presence' here is an elusive term and cannot really be understood except by contextualizing it within Heidegger's argument that the whole of western metaphysics since Aristotle has constructed an ontology which privileges presence (*Anwesenheit*) in the sense of that which is temporally present. For Heidegger, the task of philosophy was to recover a primordial form of Being: one which was not skewed by thinking the past as 'the-no-longer-now'; the future as the 'not-yet-now'; and being itself as 'essence' or the 'permanently enduring' (*ousia*).

Heidegger was working at the limits of language and trying to think (against Kant) of a mode of temporality (and hence also spatiality) that is currently concealed or covered over, and that will be disclosed or unveiled in the light of the question that he asks about Being and its relation to time. Thus, quoting Kant on 'veiled' obscurities relating to space, time and the 'I', Heidegger remarks:

> In any investigation in this field, where 'the thing itself is deeply veiled' one must take pains not to overestimate the results. For in such an inquiry one is constantly compelled to face the possibility of an even more primordial and more universal horizon from which we may draw the answer to the question, 'What is *"Being"*?' We can discuss such possibilities seriously and with positive results only if the question of Being has been reawakened and we have arrived at a field where we can come to terms with it in a way that can be controlled. (1927, H26–7, p. 49; quoting Kant, 1781/7, A88)

Heidegger's metaphors for the relationship between philosophy and truth privilege unconcealment – but also control. The primordial relationship to Being that will come if we represent time differently involves unveiling or unconcealing something that has been covered over in philosophy since the time of the Greeks.

Heidegger's project in *Being and Time* was to reform metaphysics via a process of attempting to reclaim a primordial way of Being which does not privilege 'presence'; but he still implicitly privileges unconcealment and hence, in Derrida's terms, he still remains under the spell of 'presence'. For Derrida, unlike Heidegger, the tradition of western metaphysics cannot be reformed. Instead, Derrida's way of undercutting the tradition is to note that the apparent privilege given to presence in western metaphysics is only upheld by absence – by the 'trace' of the other that disturbs and unbalances the hierarchies of western metaphysics. Derrida works to destabilize the history of western metaphysics by playfully revealing the 'other' – the excluded member of the binary – which serves to underpin the particular historical manifestation of 'presence' that is privileged in the text:

> presence of the thing to the sight as *eidos,* presence as substance/essence/ existence [*ousia*], temporal presence as point [*stigmè*] of the now or of the moment [*nun*], the self-presence of the cogito, consciousness, subjectivity, the co-presence of the other and of the self, intersubjectivity as the intentional phenomenon of the ego, and so forth. (1967, p. 12)

Being, essence, truth, identity, permanence, object, subject: according to Derrida, all are manifestations of the privilege given to presence in the history of western thought since Plato. Derrida is insistent that there is no language to speak from that is on the outside of a metaphysics of presence, and this means that he cannot deliver his message propositionally.

> There is no sense in doing without the concepts of metaphysics in order to shake metaphysics. We have no language – no syntax and no lexicon – which is foreign to this history; we can pronounce not a single destructive proposition which has not already had to slip into the form, the logic and the implicit postulations of precisely what it seeks to contest. (1966, pp. 280–1)

What has to be done, therefore, is to destabilize the system of metaphysics so as to keep 'presence' at bay. And this will be done by using the kind of tension in language that is *différance* to tip the network of signifiers and keep it in flux. Each linguistic signifier comes laced with deferrals to, and difference from, an absent 'other' – the negated binary – that is also in play. *Différance* – Derrida's term for these deferrals and differences – is not a name for a *thing*, but rather 'the movement according to which language, or any code, any system of referral in general, is constituted "historically" as a weave of differences'. Thus, the terms 'movement', 'is constituted' and 'historically' need to be understood as 'beyond the metaphysical language in which they are retained' (1968, p. 65).

Famously, Derrida allies 'woman' and the 'feminine' with *différance* and with the play of exclusions and instabilities that threaten self-present identity and the privilege given to truth, essence, substance and being in the history of the west. (See 1973; 1978; 1991, Pt 4.) For Derrida 'woman' – and, as in Lacan, this has nothing to do with *women* – is not the name of a thing. The *féminin* has no essence. Instead, 'woman' represents a boundary, an absence, a becoming and an instability that inhabits 'phallogocentric' language and that can be mobilized by language. This is why (to my mind somewhat perversely, given his claims about the ubiquitous nature of phallogocentric metaphysics), Derrida has been taken up in much poststructuralist and postmodern feminist philosophy as 'the purveyor of hope' and as an effective block to Lacan. (See Nye, 1988, p. 186.)

It is true that Derrida could be construed as optimistic in that he does invite us to think 'beyond metaphysics': to join the dance of 'woman', *différance* and becoming. But as far as metaphysics is concerned, Derrida's voice is the voice of despair – and in ways that remain puzzling. For what does it mean to claim that the whole history of western metaphysics since Plato has privileged 'presence'? When Derrida reduces the whole of the history of metaphysics to the history of 'presence' isn't he refusing to recognize differential changes in the way 'absence' and 'otherness' have been used in the history of western modernity? And isn't this historical refusal (in Derrida's own terms) a *metaphysical* move, in that it picks out 'presence' as the defining characteristic of western metaphysics, and identifies it as the permanent that persists through change?

Other commentators before me have noted this tension in Derrida's position. (See Wood, 1989, pp. 276–7.) Indeed, it is a tension that Derrida himself both explores and exploits. Thus, his whole writing strategy is designed to work with the notion that we are entangled in metaphysical structures that privilege presence: structures that we cannot escape (at least through developing a new metaphysics). It is not that a new metaphysics is possible that could return to Heidegger's primordial Being or set up an alternative to Lacan's transcendental phallus. Instead language traps us in a metaphysics which is also always already encoded with its own dissolution.

In the Temple of Isis

In what follows I will not be focusing so much on the question of the paradoxical nature of Derrida's anti-metaphysical enterprise, for this is something that Derrida himself exploits and, as such, it is containable within his system. Instead, I want to raise two related questions. Firstly, what historical differences are being covered over by Derrida's claim that there is an evolving metaphysics that always privileges presence? Secondly, I want to ask just how radical is the project of privileging the 'other' that acts as the underside of presence? Both of these questions are urgent. For spatial distancing, traces and the playful optics of concealment and disclosure have also played important roles in the containment of otherness in the history of the west. Indeed, I would argue that in the post-Kantian tradition of philosophy there is a *control* of infinite horizons (including temporal horizons), so that distance, difference and an infinite 'otherness' can entice, but also fail to disturb the masculinized self.

Derrida offers a critique of Kant in his essay 'On a Newly Arisen Apocalyptic Tone in Philosophy'. Here Derrida positions Kant as his opponent in this debate about the 'end of philosophy', and manipulates Kant into a position where the latter is proclaiming 'philosophy's finally open and unveiled future' (Derrida, 1981/3, p. 141). However, it is Heidegger (and not Kant) whose philosophical language privileges a complete unveiling of truth. Instead, Kant presents philosophy as an ever-elusive, never completable ('sublime') horizon of possibilities that lures the knowing subject forever onwards and further into the construction of the perhaps fictional – and always merely 'phenomenal' – 'real'. Thus, in Kant's own essay 'On a Newly Arisen Superior Tone in Philosophy' (1796) that Derrida is commenting on, Kant opposes those who would attempt to raise the veil of Isis and draw near to 'Mother Nature' or 'matter'.

As indicated at the end of the last chapter, Kant describes nature as a 'sublime' infinity that forever eludes the mind that constructs it. This infinity is described as a mother; she is man's other – and the necessary counterpart to his own 'I am'.

> Perhaps nothing more sublime has ever been said, or a thought ever been expressed more sublimely, than in that inscription above the temple of *Isis* (Mother Nature): 'I am all that is, that was, and that will be, and no mortal has lifted my veil.' (1790, § 49, p. 185fn.)

When Kant himself returns to the figure of a veiled Isis in 'On a Newly Arisen Superior Tone in Philosophy', it is in the context of allying himself more nearly to Aristotle, than to the neoplatonists. The essay starts with a dig at Masonic tradition (which involves ritualistic entrance into the temple of Isis), and moves on to contrast Aristotelian 'labour' with the lazy mysticism of recent neoplatonists whose philosophy prioritizes ease, passivity, inspiration and intellectual intuition for a fanciful elite (1796, 8:389, pp. 51ff). It is not a veiled Isis, nor 'metaphysical sublimation' that 'emasculates' reason, says Kant, mimicking the language of the neoplatonists with astonishing explicitness. Emasculation (*Entmannung*) comes from a false relation to the real: from making the veil of Isis thin enough for us to be able to sense what is beneath (8:399, pp. 64ff).

Instead, Kant suggests that the veiled Isis ('Mother Nature') must remain as inexhaustible labour (the sublime), and not be allied with that which is given as determinate (beauty). The sublime demands a reason that is male: unemasculated by an apparently penetrative act of intellectual intuition that merely signifies a passive and dependent relationship to matter. According to Kant, nature is a regulative idea which cannot be exhausted by any particular experience – not even by the sum of experiences. Those 'mighty men who claim to have seized the goddess by the train of her veils and overpowered her' are simply giving themselves airs (8:401fn., p. 66fn., *corr.*).[3] The truly mighty men acknowledge and kneel before 'the veiled goddess' which is 'the moral law in us, in its inviolable majesty'. They 'hear her voice' and 'understand her commandments', but they recognize the impossibility of discovering 'whether she comes from man and originates in the all-powerfulness of his own reason, or if she emanates from some other powerful being whose nature is unknown to him' (8:405, p. 71, *corr.*). Like the moral law, nature must be constructed in a way that leaves its ontological status unresolved.

The totality of 'nature' is consistent with its invention by man, the law-giver; but it is also consistent with the hypothesis of a supersensible God who is its 'noumenal' (and unknowable) creator. The 'veiling' of the ontological status of Mother Nature is integral to Kant's phenomenal reality. The status of his 'I' requires – and feeds on – this absence. Thus, Kant (like Lacan) privileges an elusive, and ever-receding 'Otherness', whilst simultaneously denying that 'Other' any power which does not derive from its role as the binary opposite of the 'I'. Nature/matter/the law/*what* is created is personified in feminine terms; the paradigmatically male 'I' that has nature as its 'other' is feminized – 'emasculated' – by any failure to regulate the distance between mind and matter. What serves as the necessary counterpart to Kant's transcendental self is not only a necessary (though regulated) distance from the transcendental object ('matter'), but also the receding infinity of the noumenal. The unity of nature, the moral law and God act as regulative ideas that have to be thought even as they exceed the capacity of human understanding.

In 'On a Newly Arisen Apocalyptic Tone in Philosophy' Derrida positions himself as 'undoing' Kant. But what is deconstructed is a Heideggerianism that thinks truth in terms of 'presence' and unveiling. Derrida attempts to destabilize Kant's system; but because he does not fully grasp the significance of 'absence' in western modernity, I would argue that Derrida's moves get trapped within a form of post-Kantianism that simultaneously celebrates and *contains* otherness. In this respect, Derrida is not unlike Lacan – or, indeed, Kant himself. Derrida's insistence that the history of metaphysics closes itself down into a single trajectory that privileges 'presence' does, in effect, *fix* otherness and *fix* becoming in ways that prevent a more radical engagement with an otherness that is not just 'feminine' excess. Thus, Derrida's deconstructive strategies serve to render invisible an alternative metaphysics of the fleshy, and of a mode of otherness in which bodies, nature and matter are more than the negation of a masculinized 'I'.

For Kant, 'matter', 'nature' and the 'object' are constructed in terms of an epistemology of the 'real' that privileges an *absence* from the gaze. This pinioned infinity remains visually and conceptually elusive, and in ways that also elude Derrida's criticisms. In part, Derrida's mispositioning of Kant could be traced to his acceptance of Heidegger's claim that the whole of western metaphysics since Aristotle needs to be understood in terms of the metaphysics of presence. Thus, for Heidegger Kant's philosophy of time and the self are understood as variants of Cartesianism (1925, p. 172; 1927, H23–4, p. 45). This claim has an element of truth, but is also seriously misleading if it is supposed that the permanent in Kant has the same ontological and epistemological status as Cartesian matter. As we saw in the last chapter, for Kant the 'permanently enduring' space/time frame is only a necessary fiction sustained by an infinitely (and forever invisible) receding horizon of nature.

Derrida broadens of the notion of 'presence', so that Heidegger is himself fitted within the confines of this ubiquitous sin of 'phallogocentric' thought. This dialogue between Heidegger and Derrida involves different attitudes to concealment and control. Thus, commenting on the passage from Heidegger's *Being and Time* that uses the metaphor of the 'thing itself' that is 'deeply veiled' (quoted above p. 90), David Wood suggests that Derrida is closer to the later Heidegger who has moved away from a model in which a subject exerts control over the primordial horizons that are unveiled.

> But where Derrida can explicitly celebrate this loss of control without
> handing over control to another responsible agent, Heidegger seems to be
> prepared to release control only because of a faith that the ends it sought
> will be more surely realized by letting language speak. A *responsible* lan-
> guage. (Wood, 1989, p. 157)

But there is more than one way of keeping control over the other.
Indeed, Derrida's apparently 'irresponsible' playing with the act of veiling and unveiling has itself a history – and one that means that this
gesture or movement has become just one more way to contain infinity
or otherness. Perhaps against his own conscious intentions, Derrida also
keeps a control over the 'other' that acts as the binary opposition that
underpins the (masculinized) self.

In reducing Kant and transcendental idealism to the metaphysics
of presence, Derrida first 'fixes' western metaphysics into a system of
phallogocentrism that is incapable of radical change. This is analogous
to Kant's own techniques for curtailing the potentialities of matter to
evolve into new structures that I explored in the last chapter. Both
philosophers fold the horizons of possibility back into epistemological
structures that leave only a 'real' that is conceptually formed. As such,
the 'object' becomes merely the 'other' of the self, and rendered incapable of radical transformation, novelty or birth. Furthermore, Derrida's
own 'metaphysical' refusals – his Heideggerian inability to register radical diversity and change within the philosophical tradition that stretches
from Aristotle to Kant – also mean that he overlooks the privilege given
to absence in post-Kantian thought. And this means that Derrida seems
to repeat some of the other moves of German Romantics who extended
the Kantian notion that the identity of the transcendental self is only
ever established in relation to the not-self. Thus, the similarity between
Derrida's position and that of Fichte and Schelling has been noted by
Peter Dews (1987, pp. 29–31). Like the Romantics also, Derrida's privileging of traces and absence repeats moves made by those Romantics
who used Kantianism to open up a space for the 'feminine', whilst also
containing and refusing the 'female'. (See Battersby, 1989, 1994.)

Beyond Deconstruction

Much 'postmodern' feminism that looks to Derrida to mobilize the
'feminine' does not move 'beyond' modernity, but merely picks up on an
instability present – and exploited – within modernity from the eighteenth
century on. Within poststructuralist, psychoanalytic and postmodern
traditions of feminist thought, the emphasis has been on displacing

the subject from the centre of knowable reality. However, this is by no means enough for a feminist philosophy if (as in Kant) that subject is already thinking its own displacement in thinking its self. To do more than destabilize the Kantian subject-position, it is necessary to think an object that falls outside the framework of embodiment that Kant's system allows. But thinking that object also entails thinking a new subject that can exist in a world in which bodies are fleshy and matter can birth.

In this book I am not arguing that we have an 'immediate' consciousness of self or of an 'objective' world. However, I am interested in what would be involved in thinking identity in terms that take the fleshy female – not 'feminine' – subject-position as norm. Derrida's deconstructive strategies entail exploring the gaps in the Kantian system and exposing the 'other' that Kant's text represses. But these gaps only bring into view the 'unrepresentable' and the powerful 'feminine' 'Isis' that acts as the construct (and limits) of the (masculinized) imagination. As such, Derrida implicitly keeps in place a model of thinking self which supposes that identity can only be established by a 'cut' from a feminized 'other'. Derrida's own move 'beyond the binary' only works by first establishing identity as resting on binaries. But this move in a sense reinforces a Lacanian metaphysics of identity that uses the self/Other binary to rework Kant's account of the transcendental subject which only establishes its identity via a 'cut' from the transcendental 'object' or 'not-self'. (See pp. 67–8 above.)

To deploy the Derridean 'feminine' as the only possible mode of disruption, it is first necessary to trap the subject within some modification of the Kantian/Lacanian frame in which both 'subject' and 'object' are oppositional, and come into existence together in the play of relationships that constitute a mode of 'truth' that is also 'fiction'. For Kant these relationships are categorial and also linked with the schemata of the imagination. For Lacan these relationships are dialectical ('I'/Mother/Other) and also a product of language (*langue*) considered as a system. For Derrida, the structuralist account of language has given way to discursive formations in which the centre is dispersed throughout the conglomerate. Instabilities in this whole (which is no longer a unified 'system' in a Kantian or Lacanian sense) are mobilized as modes of disruption. However, the 'object', 'matter' and 'nature' – and hence also 'woman', *différance* and modes of becoming – are first fixed in a posture that deflects feminist metaphysics into an epistemological cul-de-sac. What is denied is the capacity of an object (nature/matter/the other) to score the self via modes of relationship that are non-oppositional.

Deconstructive postmodernism works through a strongly despairing epistemology. It works by a paradoxical move: of claiming both that nothing can be known for certain, and also that it is evident that western metaphysics cannot escape the pervasive privilege that is accorded to presence. Derrida undertakes his deconstructive enterprise not with any intention of thinking a new metaphysics and a new model of identity that could more satisfactorily deal with 'becoming', 'woman' or with a 'matter' that is neither permanent nor hylomorphically formed. Instead, Derrida aims to undercut all metaphysics, and to leave us with an epistemology that is also unstable. Against such strategies I am arguing that Derrida is, in effect, celebrating the ruin and decay of western metaphysics in ways that involve a form of philosophical refusal – a refusal to think identity *otherwise*. Indeed, the question I would pose to Derrida is analogous to the one that Luce Irigaray poses to Lacan, Kant and to western metaphysics generally: 'But what if the "object" started to speak?' (Irigaray, 1974, p. 135).

For Lacan, in order to look, women have to adopt an oedipalized viewing position and become like men. For Lacan there is no other of the Other. This is the move that Irigaray refuses. In *Speculum of the Other Woman* (1974) she argues that in patriarchy there is:

> *Also an optical chiasmus.* The father denies the condition of specularisation / speculation. He ignores, one would say, the physical, mathematical and even dialectical co-ordinates of representation 'in the mirror'. In any case, he would know nothing of the irreducible inversion which is produced in the identification of the other, as other. (p. 301 *corr.*)[4]

Irigaray looks back at her philosophical 'masters' with a gaze that Lacan and Derrida would deem an impossibility: that of the 'object' who has not taken on the masculine parameters of self, but whose identity is not just that of man's Other. For Irigaray, this 'woman's look' cannot be that of the 'Other of the Same'. But it also cannot be a gaze that flattens reality out into a single clear 'truth'. Using the metaphor of a curved mirror or speculum, Irigaray works to represent reality in ways that allow new formations to emerge out of blur.

Within the Lacanian schema woman is merely a part of that Otherness against which male identity and western 'civilization' are secured. There can be no 'female' or 'feminine' reversal of perspective: no other of the Other. In her early work, Irigaray's solution to the paradoxical position of attempting to speak as a woman within a hostile theoretical space is to 'mimic' that theory in ways that 'jam' the analyses of both psychoanalysis and philosophy (1977, p. 78). And, since both rely on metaphors of sight and mapping to explain the relationship between 'image' and the 'real', she also seeks to 'jam' the sciences of optics and topography. She uses that jamming operation to open up the possibility of another way of mapping reality – a female optics and topography that involves a different relationship to space and time. Irigaray opposes an optics that privileges straight lines, particles and clean-cut identities. Instead, she proffers a morphology of the female body: structured by gradation, shadows, flows and intensive magnitudes.

In *Speculum* Irigaray suggests that patriarchal culture freezes fluidity into fixity in the mirror of the (M)other's eyes; but only because it has no perspectival space in which it can mimetically represent the original bond of the infant and the mother. To rethink identity (so that self is not constructed against Otherness), Irigaray will later appeal to 'the placental economy' – the 'neither one nor the other' – that regulates exchanges of fluids between foetus and mother (1990, p. 41). She also suggests that we rethink our relationship with mucus – and hence with the tacky borderline between self and not-self. (See also Whitford, 1991, p. 163.) Irigaray asks us to consider this porous boundary between one's own body and otherness not with horror or disgust (pushing Otherness away, as in Julia Kristeva's [1980b] description of abjection), but as instead providing a glorious opening onto a new form of identity construction. Skirting the terminology of the Kantian sublime – the parameters of which are explored in *Speculum* – in her later writings Irigaray terms this new opening between 'self' and 'other' the female 'divine' (1987, pp. 57–72).

In English-language reception of French feminist thought, there has been a tendency to conflate the very different strategies of three feminist theorists: Hélène Cixous, Julia Kristeva and Luce Irigaray. Of these three, it is Kristeva who remains closest to Lacan; Cixous who comes nearest to Derrida; Irigaray who escapes both of these frameworks for dealing with 'otherness'. Thus, whereas Derrida does not fundamentally disturb a metaphysics that renders woman/matter/the object that acts as the 'Other' *against* which the identity of the 'I am' is constructed, Irigaray queries Kantianism and Lacanianism in more radical terms when she suggests that there are two symbolic axes, not one, round which identity can be constructed.

Thus, whereas for Lacan it is not possible for the ego to be formed as self except by a process of visual and linguistic refusals, Irigaray rejects the model of the phallus as sole transcendental signifier. She suggests that there is not just one optical and linguistic repression in the construction of the ego: that of the Other/the mother – excess and grounding for the (masculinized) ego. A second, more profound, cultural repression involves a refusal to envisage an alternative model for identity construction: one that would take mother/daughter relations as primary, and hence entail a paradigmatically female dialectic of relation to otherness (Irigaray, 1987, pp. 9–21).

In *Speculum*, using a methodology consistent with her theory, Irigaray thus attempts two tasks simultaneously. On the one hand, there is the deconstructive task: one that is analogous to the Derridean move that dissolves identities into a play of differences. Like Derrida, Irigaray seeks to jam the established theoretical machinery for speculation and specularization. On the other hand, Irigaray also works to allow a diffuse and fluid subject-position – identity as a woman – to emerge from the shattered mirror of the specularizing gaze of western philosophy and psychoanalysis in a way that Derrida would disallow, but which also does not entail biological essentialism. Thus, Irigaray is not claiming that being born into a woman's body guarantees seeing as a woman. We are reared in a patriarchal culture which does not allow us to explore the revolutionary dimensions of mother/daughter and other female/female relationships. The gaze of the absent male intrudes even into our most intimate relationships: between mothers and daughters, and even onto our own selves. Irigaray's is an ontological claim, not one based on women's 'experience'. She is offering a counter to Lacan's claim that there is – and only ever could be – *one* symbolic: the 'father's' symbolic that employs a model of identity that is based on the 'cut' from the Other.

Different Disruptions

Irigaray's strategy for opening up the closed Lacanian system is the reverse of Julia Kristeva's. The latter looks within the symbolic order for traces of pre-linguistic – pre-oedipal – drives that link back to a gender-free stage of maternal bonding, before the 'I' was formed (Kristeva, 1980a). By contrast, Irigaray insists that the notion of a pre-oedipal psychic moment prior to the construction of sexual difference is still deeply androcentric (Irigaray, 1977, p. 142; 1987, p. 13). This is because the oedipal relationship describes first and foremost the relationship between a father and his son, with the mother as the third term. To stress the pre-oedipal is to carry on privileging the father/son rivalries that constitute the oedipal, and the feared 'cut' of castration that the boy is supposed to feel on seeing the mother's monstrous body which has 'lost' its penis. An emphasis on the pre-oedipal leaves untouched the Lacanian notion that all identity is established through a 'cut' from the Other, from the unconscious and from abjected portions of the (male) body.

Suggesting in the first part of *Speculum* that the psychoanalytic accounts simply do not manage to explore the processes of female development, Irigaray indicates that there is no sexually neutral pre-oedipal moment. Unlike Kristeva, she does not retain 'the' Lacanian symbolic, whilst adding traces of a 'lost' – 'feminine' – imaginary that stems from a time before sexual difference and before identity. Instead, Irigaray explores alternative models for thinking identity that privilege mother/ daughter relationships. And in these alternatives, self is not always and only necessarily defined by means of a binary logic (not Other/not Mother/not 'I'). Irigaray's tactics suggest an alternative symbolic: one in which identity remains in contact with otherness and does not entail a 'cut' from the Other. As such, Irigaray begins to open up an ontological alternative to a metaphysics of substance and a metaphysics of presence as she maps identities that emerge from flesh and from flux.

Viewed from an epistemological angle (the angle that is privileged in most feminist theory), it is difficult to focus on the details of Irigaray's divergences from Derrida. But viewed from the angle of metaphysics, the issues are more straightforward. Irigaray is allowing an other form of otherness, disallowed by the philosophies of Derrida and Lacan. In particular, her analysis makes it possible to see that Derrida cannot think a form of identity that is established through becoming. Patterns of fluidity can have their own forms and stabilities. Becoming does not always have to be the underside of being. Thus, to give an example which is by no means one of Irigaray's own: if the speed is great enough, water running through a colander in the sink can remain a stable 'form' – as long as the speed of flow into the vessel exceeds the flow of water out of the vessel. Flow, flux, becoming, do not always have to be envisaged in terms of a movement that is alien to persisting identity or to metaphysics itself.

A warning about Irigaray's position is, however, necessary before we move on. Although Irigaray does not view the symbolic as fixed into a necessary metaphysics of presence, she does treat western metaphysics as homogeneous, and also as concealing a 'forgotten' mode of being (that is related to birthing). As such her position is closer to that of Heidegger than to that of Derrida himself. It also means that she is forced to push the possibility of a *féminin* art and a *féminin* metaphysics onto non-western and/or pre-Platonic cultures – and towards a future that is 'still to come (or to come again?)' (1994, p. 13). Indeed, it is when Irigaray writes as if there is a primordial *féminin* future (or past) that is waiting to be unveiled that the problems with her position emerge most clearly. This is particularly evident in her later texts written after the nuclear accident at Chernobyl, in which she allies with the Italian Communist Party (PCI) to oppose androcentric 'science'. (See Irigaray, 1989.) Here she tries to draw concrete political proposals from the anti-Lacanian account of identity that she had offered in the seventies in *Speculum* and in *This Sex which is Not One*, but in so doing she gets trapped by a belief in a single '*féminin*' imaginary that has been 'forgotten'.

In contrast to Irigaray, I am not claiming that there is one 'woman-centred' ontological order that has been 'forgotten'. My claims about the need to think a female identity do, however, emphasize that there are alternative ontologies and modes of descriptive metaphysics that would be more useful for thinking female selves. These ontologies have not featured strongly in the history of the west. However, they have not been entirely absent, and that means it is not necessary to look 'outside' or 'beyond' western metaphysics to find alternatives. Unlike Irigaray, I am also making a strong distinction between the 'feminine' and the 'female'. *Women* have occupied contradictory places within the history of western modernity in respect to the 'feminine'. And this means that it is possible to utilize those historical tensions as sites of resistance. We can register these cultural variations as *within* modernity (and postmodernity) if we develop the notion of patriarchy in terms of the model of 'dissipative systems' discussed in chapter 3. Patriarchy is not homogeneous. It contains otherness within and, as such, can be modelled as itself possessing a fluid identity that is not established oppositionally, via processes of exclusion and abjection.

Writing or speaking from a female standpoint is not like writing from a position beyond the symbolic. But neither is it like speaking from the gaps within a single, synchronic language system (as Lacan would have it) or from within the diachronic flux of a homogenized metaphysics (as Derrida would have it). We need to think flux in order to think female identity; but we do not need to think of that flux as 'beyond' language, history or identity itself. The male imaginary is by no means monolithic – and it is this history that gives us the resources to think a subject-position that is female and that cannot simply be incorporated into the specularizing gaze of a metaphysics of absence.

6
Antigones of Gender

Luce Irigaray's *Speculum of the Other Woman* (1974) has been celebrated as one of the war-texts of deconstructive philosophy: mimicking, miming, mocking the delusions of the transcendental phallus. However, as I suggested at the end of the last chapter, *Speculum* can be used more positively: to think an alternative ontology in which self exists in a tacky relationship with otherness – and which does not negate the fleshy, nor a matter that can birth. It is this reading of Irigaray that Judith Butler blocks in her *Bodies that Matter* (1993). Instead, Butler annexes Irigaray for her own philosophical project – first set out fully in *Gender Trouble* (1990) – in which the overall concern is to undermine any kind of identity politics. In effect, Butler exhorts feminists to adopt a philosophical position that is beyond all identity. But how radical such a position is depends on whether or not it is possible to think identity in terms that do not take the masculinized subject – closed, autonomous, self-present, self-determining – as the norm for identity and hence, also, as paradigmatic for an identity politics.

Via masquerade, mimicry, parody and drag, Butler works to muddle the borders of the Lacanian symbolic. However, Butler has to force a return to Lacanian starting points about the 'symbolic', the 'feminine' and also about bodies before she can undertake her anarchist moves. To this end, she opens up a dialogue with Irigaray in the opening chapter of *Bodies that Matter* which neutralizes (by a kind of determined deafness) what is distinctive about Irigaray's voice (1993, pp. 27–55). Here Butler interprets Irigaray's *Speculum* in a way that enables her to close over the gap that Irigaray had opened up in the Lacanian system: a gap that allowed Irigaray to theorize a specifically *féminin* identity. It is only after all reference to a female subject-position has been blocked that

Butler will go on to effect her different – 'queer' – disturbance to the symbolic order which effects a kind of anarchy in the symbolic realm.

In the opening pages of *Gender Trouble*, Butler links an identity politics to 'the metaphysics of substance' in the following terms:

> What is the metaphysics of substance, and how does it inform thinking about the categories of sex? In the first instance, humanist conceptions of the subject tend to assume a substantive person who is the bearer of various essential and nonessential attributes. A humanist feminist position might understand gender as an *attribute* of a person who is characterized essentially as a pregendered substance or 'core,' called the person, denoting a universal capacity for reason, moral deliberation, or language. (1990, p. 10)

Butler immediately goes on to marshal Irigaray in support of her argument that 'the feminine could never be the *mark of a subject'*, instead the feminine 'eludes the very requirements of representation' (p. 10). Butler, in other words, recognizes that Irigaray is against a 'metaphysics of substance', but reads Irigaray's own comments on the 'feminine' epistemologically, not ontologically. Opposing those who regard gender as an attribute of a person, Butler moves on to use the inadequacies of a metaphysics of substance to undermine *any* metaphysics – and the notion of a 'feminine' identity, in particular.

In support of her anti-metaphysical stance, Butler appeals to Friedrich Nietzsche (pp. 20–1). However, in chapter 3 of this book, I also used Nietzsche in support of an alternative metaphysics of identity that does not entail substances and attributes. Butler determinedly resolves the ambiguity in Nietzsche's position as to whether Nietzsche is simply against a particular mode of metaphysics, or against metaphysics *per se*, and, instead, presents him as simply anti-metaphysical. What disappears is the alternative Nietzschean metaphysics that would make an organism only an (unstable and temporary) balance of energies, so that the boundaries of selves (and objects) are potentially fuzzy, and hardened only by the processes of appropriation and expansion. Instead, Butler presents Nietzsche's project in primarily epistemological terms.

Butler does not quote Nietzsche himself in support of her anti-metaphysical stance, but instead in *Gender Trouble* she uses an essay by Michel Haar in which he associates Nietzsche with an attack on all psychological categories based on the 'illusion of substantial identity'. Thus, Haar claims to find in Nietzsche an opposition to the Cartesian *cogito*:

> It was grammar (the structure of subject and predicate) that inspired Descartes' certainty that 'I' is the subject of 'think,' whereas it is rather

the thoughts that come to 'me': at bottom, faith in grammar simply
conveys the will to be the 'cause' of one's thoughts. The subject, the self,
the individual, are just so many false concepts, since they transform into
substances fictitious unities having at the start only a linguistic reality.
(Butler, 1990, p. 21; quoting Haar, 1971, pp. 17–18)

Through the quotation from Haar, Butler presents a fundamentally
linguistic gloss on Nietzsche, and reads his project in terms that might
remind us of Lacan – and also of Derrida. Although 'reality' is (presumably) 'out there', we only ever experience it as constructed via language,
the symbolic and via a form of identity construction that privileges a
'sameness' that involves a 'fictitious unity' – whether that 'false' unity
relates to the 'I', the 'person', the individual 'substance', or even to
Lacan's 'transcendental' phallus.

There is no space in this book to develop an alternative reading of
Nietzsche. It should be noted, however, that this is by no means a
'neutral' description of Nietzsche's philosophical strategy – and that a
different (more materialist) tradition that also claims Nietzsche as a precursor will emerge via the dialogue with Adorno in the next chapter of
this book. However, to understand Butler's own philosophical agenda,
it is worth quoting a part of Haar's essay, not quoted by Butler herself. And that is because Butler's own project of queering the pitch of
feminist identity politics could be described in terms almost identical to those used by Haar in his appropriation of Nietzsche for anti-
metaphysical ends:

> Contrary to Plato's method (consisting in gathering sensuous diversity
> into a unity of essence), Nietzsche's method aims at unmasking, unearth-
> ing, but in an *indefinite* way – i.e., without ever pretending to lift the last
> veil to reveal any originary identity, any primary foundation. Thus, the
> method itself manifests a deeply rooted repugnance toward any and all
> systematization. (1971, p. 7)

Haar goes on to characterize Nietzsche's world as one that is 'scattered
in pieces':

> a world made of moving and light surfaces where the incessant shifting
> of masks is named laughter, dance, game.
> Thus, Nietzsche's language and Nietzsche's method both possess an
> explosive energy: what is volatized in each case is always identity, on which
> every system rests. (p. 7)

Butler will, analogously, 'volatize' identity – laughingly, playfully, and
with an explosive energy that is also sometimes masked by her dense

writing style. Thus, in *Bodies that Matter* the 'joke' against 'substance', 'sameness' and the 'phallus' goes so far as to allow the category of lesbian males, whilst also (simultaneously) refusing 'women' and 'woman' an identity. For Butler any talk of a female identity is disallowed, since it involves reference to a body that only emerges as a (fictitious) unity within the symbolic order that is effected by language.

On one level, then, Butler sounds like Lacan; but Butler insists that the symbolic construction is only gradual, accruing over time. Indeed, she distances herself from the term 'construction', claiming instead that we need to return 'to the notion of matter, not as a site or surface, but as *a process of materialization that stabilizes over time to produce the effect of boundary, fixity, and surface we call matter*' (1993, p. 9). Now this seems to me exactly right; but, unfortunately, Butler continues to write as if this process of materialization emanated from regulatory norms that originate from within the symbolic. However, by adding in the time element to the Lacanian frame, Butler makes it possible to subvert the closed identities that Lacan's symbolic constructs. She argues, in particular, that the male body (and hence the penis) has only a fragile relationship with the phallus.

This is an interesting move – and it is one that, as we will see, in effect positions Butler as an anarchist working for permanent revolution within the symbolic order. She advocates strategic (oppositional) alliances of 'lesbians', 'women', 'black' Americans, whilst insisting on the need for a permanent revolution to overthrow the identities fixed by the Law of the Father. But whether all such alliances must be imagined as merely strategic depends on whether Butler's starting point is right. Is it necessary to link all forms of identity politics to (fictitious) closures that are effected always and everywhere in the same way – via the structures of language? Is it necessary to suppose that all metaphysics will necessarily be a metaphysics of substance? As indicated towards the end of the last chapter, it is precisely these premises that Irigaray's insistent questioning of Lacan's notion of a 'single' symbolic order would seem to deny. To understand what Butler's 'queer' rendering of Irigaray leaves out (and the relative strengths and weaknesses of their two positions), I want now to explore *Speculum* – and Judith Butler's response – in more detail.

All Done with Mirrors

Irigaray's *Speculum* divides into three roughly equal sections: the first on Freud and psychoanalysis; the third on Plato (primarily *The Republic* and *Timaeus*); and the middle section a series of shorter essays designed to reveal the continuities in the tradition of western metaphysics running from Plato to Freud. Here, Irigaray's primary philosophical targets are Plato, Plotinus, Descartes, Kant and Hegel, with a further (unsatisfactory) chapter on Aristotle (who acts as a mediator between Plato and Plotinus), and an important intervening chapter on medieval Christian mystics. Two more general chapters – one on the subject and one on the object of the metaphysics of modernity – frame this important middle section of the book.

Jacques Lacan's name is never explicitly mentioned in Irigaray's book. However, it is his methods and assumptions that are under critique – and also paradoxically imitated in ways that leave much of the psychoanalytic framework in place. Speaking primarily through quotations and ironic 'voice-overs', at times Irigaray's 'mimicry' of her 'masters' becomes so intense as to leave only pantomimic voices that explore the 'unconscious' of an androcentric tradition that thinks 'ego' by negating the 'other' that is both 'woman' and the 'id'. Since on the Lacanian model the unconscious is not a deep 'place' of the soul, but all that has to be excluded for the 'I' to set itself up as a (fictitious) unity within the domain of language, 'woman' is not a different subject-position, but simply is (man's) unconscious. As such, Irigaray's non-linear (and often grammatically ambiguous) prose seems designed to explore a different domain – one that does not obey the laws of the Lacanian symbolic.

The argument of *Speculum* thus works on a double axis of progression. On the one hand, there is a narrative impulse that moves from the present (Freud) back through the history of philosophy to find the origin of current dilemmas in Plato. On the other hand, the text itself is also structured like a curved mirror: a 'speculum'. This instrument was developed to see into the most distant reaches of the heavens, but was then employed as a gynaecological instrument to probe inside the bodies of women. *Speculum* as a whole reverses the direction of gaze, using woman's body as the apparatus through which to regard the philosophers' account of being. However, it is in the most densely philosophical essays in the middle part of the book that the reverse mirroring becomes most intense, as Irigaray works to produce a 'burning point' that would reflect back and destroy the metaphysical past. It is also in this central section that a new (blurry) image begins to come into focus: of a female subject-position that has remained unrepresented in the history of the west. It is this 'impossible' shape that Butler cannot – or will not – see.

The anti-metaphysical reading of Irigaray in Butler's *Bodies that Matter* is based almost exclusively on the chapter of *Speculum* called '*Une Mère de Glace*'. This is the part of *Speculum* that Judith Butler takes as one of the most 'trenchantly articulated' statements of Irigaray's position (1993, p. 35). In itself, this is – in every sense – a perverse reading of the Irigarayan text, in that it is precisely within this chapter that we find not a single word in Irigaray's own voice. Instead, this is where Irigaray apes her masters most consistently, speaking entirely through the mouth of Plotinus. Appropriating passages from *The Enneads* (254–70, pp. 196–212), Irigaray plays with the voice of this third-century neoplatonist. Choosing the passages – and adopting an ironic title – is the extent of Irigaray's intervention. Thus, Irigaray's title for this chapter translates as 'Mother of ice/mirrors', but '*mère*' (mother) is also homophonic with '*mer*' or 'sea'.

For Plotinus – in the pantomimic voice that Irigaray assumes – matter is an absence of form and of being; it is sterile, dead, passive, receptive, 'feminine'. Equating matter, femininity and passivity, Plotinus claims that perfection of being and of species requires formative force and what he terms 'that impregnating power which belongs only to the unchangeably masculine' (Plotinus, 254–70, p. 212; quoted Irigaray, 1974, p. 179). Plotinus thus exaggerates the tendency within Platonism to downgrade matter, to equate 'soul' with changeless 'being', and to represent the physical world as dreamlike and illusory. But Irigaray doesn't offer any commentary on this. Neither does she remark on the way that 'femininity' becomes as 'passive' as the despised matter as Plotinus reads Plato through Aristotle – nor on the centrality of Plotinus to the history of Christian (and especially Catholic) thought. Instead, Irigaray's strategy in this portion of the text is simply to quote large chunks of the Greek original. In so doing, she shows the twists and turns that Plotinus has to execute in order to retain hylomorphism and keep matter in its subordinate and entirely inactive place: as the apparently simple – but, in fact, extraordinarily complex – absence of form and of being.

It is impossible to tell from Butler's references to '*Une Mère de Glace*' that Plotinus is throughout the 'real author' of Irigaray's chapter. Butler claims, for example, that 'Irigaray accepts and rereads Plotinus's effort to read Plato through Aristotelian "matter"' (1993, p. 43). Butler also tells us that in this essay Irigaray 'writes that for Plato matter is "sterile," "female in receptivity only . . ."', and that 'Her reading establishes the cosmogony of the Forms in the *Timaeus* as a phallic phantasy of a fully self-constituted patrilineality' (p. 43). Since it is Plotinus (and not just Irigaray) who reads the Platonic forms as masculine and who writes that matter for Plato is 'sterile', Butler's remarks are, at the very least, misleading for the reader who is unfamiliar with the entirely parasitic nature of Irigaray's text at this point.

This is not a merely a quibble about the adequacy of Judith Butler's famously dense style of writing, since Butler wishes to claim that this (entirely negative and parasitic) essay is representative of what Irigaray has to say about femininity in *Speculum*. However, it is only after this entirely negative section that Irigaray's own narrative trajectory through the history of philosophy opens out to present some more positive views about a different *female* relationship with Otherness. Thus, Irigaray's chapter on female mysticism, '*La Mystérique*', introduces for the first time a different (female) voice that opens up the masculine economy of the self/other relationship from within. And the three final essays in this portion of *Speculum* – on Kant, Hegel and the metaphysics of the object – develop further the revolutionary potential of thinking self not *against* Otherness, but via a more fluid, permeable relation that takes mother/ daughter relations as primary.

Hegel's Antigone: Opening Scenes

Against Butler I would argue that it is not in the pantomimic chapter on Plotinus, but in the chapter on Hegel that we find Irigaray developing a 'trenchantly articulated' argument. The section is headed 'The Eternal Irony of the Community' and, as such, takes up Hegel's description of woman in the *Phenomenology of Spirit* (1807). Here Hegel (famously) evokes Sophocles' 'Antigone' as he focuses on the brother/sister relationship to reveal the spirit of woman in its purest form. Antigone is only mentioned by name twice, but her presence is unmistakable as he describes woman as the 'everlasting irony [in the life] of the community' – as the enemy within the *polis* which is the Greek city-state (§ 475, p. 288).[1] As we will see, this section of *Speculum* also enters into disrespectful dialogue with Lacan, whose *Seminar* of 1959–60 developed a detailed counter-Hegelian interpretation of Sophocles' play.[2]

Antigone was the final part of Sophocles' trilogy on the Theban legend (written first, in 441–2 BC, before the two prequels, *King Oedipus* and *Oedipus at Colonus*). What is at stake in this three-way debate about Sophocles' heroine between Hegel, Lacan and Irigaray is the status of woman with respect to the laws of patriarchal society. In Sophocles' play Antigone, daughter of Oedipus, obeys the (unwritten and unspoken) dictates of family and the gods, and refuses to obey the rule of the city-state of Thebes. Commanded by the king (Creon) not to bury her brother, Polynices, Antigone obeys the ethical commands of family and of the gods, rather than kingly decree. For Hegel, it is

Sophocles' portrayal of the sister/brother relation that reveals the essence
of woman most clearly. Antigone's tie is to 'blood': to the family and
(spiritualized) nature, in ways that put her outside the customs and
ethics of the state or Greek *polis*.

According to Hegel, in the early stages of society woman's concern
is properly with family. As such, she can combine a concern for the
particular with a form of universalism in ways that males cannot. In
refusing to obey the laws of the city-state Antigone is not egoistic;
rather she acts as 'woman': 'her interest is centred on the universal and
remains alien to the particularity of desire' (§ 457, p. 275). Hegel supposes that woman's bondage to 'blood' keeps her obedient to sacred
law in ways that leave her outside the duties imposed on (male) citizens.
Hegel is not saying that there are no ethical duties – 'universals' –
imposed on the males. Rather, his point is that the universals of the
males are related to the man's status as citizen (outside, and opposed
to, the family), so that 'man' and 'woman' occupy a different relationship to the duties imposed by the universals of 'blood', 'family', 'community', 'state' and 'spirituality' that develop over history. Indeed, as
ethics develops from a clan-based mode of organization to one based
round the (Greek) city-state, 'woman' provides the catalyst for further
development – but is also the traitor within:

> Since the community only gets an existence through its interference
> with the happiness of the Family, and by dissolving [individual] self-
> consciousness into the universal, it creates for itself in what it suppresses
> and what is at the same time essential to it an internal enemy – woman-
> kind in general. Womankind – the everlasting enemy [in the life] of the
> community – changes by intrigue the universal end of the government
> into a private end, transforms its activity into a work of some particular
> individual, and perverts the universal property of the state into a posses-
> sion and ornament for the Family. (§ 475, p. 288)

Thus, society, for Hegel, is in origins a male concern. Woman is other
– the enemy within – whose apparent concern with 'private' ends shows
respect for the 'universals' of blood and spiritualized nature. As such,
woman is both necessary to the existence of the society and excluded
by the society. In a passage that Irigaray will make use of in the 'irony'
chapter of *Speculum*, Hegel goes on to state that woman finds pleasure
in the brave young men who would usurp the law of the fathers (§ 475,
p. 289). Woman brings war and conflict into the (patrilineal) community; but it is a conflict that both sustains the community and which also
enables it to develop a morality that transcends that of civil society.
Antigone acts out of family duty; but the family is an ethical entity only

in so far as the 'natural' relationship between its members is taken up by spirit and functions as a universal (§ 451 pp. 268–9). Thus, the emergence of the individual subject and the eventual move beyond the individualism of modernity are both only made possible in virtue of a dialectic that requires woman's liminality. Antigone's position as the 'other' of patrilineal society is a necessary polarity *within* the development of (male/human) spirituality.

Lacan's Antigone: Strophe and Antistrophe

In his 1959–60 *Seminar* Lacan also retains Antigone, the daughter of Oedipus, as representative of woman: '*Antigone* reveals to us the line of sight that defines desire' (p. 247). But Lacan's Antigone is no longer tied to spiritualized 'nature' or to 'blood'. Indeed, Lacan explicitly argues against Hegel and employs Kant's account of the beautiful and the sublime from the *Critique of Judgment* (1790) as a means of understanding Antigone: 'what it is man wants and what he defends himself against' (1959–60, p. 240). Instead of using Hegelian universals to position 'woman' as liminal, Lacan's Antigone/woman is constructed as beautiful (as the object of desire), in order to cover over that which threatens the ego. But since on the Lacanian system what was pushed into the unconscious was those linguistic and visual signifiers that disturb the ego's fragile sense of autonomy and identity, that which is covered over is the dissolution of the ego or death. Antigone 'pushes to the limit the realization of something that might be called the pure and simple desire of death as such. She incarnates that desire' (p. 282). Antigone/woman thus represents the threat of the dissolution of the self into the Otherness that bounds it.

In Sophocles' play, Antigone acts in support of Oedipus, her father, and Polynices, his loyal son. Lacan reads her as sacrificing her own desires and her own being in order to maintain 'the essential being' of Oedipus's family – its 'destructive misfortune' or fate (*Atè*) (pp. 283, 264). Accordingly, the primary role of 'woman' in Lacan's system is to underwrite the dialectics of desire based on the son's incestuous love for his mother. Although Antigone's own desires might have the power to undo the oedipalized ego, her power is not exercised except through the patrilineal family. In this respect she is, Lacan suggests, analogous to the Kantian sublime. In the moment of the sublime the (masculinized) self confronts the infinity which has the power to wipe out its very existence; but infinity is mastered – and becomes no more than the necessary boundary of the self as constructed by the self. The sublime involves fear of the infinite, and the transcendence of fear; analogously, Antigone represents the death drive and the warding off of the death drive.

Thus, for both Hegel and Lacan 'woman' falls outside the universals of the male community. But whereas for Hegel there is another universal – spiritualized 'nature' – that woman represents, for Lacan woman is simply that Otherness against which the oedipalized/masculinized self constructs itself as self. For Hegel, 'woman' had an identity of her own, even if that identity is not really self-generated, but is constructed at the intersection of 'blood', 'spirit' and 'nature'. For Lacan, by contrast, nature no longer exists. And neither does 'woman' – except in so far as she acts as the necessary limit to the oedipalized self. Woman is merely the obscure object of desire (the beautiful) and the silver at the back of the mirror in terms of which the self constructs itself as self (the sublime). Lacan's Antigone has no identity of her own, and nature and the gods are themselves part of that Otherness that is pushed metonymically away as the self cuts itself off from its Other.

Thus, whereas Hegel's Antigone is unruly, in the Lacanian text Antigone's potential destructiveness has been harnessed; it has been transmuted into the loyal obedience of the dutiful daughter. Lacan has deprived woman of the resources from nature and the gods that Hegel's Antigone had employed to incite the brave youths to rebellion against the law of the city-state. Note, however, how even on the Hegelian model Antigone's status as 'other' only serves to aid the progression of patrilineal society, and does not fundamentally overturn patriarchal law. Like Lacan, Irigaray argues against Hegel; but she does not use Kant's theory of the beautiful and the sublime to counter Hegel in the manner of her 'master'. Instead, she develops an original treatment of Antigone – which, by giving 'woman' an identity that is more than man's 'Other', no doubt contributed to Irigaray's expulsion from the institutions of Lacanian psychoanalysis after the publication of *Speculum* in 1974.

Irigaray's Antigone: Identity without Oedipus

Irigaray returns to the subject of Antigone again and again throughout her philosophical works. But in her first treatment of this theme in *Speculum*, she uses her two 'masters' against each other – without, however, explicitly referring to Lacan by name. From Hegel she takes the notion that woman subverts the law of the fathers via her pleasure in 'brave young men'. From Lacan she takes the notion that Antigone is bonded to the death drive, *jouissance* (orgasm/ecstasy) and to the dissolution of the conscious ego. But whereas for Lacan woman's own desires were recuperated into the realm of the symbolic and existed only as the limit to the symbolic, Irigaray gives 'woman' an identity of her own. This identity places Irigaray's figuration of woman nearer to that of Hegel than to that of her more immediate 'master', Lacan. But Irigaray's woman is not bonded to the same blood as Hegel's. Instead, nature itself is split into two as Irigaray denies that woman can simply be recuperated as the necessary ground for patrilineal society, for the development of the (male) individual or for the eventual emergence of (male) spirituality.

Hegel had described the brother/sister relationship as presenting the male/female relationship in its purest form:

> They are the same blood which has, however, in them reached a state of rest and equilibrium. Therefore, they do not desire one another... they are free individualities in regard to each other. (1807, § 457, p. 274)

But Irigaray exploits the problem of what counts as the 'same' blood to disturb all sense of equilibrium and also individuality. The blood lines, the paths of desire, and the whole equilibrium of Hegel's 'spiritualized' nature is put into jeopardy, and with it also civil (patrilineal) society and (male) universals and individuality. Oedipus is Antigone's brother (the son of her mother) as well as her father. Within the Antigone myth, there is no equilibrium between the blood of the sister and the blood of her brothers.

Irigaray asks how we understand Hegel's claim that Antigone and her brothers are of 'the same blood' in the above description. Do we understand it with respect to the blood supplied by the same mother in a 'matriarchal type of lineage'? (1974, p. 216) 'Or is it rather that brother and sister share in the *same sperm*, thus giving consanguinity an (other) equilibrium. . . . ?' (p. 216). In posing these questions, Irigaray opens up a division between '*sang rouge*' (red blood, which is linked to matrilineal descent) and '*sang blanc*' (white blood/anaemic blood, which links with white sperm and patrilineality). Deciding what counts as belonging to the 'same' family' within patrilineal society involves bringing 'blood' itself within the realm of the symbolic and linking it to the 'name' of the father which forces the cut between mother and child, between self and other. 'Nature' itself becomes specularized. 'White blood'/'*le sang blanc*' turns via homophony into that which is merely '*le semblant*'/'semblance' – the merely phenomenal or phantasmic.

In the phenomenal world which is the world of 'white blood' and the world of the Lacanian symbolic, woman has no agency of her own. 'Woman' is reduced to the role of mother/wife. The conflation of the two positions is emblematized by the actual position of Jocasta, who was both wife and mother to Oedipus. The only other position for woman within the realm of the symbolic is that occupied by Antigone's sister, Ismene, who – according to Irigaray – in her 'weakness, her fear, her submissive obedience, her tears, madness, hysteria', is so over-feminized she has become a caricature of woman: the phenomenal woman; the woman of *sang blanc/semblant* (pp. 217–18). Using Lacan to posit something that is covered over – a 'real' that escapes the realm of the symbolic that is structured round the transcendental phallus – and using Hegel to posit woman's tie with blood as a subversion within the structures of patrilineality, Irigaray thus sets Hegel and Lacan to destroy each other. They fight to the death, as do Polynices and Eteocles, Oedipus's twin sons and Antigone's brothers, in the Theban legend.

In 'The Eternal Irony of the Community' Irigaray parodies Hegel, but her voice emerges above that of her masters. As such, this portion of her text is quite unlike the chapter that Judith Butler takes as typical of *Speculum*. The claim that woman is bound to spiritualized nature/blood (Hegel) is put fundamentally into question, as Irigaray argues that nature has itself been seen in terms that present it merely as that otherness that makes the development of the self, society and spirituality possible. Even more significantly, Lacan's refusal to credit woman with desires or a gaze that cannot be recuperated from with the symbolic is undermined. The over-feminized caricatured woman is a product of patriarchy and the realm of the symbolic that thinks the development of identity in masculinized terms. So also is the conflation of woman/mother/wife a product of an oedipalized reality.

Red blood/real women/unspecularized nature cannot simply be recuperated into the masculine economy. What Irigaray shows is that (in their different ways) both Hegel and Lacan cannot think female agency. Indeed, in a part of the quotations from Hegel that head Irigaray's 'Irony' chapter (p. 214) – and that the English translator inexplicably omits – we see Hegel refusing to register the active part played by the ovum in the processes of reproduction. Whether allied with 'nature', 'blood', 'the beautiful', 'the sublime', the presentation of the female as merely 'other' blanks out the possibility of a matter that might be self-shaping and that is not merely dead and inactive, 'formed' into identities by the imposition of male codes. By contrast, in the final paragraphs of this section on Hegel, Irigaray suggests that there is a 'living nature' – a 'red blood' and a form of bonding to the mother – that cannot be seen from within the systems of either Hegel or Lacan, and which can allow us to configure a different model of identity that emerges in a 'bottom-up' way.

What Irigaray is suggesting is that there are two possible symbolic orders. There is the oedipalized order in which the self can establish its identity only in terms of a cut from the Other. This is the 'white' symbolic: that in which we confront only white forms or ghosts. But there is also the 'red' order: the more revolutionary symbolism of bonding by blood, in which there is a more fluid relationship between self and its other. This appeal to nature and woman's 'red' blood is not, I think, an evocation of an unmediated access to 'the body' or 'matter'. Her (in)famous claim that 'woman "touches herself"' all the time' via her sexual organs – the 'two lips in continuous contact' – is not offering an experiential report, but a metaphor for the different model of identity that is required in order to think the specificity of women (1977, p. 24).[3] 'Being a woman' involves not self *against* Other, but thinking otherness as incorporated within the self. In this *féminin* order the self extrudes into otherness via processes analogous to birth.

Irigaray's chapter on Hegel thus ends with a reference to a different (non-masculinized) relation between eye, spirit and blood: a blood that would remain 'in its autonomous flux without reuniting itself', and an eye 'that would have no need – at least absolutely – to see, and perhaps not even the Spirit to think (itself/her)' (1974, p. 226, *corr.*). Irigaray is refusing Antigone/woman the Hegelian role of synthesizing blood and spirit, and the Lacanian role of being the object of vision/desire against which consciousness is formed into self. Irigaray is referring back to the quotations from Hegel's *Philosophy of Nature* that headed this chapter of *Speculum*. In the second of these quotations, Hegel had himself quoted Sömmering, who claimed that 'the arteries in the eye lead into finer branches which do not contain *red* blood' (quoted Irigaray, 1974, p. 214, *corr.*). In Irigaray's French rendering, the quotation from the German philosopher italicizes the red blood that stops short of the eye. Irigaray takes up this passage and plays with the absent 'redness' of blood and vision. She is querying the way that masculinized philosophy apparently keeps nature in play, but only via a form of specularization and objectification which acts as the condition for spirit (*l'esprit*) to appropriate nature/blood/woman as its/his other. Her own voice suggests a relationship with flux – and a type of red blood – that cannot be contained within the dialectics of the self/other relation as portrayed by Hegel and Lacan.

Against Hegel, Irigaray would then seem to be suggesting a less conflictual – *'féminin'* – self/other relation. If the play *'Antigone* reveals to us the line of sight that defines desire', as Lacan claimed, then Antigone's own desires reveal a different line of sight in Irigaray's text. Woman cannot be reduced to the caricature-femininity of the Lacanian symbolic (Antigone's sister, Ismene) or to the mother/daughter conflation of the oedipal family (Antigone's mother, Jocasta). Nor is woman's desire that of the Lacanian death drive which merely acts to undo the fiction of the male self that is established in opposition to Otherness. Rather, woman's desire belongs to a different (matrilineal) order: the order of red blood, in which the self's identity is neither established via an oedipalized cut from Otherness nor established via an active subjectivity working on passive matter.

Irigaray's optical/dialectical jamming demands thinking identity differently. Working from within the all-embracing system of Hegel and the all-encompassing symbolic of Lacan, it opens up a space, a desire, a direction of sight that the 'masters' themselves cannot think. In this respect, it is like the impossible space in which the heroines of her text are repeatedly enclosed: St Teresa of Avila in the section of *Speculum* entitled '*La Mystérique*'; and Antigone herself who is walled alive in a cave in a rock as a punishment for disobeying the laws of the city. These cavernous spaces – apparently mere nothingnesses in which woman must die – open out into another dimension in which woman is not suffocated by patriarchal decree, but remains alive and thrives. The female self is allied with these fluid spaces that open up within an apparently solid and dense metaphysics of closure.

Philosophy Beyond Dialectics

The final third of *Speculum* offers an extended analysis of the myth of the cave from Plato's *Republic* (*c.*375 BC). Here, again, although we seem to be presented with mere mimicry and parody, something positive emerges at the end of Irigaray's twisting and turning through the passage that gave birth to western metaphysics. This 'something positive' is also once again linked with 'red blood', 'birth' and with possible/impossible spaces that fluidly open out from within the Platonic corpus. The text ends by presenting the dialectics of philosophy as a form of body to body wrestling in which the male philosophers seek to destroy each other, but within which blood flows in ways reminiscent of a different 'body to body' relationship: 'blood that recalls once more (*encore*) a very ancient relationship with the mother' (p. 364, *corr.*).[4]

In talking about this 'recall' of a different mode of relationship, Irigaray uses the adverb '*encore*' – thus also recalling Lacan's (in)famous *Seminar*

20 (1972–3) in which he linked the mystical/sexual/'feminine' *jouissance* of St Teresa with the desire to be penetrated again and again (*encore*) by God and the transcendental phallus. However, for Lacan this feminine '*encore*' represents a spatio-temporal order in which there is never closure. Woman's polymorphous and insatiable pleasure poses a threat to the masculine illusion of contained identity. As such, the Lacanian '*encore*' belongs with the always unobtainable 'real' – and constitutes the zero point that falls outside the (illusory, but necessary) identity constructions of the symbolic. For Irigaray, by contrast, the zero point is not merely negative, but an opening on to a different topology for identity construction.

In positing this 'body to body' relationship with the mother, Irigaray seems once again to be drawing on accounts of the origins of western philosophy in ancient Greece. In particular, the rules of Aristotelian logic involved a formalization of the elaborate rules that governed a form of verbal duelling – *eristic* – in which the object of the game was to trap the opponent in a form of self-contradiction, logical clinch or *elenchus* from which it was impossible to escape (Ryle, 1965). As such, logic was the verbal equivalent of a form of physical competition (*agon*) that was also a common sport in ancient Greece – one that involved elaborately staged body to body contests between two male wrestlers. Thus, behind the contact with the physical body of the two males which the philosophers mime (via the stylized combat of dialectics) is another less agonistic body to body contact with the mother. This commingling of bodies provides another 'origin' for philosophy which is hidden, but which Irigaray seeks to bring back into play as the appropriate methodology for her philosophy of the *féminin*.

For Plato, the body was associated with the merely phenomenal world; reality was bonded to the perfect, eternally unchanging world of Ideas or Forms that underlies matter. Via dialectics the Platonic philosopher approaches (as nearly as possible) to knowledge of the world of pure Form. And this knowledge is described as a mode of recollection of a state of being that existed prior to birth. In Platonic myths we 'fall' into body via the processes of birth and we regain the purity of soul after death (Plato, *c*.370 BC, 248c–249c). In *Speculum*, by contrast, there is an upside-down reality in which the phenomenal world of becoming is privileged. Bodies and birth are what Plato himself has repressed, and thus cannot 'recollect'. However, Irigaray's own privileging of this other (bodily) 'real' does not involve intuition or a sudden flash of light or inner vision, as in Platonic 'recollection'. Instead, the bodily 'becoming' is accessed via the work of intermingling philosophical voices and personae. As such, it does not involve recollection of the moment of birth, but mimes the process of birth itself: conjoined blood and corporeal fluids, body to body contacts, and the reproductive labour of the mother.

There is an addendum to *Speculum*: a footnote, printed in the French in small type and after a blank page. Indirectly referring to Plato's representation of Socrates as the 'midwife' of knowledge, the note indicates that Irigaray hopes her text has produced 'the discomfort of a distortion, if possible irreductible' (p. 365, *corr.*). Irigaray has tried to produce the effect of a twist in the position of the female organs that the 'midwife' of knowledge can't treat. Such a distortion would not be merely negative. Nor is it merely an optical distortion. Instead, this distortion is also related to birth and the processes of reproductive labour. If it has been felt, then 'Something of the difference between the sexes would have taken place also in language' (p. 365, *corr.*).

The end of *Speculum* thus suggests that something positive will emerge from the processes of jamming the procedures for speculation and specularization. *Speculum* is not just a parodic or deconstructive text. The body that is covered up by the dialectics of philosophy is not alien to philosophical discourse *per se*. Rather, contact with the mother can be reaccessed via putting philosophical tradition in semi-mimetic opposition to itself, and by showing the female blood that is spilt in the male philosophers' fights – as in the struggle over Antigone between Lacan and Hegel. By suggesting that identities can gradually emerge from a commingling of self and other, Irigaray presents a 'positive' project for thinking identity in female terms. In this respect, her philosophical procedures mimic – but also in another sense undermine – the dialectical movements that Hegel makes in charting the unfolding of spirit through the antinomies of philosophy. Thus, Irigaray splits 'nature' into two; she sets out her project for thinking matter, nature and blood not simply in terms of the role that they play in a monolithic 'symbolic' or a single developmental history, but in terms of two intermingled symbolic 'languages' which mark out identities. The red and the white.

A Queer Antigone

From Irigaray I wish to retain the notion that by thinking the embodied female self new philosophical possibilities will be birthed that will allow us to think in ways that prioritize women. However, without also thinking the way that women (not 'woman') already live with – and in – unequal power relations, Irigaray's position remains somewhat of a trap. And it is here that I find Judith Butler's parodic 'drag' most useful for thinking strategies for conceptual change. As a lesbian excluded from those regulative practices which valorize women in their roles as mothers and child-carers, Judith Butler has an intimate understanding of the way the normative values of pregnancy and of motherhood serve to marginalize women in varying degrees from the exercise of power. Her sceptical, often mocking, 'ironic' laughter serves to disrupt Irigaray's too easy complacency about the joys – and the *jouissance* – of the female subject-position.

Thus, I would not wish to follow Irigaray into the kind of 'revivalist' comments on the female imaginary that she makes in some of her late essays. As indicated in earlier chapters, it is a mistake to interpret the 'feminine imaginary' (and female identity) as something which has not existed in patriarchal modernity. It is a mistake to homogenize the history of western metaphysics in ways reminiscent of Heidegger, and in ways that close down the philosophical potentials opened up by the end of *Speculum*. In her late works, the weaknesses of Irigaray's position emerge most clearly as she cuts to a minimum the philosophical frame and tries to address women in simpler terms.[5] Here it becomes apparent that Irigaray is once again regarding 'the symbolic' as linked to the structure of language. As a consequence she can only conceive of utopian – and highly unrealistic devices – for reforming 'the rule of the fathers'. Thus, in these late pieces, it is suggested that revolution might come through hanging up pictures of St Anne or revising the gender operation of certain grammatical laws (Irigaray, 1990, pp. 47, 29–36).

Irigaray herself tends to sentimentalize 'woman' – and even the unequal power relations that exist between women. Indeed, it is this aspect of Irigaray's theories that has been used as a basis for the (harmful) practices of 'entrustment' (*affidamento*) in the Italian feminist communities of 'Diotima' (based in Verona) and the 'Milan Women's Bookstore Collective'. The supposed need of each woman to acknowledge her status as daughter – and to render in public 'a symbolic debt' to the mother – has led to political practices structured around the need to choose (and obey) a symbolic mother who is not one's natural mother.[6] In *affidamento* the emphasis is on a symbolic revolution via a kind of 'social contract' between women. But *affidamento* operates as if patriarchy were a closed system. It valorizes 'woman' as symbolic mother without giving due weight to the ways in which issues of race, class, history, sexuality and upbringing contribute to power differentials between women that would render suspect any such 'contract'. As such, *affidamento* can offer little to those (many) immigrant women who act as domestic workers within Italy – and who would be ill advised to position themselves either as the symbolic 'mothers' or 'daughters' of their female/feminist employers.

By contrast, Butler knows that it is a mistake to overlook issues of race and sexual preference that have also remained unrepresented in the history of the west. She reminds us that the category 'woman' disguises the hybridity of 'women' who must occupy a subject-position that is always split – and that is marked as much by race, class, sexual preference, geography, as by being assigned to the category 'female'. Butler also has a much stronger sense than Irigaray of the possibilities of employing the dialectics of history to subvert the law of the fathers, in ways that doubtless come from her Hegelian past. For Butler is, in origins, a Hegelian. And it is significant in this respect that the essay by Michel Haar quoted above – and used by Butler in *Gender Trouble* to establish Nietzsche as an anti-metaphysical thinker – goes on to describe Nietzsche as providing a block to Hegel (Haar, 1971, pp. 21, 33).

Blocking Hegel is also Butler's project. Her very first book, *Subjects of Desire*, looks at the impact of Hegelianism on French philosophies, but ends with a 'laugh of recognition': 'From Hegel through Foucault, it appears that desire makes us into strangely fictive beings' (Butler, 1987, p. 238). It is this (Nietzschean) 'laugh of recognition' that echoes through Butler's later books and essays. As I noted in chapter 5, in Foucault this Nietzschean 'return of masks' as man's face 'explodes in laughter' has its origins in a dialogue with Kant.[7] However, in Butler this laughter is pitted against the Hegelian dialectic, but in ways that mean that she remains caught up with Hegel's figure of woman as the 'everlasting irony (in the life) of the community'. With her commitment to permanent revolution, Butler functions as a Maoist of the symbolic order. Her Hegelian legacy has made it impossible for her to think 'woman' except in oppositional terms.

Like Irigaray, Butler uses Lacan against Hegel, and Hegel against Lacan, but with different results. To prevent woman being simply reincorporated into Hegelian 'nature' and 'blood', Butler, in effect, accepts the strongest version of Lacanianism which gives us access only to that which is symbolically constructed via a logic of relationship that privileges the phallus. Then, in ways that also block Lacan's incorporation of woman into 'the sublime' (that which exceeds the symbolic from a position within the symbolic), she argues that the borders of the symbolic are not established via a single act (or set of acts) that 'cuts' self from Other.[8] What is – and what is not – included within the symbolic domain is established only gradually over time and by speech acts and other 'performatives' that make it impossible to enforce closure of the system. 'Drag', parody, mimicry, ridicule thus have the potential for preventing symbolic closure.

Butler does not discuss Antigone – even her book on the Hegelian tradition in France focuses instead on the master/slave dialectic. 'Irony' is a word that she also seems to avoid. However, I interpret her strategy of philosophical 'drag' and 'parody' as a reworking of Antigone's marginality – to prevent the reincorporation of 'woman' into the 'system' or the 'symbolic' in the manner of Hegel or Lacan. In effect, Butler exhorts all women, blacks, gays and lesbians (of whatever sex) to become 'Antigones', living in a state of eternal irony – subverting the symbolic from the borders within. For Butler, 'woman' becomes once again the merely phenomenal woman – Irigaray's 'white'/'bloodless' woman – all that is metonymically displaced by the Lacanian self in order to produce its own boundaries from Otherness. But living this parodic caricature becomes a positive act, as the caricature works to reveal itself as caricature. Thus, Butler functions as a non-necessary (but nevertheless useful) irony at the edge of'the female community – both inside and outside 'our' sex.

A Maoist of the Symbolic Order

Butler argues that we (who?) can continue to identify as 'women'; but always and only through a 'double movement' that invokes the category whilst, at the same time, undoing it by resisting its closure (1993, p. 222). And this is because:

> To understand 'women' as a permanent site of contest, or as a feminist site of agonistic struggle, is to presume that there can be no closure on the category and that, for politically significant reasons, there ought never to be. That the category can never be descriptive is the very condition of its political efficacy. (p. 221)

Butler has reversed and infinitized Lacan's symbolic by subjecting it to doubling, to permanent revolution, and by decentring the transcendental subject. Thus, in *Bodies that Matter* she conducts most of the debate about what is involved in being consigned to the female sex in Lacanian terms as if all that mattered were relation to the (transcendental) phallus – with the only alternative discussed in any detail being the having of a body that is penetrable. But this is precisely to reinforce age-old philosophical orthodoxies that equate the 'feminine' and 'matter' with that which is inscribed and with that which cannot be self-forming. Butler 'twists' the penetrable body back on itself, as she operates as 'the enemy within', and subjects the patriarchal tradition to continual disruption. But what she also refuses to explore is a new metaphysics that would use the 'wombed' and fleshy, female body to think a different model of self and object.

As such, she parodies, mimes and 'drags' the female and male subject-positions as delineated in Lacanian terms. But since there are only caricature-women in the Lacanian sphere, it becomes necessary to ask just how radical Butler's project is in political terms. Won't this rebellion simply be reincorporated into the Lacanian system? Butler's ironic laughter offers political hope, but only through the acceptance of too much despair. Thus her claim that the category of 'women' *ought to be* left undefined for political reasons accepts too readily the prohibitions on an 'essence' of the becoming or of the feminine laid down in the tradition of philosophy in the manner of Aristotle and Plotinus. And Butler's claim that 'women' can only remain an oppositional category in effect places woman/Antigone back within the framework of a single developmental (Hegelian) history that both requires and yet also contains woman's revolutionary potential.

In Butler's early book on the Hegelian tradition in French thought, she remarks:

> Throughout my inquiry I will be concerned with the dissolution of Hegelianism as well as the peculiar forms of its insistent reemergence, its reformulation, and its inadvertent reappearance even when subject to its most vehement opposition. (Butler, 1987, p. 15)

I am suggesting Hegel has reappeared in Butler's own later texts – and that this is something of which Butler herself is only too aware. Her Nietzschean laughter is valuable, as is also her emphasis on differences between women, but we need to ask if Butler is correct in limiting woman's revolutionary potential to parodying '*the*' system of masculinized identity construction. Isn't that granting too much to Hegel and Lacan?

Thus, against Butler's subversive techniques I would argue – as I also insisted in chapter 2 – that registering differences within the category of 'woman' or 'women' does not entail that the female subject-position cannot be described, nor that it is necessary for political action to ensure that these concepts are left undescribed. Instead, we can seek to combine a Butlerian emphasis on power differences between women with Irigaray's own (early) concern with a different (non-oedipal) model of ego formation. And here it is necessary to posit identity as emerging not through 'symbolic' codes traced on a matter (women's bodies) that remains inactive, passively traced from outside and above. Instead, we need to think identities emerging through non-dialectical contact between forces, in which 'self' and 'other' are not antagonistic categories. Thinking the female body that is normatively not simply 'penetrable', but also fleshy and 'wombed' allows us to register an 'otherness' that can exist within the self itself. As we saw in chapters 2 and 3, to think 'identity' in terms that take the female subject-position as norm we do not have to think in terms of a closed, autonomous and self-contained system that can maintain 'sameness' only by the abjection of otherness, nor in terms that rigidly exclude all change and all difference.

Instead, we can productively think identity – and also patriarchy itself – as a dissipative system, with features that are not shaped in a top-down way, via the imposition of an artificial 'symbolic' order onto previously chaotic and inert material. If patriarchy is (like matter) capable of formation and configuration by a variety of interchanges between 'self' and 'other' that occur over time, then why should we limit these interchanges to those 'imposed' by '*the*' Lacanian symbolic – or even to those imposed by a symbolic fashioned gradually, over time, in good Hegelian fashion? Profound consequences stem from a refusal of Butler's starting points about language and the so-called 'metaphysics of substance' imposed by grammar. Once we deny that language or 'the symbolic' always everywhere fixes – and closes – identities in a top-down way, then we can also escape Butler's conclusion about the need to reject all models of identity, and all metaphysics. We need not conclude that there can be no (fluid, shifting) 'essence' of woman, nor that feminist theory and metaphysics are incompatible projects. In other words, not every identity politics need fail to register difference amongst women.

Thinking patriarchy as a dissipative system means thinking it in terms of a long-lasting – but nevertheless, in principle, temporary – pattern of forces, with boundaries that are variable and that can include other structures of power as operating within, as well as outside, the structures that position the male as norm in the exercise of power. As such, a variety of regulative structures (androcentrism, colonialisms, postcolonialisms, heterosexualism, nationalisms, et cetera) will together mark – but also themselves be marked by – specific groupings of humans, as well as marking and being marked by the specificity of the individual self. And this means that there will be many different modes of patriarchy – not a single model that everywhere betrays its origins in a metaphysics of substance. But that, in its turn, means that there will also be modes of gender-revolution disallowed by Judith Butler's own ironic gesture that leaves 'woman' and 'women' the eternal enemy within the Lacanian and Hegelian communities of 'man'.

Remodelling identity in terms of a metaphysics of becoming allows us to register differences and changes occurring within a single category, and allows us to register power differentials and differences amongst women themselves. As such, an identity politics need not entail homogenizing 'woman' or 'women' into Irigaray's 'other of the Other'. Nor need we spend all our oppositional energies in continually fixing and unfixing 'woman' to Hegel's 'eternal irony in the community' or to Lacan's 'Other of the Same'. We can move beyond Butlerian parody and deconstruction, but also beyond the modes of utopian remembrance that characterize the late Irigaray. Instead, we will need to ally a metaphysics of becoming with an account of the historical and cultural factors that help configure the female subject-position in its diverse specificities. As such, the question of an *other* kind of identity politics becomes once again a not disreputable dream.

7
Flesh with Trimmings:
Adorno and Difference

In his *Logical Investigations* Edmund Husserl, the founder of philosophical phenomenology, follows Kant in rejecting the notion of a reality that exists prior to all experience and which shines into a room of consciousness. According to Husserl, the mind does not respond passively to the world; but neither is the world constructed by the mind via a kind of peephole in the way that Kant himself seems to suggest. Instead, Husserl claims that reality forms itself as we move through our environment and walk along spatio-temporal corridors peopled with forms. Husserl goes on:

> Wandering about in the Panopticum Waxworks we meet on the stairs a charming lady whom we do not know and who seems to know us, and who is in fact the well-known joke of the place: we have for a moment been tricked by a waxwork figure. As long as we *are* tricked, we experience a perfectly good percept: we see a lady and not a waxwork figure. When the illusion vanishes, we see exactly the opposite, a waxwork figure that only *represents* a lady. (1900–1, vol. 2, p. 609)

The post-Kantian tradition of idealism is like the Husserlian waxwork museum – with a lady ('mother nature', 'matter', the 'other') that appears and disappears as the male philosopher patrols its corridors. This 'nature' looks real enough; but whenever we meet her she is just a representation of the living. Her waxy flesh is just a constrained infinity that represents nature only by being kept at a regulated (and ever-receding) distance from the (masculinized) 'I' that constructs her as the counterpart to his own self-identical self. Against this tradition Theodor W. Adorno provides an account of 'matter' and the 'object' that does not simply function as the specularized 'other' of the consciousness that constructs it. And Adorno argues that even Husserl has failed to escape the 'waxifying' of nature that fixes it as dead and thing-like matter. Thus, in *Against Epistemology* (1956) Adorno provides a critique of the above passage from Husserl, and argues that it is a mistake to begin an analysis of the objective world via an exploration of the 'subject' of knowledge (pp. 218–19). More broadly, he maintains:

> It is impossible to correct a mistake of idealistic epistemology without neces-sarily producing another error. One concept is evolved out of another so that contradictions may be corrected in ordered succession, but none would come closer to the 'thing' than the first one. Indeed each falls deeper into the thicket of invention. (Adorno, 1956, p. 211)

Later in this chapter, I will argue that Adorno himself cannot deal adequately with flesh, partly as a consequence of the fact that he also cannot deal with bodies that are female. However, Adorno's critique of specularized nature will be useful in indicating further what is wrong with Butler's position, as well as with that of Irigaray. If we start from within an idealist frame (in which the 'outer' world is simply constructed as the counterpart – the 'other' – of the subject), it is not possible to speak coherently of a 'real' that falls outside that conceptual frame. If feminist and poststructuralist theorists start from Lacan, they will remain trapped within the dialectics of the self/other relationship that Lacan sets out.

In effect, Butler treats bodies via a kind of idealist 'peephole': 'mat-ter' becomes a product of discursive formations in a way that 'falls deeper into the thicket of invention' originally marked out by the ide-alist philosophies of Kant and Hegel. For Irigaray, by contrast, matter is not just socially and culturally constructed. However, her failure to think difference historically means that she moves erratically through the corridors of philosophy's 'Panopticum Waxworks', opening out hid-den spaces and concealed passageways, but without an adequate model of historical change.

Adorno's concern to politicize philosophy – a concern worked through in the triple shadow of Kierkegaard, Hegel and Kant – means that he develops a position which has been described as that of a 'metaphysi-cian in an antimetaphysical age' and as attracted to 'nonmetaphysical metaphysics' (Buck-Morss, 1977, p. 93). Adorno describes how his own methodology of negative dialectics emerges historically: out of the break-down in metaphysical categories that occurred after the Enlightenment. As metaphysical truth is made subordinate to the 'subject' of know-ledge, it moves from the centre of philosophical debate, becoming 'smaller and smaller' as it recedes (but never completely attains) complete insignificance. Negative dialectics emerges as 'metaphysics immigrates into micrology. Micrology is the place where metaphysics finds a haven from totality' (Adorno, 1966, p. 407).

The position adopted in this book could be described in analogous terms, as involving a type of 'nonmetaphysical metaphysics' appropriate to a discipline (feminist theory) which has developed in anti-metaphysical ways. Thus, within feminist theory epistemology has been allocated a privileged place. Whereas metaphysics has been supposed complicit with an 'essentialism' that feminism can neither allow nor develop, epistemology has been portrayed as open to feminist interventions. To quote the introduction of a recent book in this field, the link between issues of knowledge and issues of power has moved epistemology 'from the world of somewhat esoteric philosophy to the centre-stage of contemporary culture. Not only philosophers, but also social scientists, political theorists, historians and literary theorists are now urgently addressing epistemological questions' (Lennon and Whitford, 1994, p. 1).

My own opposition to the project of 'feminist epistemology' does not indicate a disagreement with all of the work that has gone on under this heading. But I am arguing that the fundamental feminist revisions in the sciences and in philosophy that feminist theory has as its goal cannot be secured by privileging an epistemology of the subject, rather than a metaphysics of the object. Most poststructuralist and postmodern feminists take Descartes as typical of modernity, and therefore read modernity as caught up with an 'I' that deludes itself with certainties relating to that 'I' and to knowledge. However, as I argued also in chapter 5, Descartes's self-certainty was far less typical of modernity than Kant's complex 'proof' of the transcendental subject that exists only as a counterpart to the so-called 'transcendental object'. In this book I have been suggesting that the urgent problem for feminist theory to address is not the problem of the subject, but the problem of the *object*. We require models of essence that allow us to register both difference and sameness, and models of identity that allow us to think the morphological transformations of matter and bodies that birth. However, rethinking this 'object' will produce changes in the 'subject' also.

Historical Reversals

Adorno's analysis of modernity agrees broadly with my own. He emphasizes not epistemological questions, but the subject/object dualism, and the limitations in Kantian (and post-Kantian) modes of thinking 'objects', bodies and the 'not-I'. For Adorno, the problems of contemporary philosophy do not relate to the question of the 'certainty' of the self, but instead stem from the delusion that the ontological or epistemological priority of the mind (or spirit) can be addressed without also considering the historical circumstances within which the question of the subject comes to be posed. Thus, Adorno argues 'against epistemology' and also against metaphysics considered as an objective account of 'being'. His own methodology of 'negative dialectics' rests on the claim that we need to register how 'object' and 'subject' belong together – and change together as the position of the bourgeois subject changes in the period of modernity.

In *Dialectic of Enlightenment* (1944) – written together with Max Horkheimer – Adorno argues that the characteristics of modernity have roots in the distant part of (western) history. Instrumental reason takes two forms, both of which are modes of domination. There is technological reason (which dominates nature) and social reason (which is directed towards the domination of other human beings in the social sphere). It was the drive to dominate nature that led at first to the reification of nature – reducing it merely to the 'other', to be controlled and manipulated by the 'subject'. But in order to control that 'object' and manipulate it, nature has to be stripped of all its qualities and represented as a 'unity' and as mere matter:

> Bourgeois society is ruled by equivalence. It makes the dissimilar comparable by reducing it to abstract quantities. To the Enlightenment, that which does not reduce to numbers, and ultimately to the one, becomes illusion; modern positivism writes it off as literature. Unity is the slogan from Parmenides to Russell. The destruction of gods and qualities alike is insisted upon. (1944, pp. 7–8)

Little by little, this drive for abstract (and quality-free) 'equivalence' which is a feature of instrumental reason comes to pervade all aspects of human life.

Instrumental reason drives us to reduce the world to 'thing-like' equivalences, judging objects (and also other subjects) only in terms of material use-values. Adorno terms this collection of objects 'second nature', in ways that might remind us of Lacan's (and Irigaray's) account of 'specularized nature'. But for Lacan it was language as a system (*langue*) that was the basis of the specularization, and in ways that made one individualized subject identical to another individualized subject at least in terms of the model of ego formation. For Lacan, the incursions that come from beyond the self are those that threaten its (fragile) sense of itself as autonomous and whole; they are not those that come from contact with different (historical and cultural) 'realities' and 'histories'. Therefore, for Lacan what threatens the ego – through incursions from the 'real' or from the 'fringes' of vision – cannot be articulated within a language in which there is an ego. By contrast, for Adorno there is not just *one* type of ego, but egos – and not just *one* type of object that exists over and against the 'I' but different 'objects' and different 'realities'. We have, at least in principle, access to realities outside the norm in ways that are speakable.

For Adorno it is Kant who represents the norm for modernity, and who stands at the peak of 'Enlightenment' thought. He emphasizes how in Kant's moral philosophy all differences between individuals have to be set to one side, so that moral duty involves subjecting individuals to the 'universal'. Furthermore, in a passage explicitly linked with Kant's epistemology (and the role of the schematism in imposing spatio-temporal 'rules' on the material presented by the senses), Adorno and Horkheimer note that instrumental reason 'recognizes no function other than the preparation of the object from mere sensory material in order to make it the material of subjugation' (1944, p. 84). Thus, on the one hand, Adorno explicitly binds the 'instrumental' use of reason in Kant's philosophy with the tendency to treat 'persons' as equivalents. On the other hand, he also links the over-emphasis on the subject and its reification of the object in the bourgeois era with Kant's tendency to treat matter as a mere *thing* that can be mastered by reason.

But if it is Kant who exemplifies the era of bourgeois philosophy for Adorno, it is not part of his thesis that there have been no changes in the 'subject' and the 'object' during the last two hundred years. For Adorno, 'high' capitalism (modernity) is in decline. Furthermore, the decline is presented as historically necessary, in so far as the emphasis on equivalence means that people's 'overall condition moves towards apersonality in the sense of anonymity' (1966, p. 280). It no longer is the case that society functions as a sphere within which the individual exercises his (supposed) freedom of action. Instead, 'humankind' as a whole has come to subjugate itself to instrumental and quantitative modes of thought, so that the singularity of individuals is lost and we are faced with 'pseudo-individuals'. 'Dwelling in the core of the subject are the objective conditions it must deny for the sake of its uncondi-tional rule' (p. 281).

According to Adorno, after Kant and the period of 'high' capitalism, the self became reified into an abstract 'thing'. Whereas there were originally two distinct spheres within which reason was exercised – that of social 'community' and that of instrumental reason – modernity has seen a breakdown in the notion of an individual who exercises his 'free' choice within a community of like 'persons'. There has been a breakdown of communities and shared value-systems. Furthermore, the (rational) goal of self-preservation has become inflated and over-weening, but in ways that are self-defeating and irrational in so far as they entail a homogenization of the individual and the social sphere within which the 'pseudo-individual' operates.

As Adorno explores the way that the rational individual of the Kantian era has been replaced by the 'pseudo-rational' (and *prima facie*) 'irra-tional' self, there is a degree of recognition that the boundary between 'self' and 'other' has become blurred in late-capitalist societies. How-ever, Adorno regards this blurring in negative terms and not as an open-ing for devising a new metaphysics of self. It is not that Adorno endorses the notion of the self as autonomous; but Adorno's goal is not to break down the self/object binary, but to 'point out' how in modern societies the actions of 'pseudo-individual' agents are being directed from with-out in accordance with 'magical', 'authoritarian' and fascistic scripts which show the contradictions in the notion of the subject that has come to dominate 'post-Enlightenment' thought.

Adorno is both fatalistic and nostalgic for a state in which objects had not become commodified by instrumental reason – and individuals had not turned into 'pseudo-individuals' by being stripped of their sin-gular qualities. He stresses history, whilst also seeing it as a mistake to try to escape from history and discuss the 'real' essence of the object or the 'real' subject outside of the dialectics of history:

> the difference of subject and object cannot simply be negated. They are neither an ultimate duality nor a screen hiding ultimate unity. They con-stitute one another as much as – by virtue of such constitution – they depart from each other. (1966, p. 174)

Insisting that the polarity of subject and object is no more than a dialectical formula for something which is neither primary, nor a unity, nor positive – 'but negative throughout' (p. 174) – Adorno suggests that the 'spell' of selfhood is a necessary illusion for modern man. His own aim is to offer an endless critique that will dissolve conceptual forms before they harden into lenses capable of specularizing nature into another (fake) 'real'. Where conceptual analysis fails us, it is in our response to avant-garde art (primarily music) that we can elude the instrumental relationship between the 'subject' and its reified 'objects' that act as a 'thing-like' – and antagonistic – 'other' of the self.

Axial Turns

Adorno reworks Kant's subject/object divide by emphasizing the dependence of the subject on the object. Adorno attempts to give the 'Copernican Revolution' that placed the Kantian 'I' at the centre of the (knowable) world 'an axial turn' (Adorno, 1966, p. xx). Irigaray also makes a similar move when she demands a 'turn' in Kant's Copernican revolution which 'has not yet produced all its effects in the masculine imaginary' (1974, p. 133, *corr.*). However, for Adorno this 'axial turn' involves not a sexually differentiated subject, but a historical twist. Adorno historicizes the notion of the subject, so that it becomes 'not ahistorically identical and transcendental, but assumes with history changing and historically revealing forms' (1931, p. 333).

Thus, in Adorno's writings the individual subject does not disappear, as it does so often in post-Hegelian thought. As Susan Buck-Morss puts it, the foundations of Adorno's philosophical enterprise can be summed up in a phrase taken from Ernst Bloch: 'to let Kant burn through Hegel, the "I" must always be maintained' (Buck-Morss, 1977, p. 82). However, the 'I' that Adorno's system keeps in play is no longer a Kantian 'I' that fully controls and synthesizes the 'phenomenal' world via the synthesis of intuitions under necessary concepts that are always the same, and that remain unaltered through history. Instead, Adorno allows the unconscious an important role in the generation of new 'realities' that could, in principle, emerge as the relationships between 'subject' and 'object' also change. Furthermore, for Adorno the unconscious that shapes the shifting 'real' is itself shaped by the forces of history, not through universal and unchanging psychic structures or mechanisms.

We see this in Adorno's critique of Bergson in *Against Epistemology*. According to Bergson, there are privileged moments of temporal awareness of duration (*durée*) in which the 'normal' spatialized model of time breaks apart. Since the 'normal' time-order involves a linear linking of 'objects' in space, Bergson's move does, in effect, offer a disruption to the ontological groundwork of Kant's 'phenomenal' world. But it is a disruption that is rooted in sudden intuitions – not in memory or history – and, as such, is viewed by Adorno as involving an (unnecessary) appeal to 'irrationalism': 'Unconscious knowledge not entirely subject to mechanisms of control explodes in inspiration and bursts through the wall of conventionalized judgements "fitting reality"' (1956, p. 46).

Against Bergson, Adorno insists that this 'ego-alien' knowledge that passively and spontaneously wells up out of the unconscious is not 'rhapsodical', and is instead governed by a kind of logic. Repressed memories from the unconscious impose, and de-synthesize, the unity of Kant's orderly (and always homogeneous) space-time world that is constructed as 'objective'. These memories 'unwaxify' nature and recall the 'sheer scandal in things', so that this supposedly 'objective reality' is no longer simply the 'other' of the subject that forms it according to rules and principles that are always, everywhere the same. This scandalous irruption comes not simply from intuition, but (as we will see in more detail later) from the recollection of the manifold, and hence also of difference:

> In intuitions *ratio* recollects what it forgot. In this sense, which he certainly hardly intended, Freud was in a sense right when he attributed its own sort of rationality to the unconscious.
>   Intuition is not a simple antithesis to logic. Intuition belongs to logic, and reminds it of its moment of untruth. As the blind spots in the process of cognition – from which they still cannot escape – intuitions prevent reason from reflecting on itself as a mere form of reflection or arbitrariness, in order to prepare an end for arbitrariness. (pp. 46–7)

Adorno's talk of the 'blind spots' of reason – and of what Freud forgot to say about the processes of recollection – might remind us of Irigaray. However, Adorno's blind spots are historically – and not transcendentally – grounded. They are not integral to the structures of the psyche, as are the blind spots of the 'I' on Lacan's and Irigaray's models. And that means that Adorno can propose different means for disturbing the blind spots of reason and recollection than Irigaray's technique of 'jamming' the desires and categorial understanding of the (masculinized) self.

As we have seen, for Lacan there is only one logic of identity construction, and the relationship between (masculinized) 'self' and its (feminine) 'Other' ('it' or 'id') is forever fixed – at least if selves are to remain sane. All that threatens the ego's illusion of autonomy has to be refused for the 'I' to establish its fragile identity. Moreover, as Irigaray suggests, in the Lacanian system 'woman' acts as the 'id' or the repressed 'unconscious' of man. (See Irigaray, 1991, pp. 89–90.) Irigaray places pressure on the Lacanian notion of the unconscious or the 'Other' and (like Adorno) thereby disturbs the Kantian model of the subject that attains its identity through differentiating itself from (spatio-temporal) 'objects'.

In Irigaray's counter-Kantian (and counter-Copernican) revolution, 'woman' 'earth' and the matrix of 'matter' are gradually established as dominant counter-poles to the masculinized subject who sets himself up as 'the "sun" if it is around this that things turn, a pole of attraction stronger than the "earth"'. Like Adorno, Irigaray also privileges the object: her 'woman' 'also turns upon herself' and 'knows how to re-turn (upon herself), without seeking outside for identity within the other' (Irigaray, 1974, p. 134, *corr.*) Irigaray's position is ontologically rich, in that it suggests the 'object' is constructed not by the 'subject', but through patterns of movement.

Irigaray's 'woman' is 'never exactly the same'; but instead emerges through rhythmic cycles in the 'object' which direct the 'subject' that supposes itself in control: 'In effect, with all rigour she is never exactly the same. Always whirling, closer or farther from the sun whose rays she captures, curving them to and fro in turn with her cycles' (p. 134, *corr.*). Irigaray's grammatically ambiguous language – so difficult to translate – is entirely appropriate, in that she also allies this new order that privileges the 'female' and 'matter' with the breakdown of identities in the 'system' of language as delineated by Lacan. As such, her position also entails a disintegration of the ability to distinguish 'subject' and 'object' within grammatical sentences, and through the system of conceptual categories as outlined by Kant.

There is a problem with Irigaray's position, however, which comes from her attempts to counter a model in which the 'I' is only established as such through the abjection of all that is 'Other'. In her attempt to 'correct' her 'masters', Irigaray outlines a mode of thinking identity as emerging out of movement – but represents these 'movements' in curiously abstract and universal terms. Indeed, she is forced to privilege 'the' feminine that falls outside 'the' masculine symbolic, and outside language itself. By contrast, starting from Adorno's more historical perspective, the conceptual blind spots do not involve grammatical or linguistic breakdown, and historical change can generate an irruption of a variety of registered (but also forgotten) elements of sense experience.

A Different Blind Spot

For Adorno the manifold of experience is brought under concepts (as in Kant), but is not governed by the necessary and universal categories that Kant lays down. It follows that sexual, racial and ethnic differences are, in principle, graspable, along with other 'forgotten' singularities that also emerge from the unstable groupings of schematized particulars which Adorno – along with Walter Benjamin – terms 'constellations'. As 'subject' and 'object' (together) undergo historical change, forgotten singularities and patternings emerge from within the 'constellations' of thought. As such, registering and expressing female specificity becomes less of a conceptual impossibility and more of a historical potentiality.

Adorno himself does not exploit this potentiality, however. Although he describes 'universal' human nature as an ideological illusion, his methodology commits him to another kind of universal – the myth of 'instrumental reason' – which also makes it impossible to focus on female subjects and their relation to objects. Thus, towards the end of *Dialectic of Enlightenment*, Adorno and Horkheimer note that women stand in a different relationship to instrumental reason (and hence modernity) than do men:

> Women have no personal part in the efficiency on which this civilization is based. It is man who has to go out into an unfriendly world, who has to struggle and produce. Woman is not a being in her own right, a subject. She produces nothing but looks after those who do; she is a living monument to a long-vanished era when the domestic economy was self-contained. The division of labour imposed on her by man brought her little that was worthwhile. She became the embodiment of the biological function, the image of nature, the subjugation of which constituted that civilization's title to fame. (1944, pp. 247–8)

Adorno and Horkheimer provide an account of the self and its objects which is formed by man's relationship to instrumental reason and to the modes of production, but then observe (as a kind of afterthought in the unsystematized 'Notes and Drafts' appended to their text) that the whole analysis works only for males. As such, Adorno and Horkheimer are constrained to position woman as part of 'second nature' – a specularized 'object' (to use Irigarayan language) – not a subject capable of synthesizing a different reality via her different relationship to work and in respect to her role as 'carer' of man. Their 'woman' escapes the parameters of the 'Enlightenment' self; but the two authors do not seek to build on this basis an alternative account of the self/other, mind/body, subject/object relationships.

Sexual difference is registered by Adorno, but it is something that his own theory works to forget. Instead, women are represented in the most abstract terms, and Adorno fails to note that their primary historical roles in western modernity – as 'carers' and 'consumers' – work against each other. As 'carer', woman undermines the privileged role assigned to instrumental reason in Adorno's model, since the 'carer' functions by treating her children/partner/parents not as equivalents – as commodities, capable of exchange – but as singularities, with unique and irreplaceable qualities that have to be nurtured and preserved. The 'caring' role is not, of course, the unique prerogative of women; but historically women have acted as a resource *within* Adorno's so-called 'bourgeois' society – and provide a neglected opening within Adorno's negative dialectics for envisaging a more positive mode of social and historical change.

Adorno both complains of the 'Enlightenment' tendency to reduce a multiplicity to 'unity' and yet also himself performs an 'Enlightenment' abstraction as he strips woman of the singularity of her position and reduces 'bourgeois society' and bourgeois subjects to one (evolving) homogeneity. 'Enlightenment' is treated as a continuous historical development (running from Parmenides to Bertrand Russell): one that reaches its apogee in 'high' or 'liberal' capitalism, in which objects in nature are treated as mere 'things', capable of alignment and exchange with other 'things'. Thus, Adorno has a model that can recognize – and build on – historical and cultural differences between humans. But his account of recollection still 'forgets' the puzzles posed by women, and their lived experiences.

Adorno portrays selfhood and identity as illusions. However, he also argues that what cannot and must not be broken are the dialectical processes of history which constitute the self/other relation as a belonging together in the antinomies of thought. Philosophy must proceed dialectically, allowing illusions to play off each other, not seeking to eliminate the (historically necessary) antinomies of thought (1966, pp. 211ff). Adorno thus traps (modern) man into a necessary dialectics which can only ever work negatively as a critique of reason. However, the attempt to bring all of (western) history within a historical development that 'unifies' it in accordance with the parameters of instrumental reason is undercut by 'women' in ways that suggest that Adorno was also wrong to suggest that the (bourgeois) subject stands in an antagonistic relationship to his (reified) objects in ways that cannot be overcome, but that must nevertheless be endlessly subjected to negative critique.

Adorno insists on retaining the antagonism between subject and object (until historical circumstances work to break down this antagonism) – and this is, at least in part, what makes his position so different from my own. Whereas in this book I have been arguing for a need to displace the Kantian notion that subject and object can only ever be defined antagonistically (by thinking the object as the other that is spatially always outside the self), Adorno insists that the task of 'negative dialectics' is to show how subject and object always belong together in an antagonistic relationship that is a product of history. Adorno does not seek to get rid of the notion of the subject, but instead claims that 'even when we merely limit the subject, we put an end to its power' (1966,

p. 183). Instead of freeing us from the subject/object dualisms of Kantian thinking, Adorno locks us into this dualism, but in ways that involve privileging the object whilst simultaneously keeping the subject/object binary in play.

There are, thus, significant differences between the use of 'history' as conceptualized by Adorno and my own turn to 'history' that emerges from the perspective of contemporary debates within feminist theory. Throughout this book I have suggested that the 'singularity' of the female subject-position could be used to blow apart the 'universals' of Kantian judgement and nature in such a way as to allow us to think a subject that is both individual and non-autonomous. This paradigmatic female subject would exercise her freedom within unequal relationships of power and dependence (appropriate to those who might birth and who are born). Furthermore, to think her positioning within patriarchal modernity, it will be necessary to think modernity and patriarchy as dissipative structures: with 'others' within, as well as without – and with identities emerging from the transitional (and also non-dialectical) inter-actions of self and not-self.

Remembering Nietzsche

Adorno's own analysis of the self produces a new blind spot relating to 'woman' and 'women'. However, because this blindness can be explained historically (and in accordance with his own methodology), it is a more productive mode of blindness than that which comes from Lacanian psychoanalysis and other types of poststructuralism and post-modernism that emphasize epistemology – and the way that identity is established by the blocking out of difference. This point will emerge more clearly if we briefly compare the use made of Nietzsche by Adorno to radicalize the 'real', and that employed by Judith Butler in her cri-tique of the 'metaphysics of substance' that I considered in the last chapter.

As we have seen, in the opening pages of *Gender Trouble* (1990, pp. 20–1), Butler establishes her Nietzsche through a quote from Michel Haar which positions Nietzsche as claiming that the illusion of being an individual self ultimately derives from 'the belief in language and, more precisely, in the truth of grammatical categories'. According to this Nietzsche, all the mistakes of metaphysics derive from the lin-guistic 'structure of subject and predicate'. It was grammar that tricked

Descartes into a 'certainty' that there is an 'I' that thinks. By contrast, 'the subject, the self, the individual are just so many false concepts, since they transform into substances fictitious unities having at the start only a linguistic reality' (Haar, 1971, pp. 17–18).

Butler has been influenced by Derrida, and in *Of Grammatology* and elsewhere Derrida also appeals to Nietzsche as a (linguistic) ally in the attempt to counter the 'metaphysics of presence' which is both ubiquitous and closely tied to the structures of grammar (1967, p. 19). As Robert Scholes sums up Derrida's overall position:

> What he has helped us understand goes something like this: No world without things. No things without differences. No differences without language. No language without nouns. No nouns without categories. No categories without metaphysics, logocentrism, and all the mechanisms of subjection. The outline of this position is already there in Nietzsche . . . [who] plays a crucial role in Derrida's *Éperons* [*Spurs*]. (Scholes, 1994, p. 119)

Thus, in the deconstructive tradition that takes its impetus from Derrida, Nietzsche emerges as a precursor: as a textual – and stylistic – rebel against an ontology of 'being'.

For Haar and Butler, as also for Derrida, Nietzsche's revolutionary potential is linked to his attack on language and grammar as the source of the 'illusion' of the ego – and Descartes is taken as typical of the modernity that Nietzsche opposes. The 'I' that is under attack here is an illusion generated by grammar: the linguistically defined subject of the phrase 'I think (therefore I am)'. By contrast, in *Against Epistemology* (1956, pp. 18–20) Adorno links Nietzsche's revolutionary potential to modes of *historical* forgetting – and it is this forgetting that then generates the potential for remembering difference. Although it is possible to find support within Nietzsche's (often contradictory) corpus for the poststructuralists' interpretation, there are interestingly different consequences if we read Nietzsche in the way suggested by Adorno. For if the illusions of the self are ascribed to language, then it will not be possible to escape them except by abandoning grammatical (and propositional) language, or by disturbing its systematic operation via parody or word-play. But if these same illusions are due to history, then other ways of thinking the self (and identity) become possible – and speakable/writable – within the evolutions and revolutions (and different temporalities) of the constellations of ideas that constitute the 'real'.

In an early essay, 'On the Truth and Lies in a Nonmoral Sense' (1873), Nietzsche points out that words become concepts not through standing for a 'unique and entirely individualized original experience', but by being extended to 'fit countless more or less similar cases', which means that the original experience (and hence individuation) gets lost (p. 83). Nietzsche continues:

> Every concept arises through the equation of unequal things. Just as it is certain that one leaf is never totally the same as another, so it is certain that the concept 'leaf' is formed by arbitrarily discarding these individual differences and by forgetting the distinguishing aspects. This awakens the idea that, in addition to the leaves, there exists in nature the 'leaf': the original model according to which all the leaves were perhaps woven, sketched, measured, coloured, curled, and painted – but by incompetent hands, so that no specimen has turned out to be a correct, trustworthy, and faithful likeness of the original model. . . . We obtain the concept, as we do the form, by overlooking what is individual and actual; whereas nature is acquainted with no form and no concepts, and likewise with no species, but only with an X which remains inaccessible and undefinable for us. (p. 83)[1]

Nietzsche suggests that when the mind 'forgets' the other individuals in the formation of the concept of the leaf, those other experiences (of individual differences) are not simply negated. Instead, there can be no sameness without a difference that is covered over. Then, in another early essay, 'The Use and Abuse of History' (1874), Nietzsche considers what our relation to 'forgetfulness' should be. Although the essay as a whole praises the 'unhistorical' attitude that is characterized by willed forgetfulness, Nietzsche's polemic against (Hegelian) history also makes it clear that difference is threatening because it retains the capacity to dislodge the fictions of the 'I'. Indeed, the essay ends with the hope that we moderns 'may again become healthy enough to study history anew, and under the guidance of life make use of the past in that threefold way – monumental, antiquarian, or critical' (p. 71).

Such a productive use of history would involve registering and organizing the 'chaos' within our selves in ways that will allow us 'to revolt against secondhand thought, secondhand learning, secondhand action' (p. 72). 'Forgetting' is an important moment in the construction of the self on this early Nietzschean model which retains a problematic concept of a self with 'true needs', discoverable behind the 'chaos' of false and inherited concepts (p. 72). But 'chaos' is not simply the reverse of order. Instead, difference (chaos) has to be organized if we are to counter (false) remembrance and what Nietzsche terms the 'concealment and disfiguring' of life. There are clear analogies here with Adorno's concept of 'second nature' – 'waxified' and 'specularized' by supposedly 'object-ive' needs that involve an internalization of the standards of instrumental reason. As such, Nietzsche's attack on 'modern' uses of history bears a family resemblance to Adorno's critique of 'modern' reason, and also to the notion of 'constellations' that Adorno appropriated and adapted from his friend and colleague, Walter Benjamin.

Of Essence and Lace Trimmings

For Adorno particulars stand in a pattern of relations to other particulars via historically sedimented 'constellations' that are used to define identity. These patternings of individual differences in the 'constellation' are not lost, but remain in ways that allow them to impinge on consciousness in flashes of so-called 'intuition' in which what re-emerges is those differences that reason 'forgot'. In an essay on Walter Benjamin, Adorno compares these forgotten differences to the 'lace trimming on a dress' in terms that situate Benjamin's project against Nietzsche's later works. As Adorno puts it:

> The later Nietzsche's critical insight that truth is not identical with a timeless *universal*, but rather that it is solely the historical which yields the figure of the absolute, became, perhaps without [Benjamin's] knowing it, the canon of his practice. The programme is formulated in a note to his fragmentary main work, that 'in any case the eternal is more like the lace trimmings on a dress than like an idea'. (1955, p. 231)

For Benjamin, the eternal is more 'like lace trimmings on a dress' than a Platonic idea. The eternal can be grasped through the 'trimmings'; indeed the eternal cannot exist except in relation to 'trimmings'. This move is not just anti-Platonic, it is also anti-Kantian, since tying the eternal to temporal 'trimmings' entails a denial of any radical difference between being and becoming, and also between the (Kantian) noumenal and the (Kantian) phenomenal.

As Susan Buck-Morss has also argued, Adorno's comments on the 'canon' of his dead friend and colleague also give us a strong clue to Adorno's own methodology, as well as to that of other members of 'The Frankfurt School' (Buck-Morss, 1977, pp. 90–101). What she does not point out is that '*adorno*' means 'adornment' in Portuguese and 'trimmings' in Spanish, and in Italian is also a verb and an adjective with the same set of meanings. Why this is relevant is because Corsican is a dialect of Italian, and Theodor Wiesengrund Adorno changed his name from his Jewish-German patronymic (Wiesengrund) to the Corsican-Genoese matronymic (Adorno) by a gradual process of transition from the 1920s on. Thus, Theodor first started to sign articles Wiesengrund-Adorno, then assigned the Wiesengrund to the status of a middle name when he came to join the exiled Institute for Social Research in New York in 1938. This name change appropriately symbolizes the fact that the notion of 'trimmings' is key to Adorno's own methodology, as well as to that of Walter Benjamin himself.

It is the productive use of these 'trimmings' – *adorno* – to construct a new relation to 'being' that makes Adorno's Nietzsche so subtly different from the Nietzsche that we encountered in the anti-metaphysical tradition of poststructuralist theory proffered by Judith Butler. For Adorno 'being' is an illusion; but his use of Nietzsche (taken from Benjamin) allows us to chart shifting essences in ways that might remind us once more of Bergson, of Spinoza, and of a metaphysics in which being emerges out of the flow of becoming. Now being is reshaped by its relation to the tangential and the liminal: the 'trimmings'.

For Judith Butler, any talk of identity is an illusion – and we must use parodic speech-acts to attack notions of 'essence' and 'eternal' forms. As such, any talk of essence as bound up with 'lace trimmings' would make little sense. By contrast, the Nietzsche offered us by Adorno and Benjamin has a subversive memory and an attention to forgotten differences that act as more than a linguistic 'trace' that disrupts all talk of identity. As new (provisional) 'forms' emerge over time from forgotten patterns of difference, Adorno allows us to see that is not just *the* 'symbolic' which needs to be *de*-centred or disturbed by the play of *différance* or the operations of parody. Whereas the deconstructionist tradition gives up on metaphysics, different times and spaces (different ontological 'realities') become possible as Adorno claims that both subject and 'object' change (together) across time.

Even though thinking the female does not provide a historical opening that Adorno himself is able to explore, he allows us to see that the female subject-position need not be conceptualized as one that is always and necessarily at odds with a homogeneous tradition that is 'phallogocentric' metaphysics. He also enables us to understand how an emphasis on the female can be understood as a type of insight that is given by history – alongside other 'recollections' of 'race', 'ethnicity', 'class' and sexual orientation. Thus, in terms of the current debates that mark feminist theory, what is important about Adorno's move is the insistence that the 'trimmings' that can give access to 'recollection' of reason's 'blind spots' are not outside history, but themselves implicated in history.

As Adorno himself puts it: 'Kant's epistemological question, "How is metaphysics possible?" yields to a question from the philosophy of history: "Is it still possible to have a metaphysical experience?"' (1966,

p. 372). And, as Peter Osborne has argued, Adorno's answer to this question is a (qualified and paradoxical) 'yes', in ways that mean that his position should best be described as a '*materialist metaphysic of modernity*; rather than, for example, either a negative *theology* or a mere *sociology* of illusion' (Osborne, 1989, p. 23). As such, Adorno provides hints of a route for escaping the epistemological cul-de-sac into which the deconstructive modes of postmodernism divert us. His 'non-metaphysical metaphysics' promises a way forward that does not start from a game of subverting grammar, language or signs.

Disrupting Modernities

Although Adorno does not himself develop an analysis of postmodernity, his account of modernity also allows a different – less epistemological – understanding of postmodernism than that currently dominant within feminist theory. If we follow David Harvey (1990) and define 'postmodernism' not in terms of the epistemological relativism or metaphysical scepticism that was considered in chapter 5, but as involving a change in the relation between 'subjects' and 'objects' that has occurred as a consequence of developments in modes of capitalist production, then postmodernism does not entail a refusal of new ontologies. The so-called 'post-Fordist' changes and 'Just-in-Time' work practices that Harvey describes have brought with them breakdowns in the work practices that have shaped modern western societies, and which also mark out sexed identities within the state. Registering these social changes makes it possible to us to explain why we can adapt Adorno's own account to register the female subject that Adorno and Horkheimer's 1944 history of western modernity still works to 'forget'.

Despite Adorno's failure to theorize either postmodernism or sexual difference, his move is thus important for feminist theorists who are attempting to think a multiplicity of differences relating to gender, race, ethnicity, disability and sexual preference. And it is significant in this respect that Jane Flax – the feminist postmodernist who strikes me as offering the best way forward for thinking difference within a psychoanalytic frame – has been profoundly influenced by Theodor Adorno. (See Flax, 1993, pp. 10ff.) Flax presents herself as having turned to postmodernism as a way of countering the pessimism of critical theorists such as Adorno. However, her (unusual) variety of psychoanalytic postmodernism retains important features of the tradition she abandoned. Instead of looking to Freud and Lacan for a definition of the unconscious (which would make the unconscious, by definition, inaccessible to conscious thought), Flax turns to the 'object-relations' theory of D. W. Winnicott which stresses instead the notion of an intersubjective 'transitional space' which emerges at the intersection of self/other relations (1993, pp. 16–17, 117ff). This means that Flax can emphasize power relations and theorize other differences apart from sexual difference. She can also resist the temptation to place difference outside the horizons of that which can be represented or known.

There is revolutionary potential in Adorno's position. However, in practice his philosophical method involved presenting 'constellations' of ideas in ways that allow us to observe that the philosophical, artistic and cultural problematics are historically constructed, but in a way that cannot simply be negated. Absolute wisdom/epistemology is alien to Adorno's project; instead historical procedures of analysis and synthesis come to replace the conceptual procedures of analysis and synthesis that Kant and the idealists had developed. For Adorno, we are all 'modern' subjects, and modernity involves an instrumental use of reason that renders man a 'pseudo-individual' lacking in qualities and in singularity. But Adorno credits avant-garde art with the capacity to break open the everyday (Kantian) structures of 'space', 'time' and 'self'.

Thus, whereas Adorno and Horkheimer describe 'the culture industry' (popular culture) in *Dialectic of Enlightenment* as working towards the 'complete quantification' of individuals in statistics on types of consumers, Adorno also asserts that avant-garde art resists the generalized tendency. Such art is out of step with the instrumental rationality that underpins a society in which 'Everybody must behave (as if spontaneously) in accordance with his previously determined and indexed level, and choose the category of mass product turned out for his type' (1944, p. 123). For Adorno, it is 'art' and not 'woman' which bears within it the seeds of a singular subject-position that eludes the quantifying equivalences of the Enlightenment self.

Adorno regards avant-garde art as antithetical to a social 'reality' that deals in 'things', in that it conjures an emotional and cognitive response that is not centred on interchangeable commodities. However, at the same time he suggests that this social reality cannot be changed by the actions of any individual artist. From his work on music (which privileges the music of Schoenberg over that of Stravinsky, and which is dismissive of jazz) to his essays on the literature of surrealism and the theatre of Brecht, Adorno valorizes *modernist* art as a mode of resistance that retains its power to disturb as long as it remains negative (1970, pp. 320ff). Since for Adorno it is the oppositional status of avant-garde art that accords it its revolutionary status, he also opposes any attempt to re-educate the audience so as to realign the tastes of the bourgeois with avant-garde art. There is thus a deep pessimism about social change in Adorno's work. Art must remain a mode of resistance to instrumental reason and, as such, requires the bourgeois man as its oppositional pole.

Cynical Critique

In his *Critique of Cynical Reason* (1983) Peter Sloterdijk has accused Adorno of taking a kind of pleasure in his despair at the ineffectual nature of intellectual and artistic revolutionary elites. The whole of Sloterdijk's *Critique* can be read as a (rude, but nevertheless respectful) 'response' to both Kant and Adorno. From Adorno, Sloterdijk retains the notion that the subject isn't trapped in his subjectivity in the manner of Kant's three *Critiques*. From Kant, however, Sloterdijk retains the thought that the individual is not unable to change the course of history, and that Adorno's pessimistic conclusions about the inability of reason to work except via negative critique are unduly cynical and flawed. Sloterdijk ends by advocating a return to Kant's motto for 'Enlightenment man': ' "Sapere aude!" Have the courage to use your *own* understanding!' – even if Sloterdijk's anti-intellectual 'courage' is very different from Kant's. Sloterdijk is advocating not Adorno's philosophical 'cynicism', but 'kynicism'; and 'a courage that is alien to the modern despair about the "state of affairs" ' (1983, p. 545).

According to Sloterdijk, philosophical cynicism involves a disillusionment with reason. It involves irony and sarcasm, but it is all a matter of 'cleverness' and – because it does not seek to change the disease of modernity, but functions as a part of modernity – it remains '*enlightened false consciousness*' which is no more than 'a hard-boiled shadowy cleverness that has split courage off from itself' (p. 546). Philosophical cynicism is knowing, and worldly-wise; it is 'well-mannered rationality' – 'all in the head'. Kynicism, however, is an attitude towards reason that has been forgotten by history and can be reclaimed from history (here Sloterdijk uses Adorno against himself). It involves celebrating the ridiculous – the body and its waste matters – as a way of mocking the pretensions of reason. Diogenes – unkempt, masturbating, and living disgustingly in his barrel – is a kynic; Adorno is a cynic who *pretends* to be a kynic in that he rationalizes an object that has the power to shock the subject out of himself. In contrast to Adorno, Sloterdijk advocates kynicism; he seeks a relationship to matter that can move reason on, past the melancholy and nostalgia that he regards as characteristic of Adorno's pseudo-kynicism.

In order to characterize the weaknesses of Adorno's account of the relationship between the object and the subject, Sloterdijk represents Adorno as unable to deal with unreified nature (and female flesh) whilst, nevertheless, remaining on the side of the 'feminine'. Sloterdijk twice refers to an incident that happened in 1969 – a year after the student riots that disrupted the social fabric of Germany and France.

> Shortly before Adorno died there was a scene in a lecture hall at Frankfurt University that fits like a key into the analysis of cynicism begun here. The philosopher was just about to begin his lecture when a group of demonstrators prevented him from mounting the podium. Such scenes were not unusual in 1969. On this occasion something happened that required a closer look. Among the disrupters were some female students who, in protest, attracted attention to themselves by exposing their breasts to the thinker. Here, on one side, stood naked flesh, exercising 'critique'; there, on the other side, stood the bitterly disappointed man without whom scarcely any of those present would have known what critique meant – cynicism in action. (p. xxxvii)

There is a deep irony implicit in Sloterdijk's observation, since in *Against Epistemology* Adorno had criticized Husserl for the passage from *Logical Investigations* quoted at the start of this chapter: the one that represented 'mother nature' in terms of a 'waxwork figure' on the stairs in the 'Panopticum Waxworks'. Adorno's critique suggested that he himself had access to flesh which is more than a constrained (waxy) infinity, and which is something more than the 'second nature' which acts as the counterpart to Husserl's epistemology of the subject. It is, therefore, very clever of Sloterdijk to use Adorno's silence when confronted with real-life female flesh to show the inadequacy of a cynicism that merely pretended to be kynicism:

> Now, their baring was no run-of-the-mill erotic-cheeky argument with female skin. They were, almost in the ancient sense, kynically bared bodies, bodies as arguments, bodies as weapons. Their showing themselves, independently of the private motives of the demonstrators, was an antitheoretical action. In some sort of confused sense, they may have understood their act as a 'praxis of social change,' in any case, as something more than lectures and philosophical seminars. Adorno, in a tragic but understandable way, had slipped into the position of the idealistic Socrates, and the women into the position of the unruly Diogenes. (1983, pp. 109–10)

Faced with the disruptive activities of the student revolt of 1968, Adorno offered no theoretical (or practical) support. This critic of 'bourgeois' society felt unable to encourage a revolution that did not stem from material changes in the processes of production. His cynicism was a form of fatalism – what Sloterdijk refers to as 'bitter disappointment' and 'tragic idealism' – which prevented 'a praxis of social change' accompanying his theoretical analyses.

Bodily Arguments

For all the cleverness of Sloterdijk's critique of Adorno, it is also, however, flawed in respect to issues of sexual difference. Thus, in the above passage the motives of the individual women who bared their breasts are left out of account. Indeed, the women are represented as acting politically 'in some confused sense', even though by 1969 the German feminist movement had accused the radical left of being itself confused when it ignored the politics of sexual specificity. The feminist agenda had been announced in another Frankfurt lecture hall in the autumn of 1968 when left-wing women disrupted the proceedings of the Sozialistischer Deutscher Studentenbund (SDS) with a hail of tomatoes, eggs and feminist pamphlets. In Sloterdijk's narration of the 'silencing' of Adorno, the motives that might have rendered this bodily display a radical *female* gesture are left to one side. Instead, women's political gestures are read as just another form of kynicism that is gender-neutral – even at the moment when a female breast is bared. The representation of the political sphere as gender-homogeneous (by both Sloterdijk and Adorno) means that the female body is appropriated for a model of identity (and the subverting of identity) in which female difference is left out of account.

According to Sloterdijk, kynical reason inverts the old values, and celebrates the ridiculous (the body/matter) that merely 'cynical' reason bewails. His own book emphasizes bodily acts and functions as a theoretical substitute for the naked flesh of these *de*-gendered students in the face of Adorno's world-weary critique. Sloterdijk's solution to the 'disease' of modern cynicism is to flaunt the body in the face of 'pure' reason and 'pure' cynicism; to allow flesh to perform a revolutionary gesture that will move philosophy on past the stage of 'enlightened false consciousness' and towards revolutionary praxis. But it is a curiously abstract – and gender-free – body that gets bared in the sections of the *Critique of Cynical Reason* entitled 'Eye Gazes, Eye Blinkers', 'Breasts', 'Arses', 'Fart', 'Shit, Refuse', 'Genitals'.

Although not exactly male, these bodies do not menstruate and they also do not give birth. Breasts do not give milk; instead they are caught between commodified objects of attraction, or attain freedom in being like 'the sweetness of ripe pears that have become so heavy and friendly toward themselves that, on an appropriate occasion, they fall from the tree into a hand they feel recognizes them' (1983, p. 147). Everything is regarded from a male perspective, but a perspective that none the less seeks to disguise its own maleness and describes bodies as if they were sexed and sexy, but nevertheless somehow also gender-neutral. And this is a serious matter, as Andreas Huyssen also notes in his foreword to the English translation (p. xx). However, whereas Huyssen suggests that attention to feminism could have strengthened Sloterdijk's philosophy, I do not see how. Despite Sloterdijk's appropriation of the rude *female* gesture of baring the breasts, male and female bodies do not stand as equivalents in the history of western thought. Sloterdijk pretends gender-neutrality, but his determined masculinism is, in fact, integral to his argument that employs bodily gestures as kynical critique.

Thus, part of Sloterdijk's critique of Adorno is that the latter is 'feminine'. Sloterdijk claims that Adorno's 'emotional-epistemological secret' is tied up with nostalgia for a lost other/the lost mother. For Adorno 'tears and knowing are connected', Sloterdijk asserts. Adorno loves (and cries over) Schubert's music 'because we are not like it, not something complete':

> Happiness can only be thought of as something lost, as a *beautiful alien*. It cannot be anything more than a premonition that we approach without ever reaching it. Everything else belongs to 'false living' anyway. What dominates is the world of the fathers, who are always appallingly in agreement with the granite of abstractions, now solidified into a system. With Adorno, the denial of the masculine went so far that he retained only one letter from his father's name, *W*. (p. xxxv)

Sloterdijk represents nostalgia for the lost mother as feminizing the male. Like Gilles Deleuze and Michel Foucault (and unlike Lacan), Sloterdijk himself represents desire not in terms of lack, but as a positive force capable of instigating social change. It is thus doubly ironic that Sloterdijk seems blind to any sexually differentiated desire, and cannot think of female desire except in terms that make it equivalent to that of the male. Indeed, Sloterdijk uses the embodied *maleness* of his own kynical position against the (supposedly) 'effeminate' affectivity of Adorno's attitude to avant-garde art. Adorno allies himself with the world of 'woman', but cannot think the female. Sloterdijk is masculinist, but cannot recognize that it is male bodies that he requires for his argument to work. Sloterdijk's mistake is to suppose that there can be a simple reinsertion of the body to counter the 'effeminization' of reason, and that we can reverse the Kantian gesture which represented it as 'emasculating' to have contact with matter and seek to penetrate 'the veil of Isis' that covers nature.

The body *per se* cannot be used as the counterpole to male philosophy. To rewrite Lacan: '*the*' body does not exist. We cannot treat all bodies as equivalents, and suppose that the use of *any* body – that is, no particular body – has the power to unsettle reason in analogous ways. However, the lesson that we can draw from Sloterdijk is analogous to the lace trimmings – *adorno* – on the bras discarded by those German women students. A return to past philosophical texts reveals features of the philosophical theories that were 'forgotten' by their authors and that can be used not merely to deconstruct the author's philosophical conclusions, but to *re*construct a nonmetaphysical metaphysics that is alive to issues of difference. It is these trimmings – *adorno* – that help us think the 'subject' in terms that privilege the female: as no hermetically closed unity, but one that is open to radical novelty and to 'objects' in ways that can facilitate social (and philosophical) change.

8
Kierkegaard, Woman and the Workshop of Possibilities

The black novelist Richard Wright (born in Mississippi in 1908) boasted that he knew everything that Kierkegaard had written before he came to read his books. However, as Paul Gilroy has pointed out, 'Wright's apparently intuitive foreknowledge of the issues raised by Kierkegaard was not intuitive at all', but was a part of the experience of an American black man in the 1930s (Gilroy, 1993, p. 159).[1] For those living with the status of almost-persons in a society that thinks the human in terms of the autonomous (white) male subject, it is Kierkegaard who captures the internal divisions and conflicting demands of the subject of modernity – and not Adorno, who was profoundly influenced by Kierkegaard, but who also neutralizes Kierkegaard, so that he becomes just another idealist who is also a theorist of 'bourgeois' thought.

As we saw in the last chapter, Adorno's account of historical 'forgetting' and memory is useful for escaping the implicit idealism of those feminist, deconstructionist and psychoanalytic thinkers who approach the question of self and its others through an epistemological frame. For Adorno, material differences and singularities erupt via the unconscious, and impinge on knowledge as the relationship between self and object undergoes historical change. Through allocating power to a historically fluctuating 'matter' Adorno disrupts Kant's 'Enlightenment' control of the 'object' – a control that remains present in Lacan, Derrida and those varieties of feminisms that present the body as a discursive, psychic or linguistic construct, or that present the 'other' as the limits of the self. However, as we have also seen, Adorno's account of the embodied self – and of past and of future possibilities – is too monolithic (too Hegelian), and is particularly weak when it comes to registering female difference.

To think how to deal more adequately with female singularity, it will be useful to go further back into the history of philosophy and look in more detail at the author who was the subject of Adorno's doctoral thesis. (See Adorno, 1933/62.) I will be suggesting that Søren Kierkegaard offers a model for rethinking temporality – and hence also identity within spatio-temporal worlds – that offers more revolutionary potential than anything offered by Adorno himself. Kierkegaard is particularly relevant in this context, since he ties his reworking of temporalities and identities to a prolonged exploration of the positioning of 'woman'. Kierkegaard is one of the few philosophers whose writings do not simply ignore the issue of sexual difference – or use the concept of 'woman' in a merely negative fashion.

Partly because Kierkegaard wants to use woman's relationship to man as a model for a different understanding of man's relationship to God, he has bothered to think how paradoxical it is to exist as a woman. Kierkegaard writes for a specific – and sometimes also hypothetical – female reader, based on Regine, the fiancée whom he jilted whilst remaining (forever) in love. He frequently presents his own predicament through 'silhouettes' of female characters, moved by their grief to the centre of the stage. Thus, with a sideways swipe at Hegel, he rewrites *Antigone* so as to make Sophocles' heroine the embodiment of the subject-position of the modern 'singular individual' – and also of his own wilfully/passively 'singular' self.

This author whose own *Journals* are dominated by an autocratic father – and in whose many thousands of entries there is no mention of his mother – has a philosophical enterprise that proceeds by making woman typical, and by dramatizing woman's predicament with all its humour and tragedy. Kierkegaard offers an account of the self which privileges vertical relationships – relationships between unequals – between the seducer and the seduced; the father and his daughter; the father and his son. Although he doesn't write about motherhood, he frequently uses images of childhood, of wombs and of weaning in order to stress what is inherited from the past. But that past is not simply a 'given', and neither is it negated: it is a part of finding oneself as a self by living through – and with – dependence. 'Woman' – and the male/female relationship – becomes emblematic of masculine illusions about autonomy of the ego. And in writing in this way, this philosopher (who is, of course, by no means a feminist) often prefigures uncannily some of the current discourse about 'woman' in the postmodern and post-structuralist traditions.

Until very recently it was conventional to represent Kierkegaard as an 'existentialist' philosopher: as stressing subjectivity, authenticity and freedom, without emphasizing the radical attack on all three notions that he simultaneously develops. This is, indeed, how Kierkegaard was appropriated by Simone de Beauvoir, who uses Kierkegaard as a precursor in *The Ethics of Ambiguity*, where she suggests that his problem about the nature of individual freedom is fundamentally the same as hers (1947, pp. 9–10). She also makes similar moves in *The Second Sex* (1949), where Kierkegaard's *Stages on Life's Way* (1845) is quoted approvingly four times.[2] Her own theory that woman is other, even to herself, was fundamentally influenced by her reading of Kierkegaard, despite her later pretence to have drawn her ontology solely from Sartre.

However, the analogies between what Kierkegaard says and what feminists say is often at its most extreme amongst those varieties of feminist theorists who stress female 'difference' and who would see themselves as opposed to the essentially Enlightenment ideals of Beauvoir. Indeed, although it is Nietzsche – or, rather, a particular Derridean reading of Nietzsche – whom these theorists of 'difference' have most often coerced into the role of 'father', it is to my mind Kierkegaard's explicit writing about woman as both real and yet bearing 'a world of desire within her' that has the greater potential for a feminist metaphysics (Kierkegaard, 1845, p. 77).[3]

This is not only because Kierkegaard uses the concept of 'woman' as a lever with which to break open Enlightenment ideals of autonomy, free-will and personhood, but also because he is not simply content with this act of deconstruction. His position is between that of Beauvoir – whose existentialist concerns lead to a stress on the authenticity and subjectivity of the individual consciousness or 'for itself' – and those varieties of postmodern and poststructuralist feminists who would dispense with selves entirely. Having explored the 'paradox' implicit in the concept of woman, Kierkegaard moves on to reconstruct a subject-position in which the self is fractured into personae which function as a unity always and only in relation to an embedded (but ambiguous) past and to other (non-equal) selves. An (uncertain) past gives the Kierkegaardian self a kind of permanence; but that permanence is no more than a temporary stability in the flow of intersecting systems and lives.

The Kierkegaardian self persists through time; but this is not the deterministic, serialized time of the Kantian world, nor is it the progressive onward movement of Hegelian history. Nor does Kierkegaard, like Nietzsche, deepen time by reference to a notion of the eternal recurrence of the 'now' in which this reality will repeat itself in an infinity of cycles. (See Wood, 1989.) However, like Nietzsche, Kierkegaard does make it impossible to think of 'the moment' in terms of a single, linear series of 'nows' that are linked together through one uniting history. As we will see in this chapter and the next, for Kierkegaard the present is birthed within a multiple play of possibilities. The 'now' emerges in a 'nook' of intersecting paths, all of which contribute to the present and to the individualized egos and objects that emerge in this meeting (1845, p. 16).

As identities are scored into specificity by repeated movements which pattern the complex possibilities into actuality, 'self' and 'other' take shape together. In a Kierkegaardian world, birth (and radical novelty) is the norm, not a strange barely conceptualized possibility. Indeed, for Kierkegaard identity emerges out of movement; movement is not simply something that 'happens' to substances. Furthermore, the complexity of these movements is such that it is 'woman' – and not 'man' – that provides the key to his new understanding of self. As we will see, Kierkegaard uses 'woman' to construct a metaphysics that needs neither underlying substances, nor hylomorphism. Instead, Kierkegaardian reality involves a dynamic interrelation of past and present; self and (symbiotic) other.

A Modernized Antigone: 'Discipline and Punish'

'Woman' is used as a kind of leitmotiv in Kierkegaard's many and various writings. Indeed, his very first essay (published in 1834, whilst Kierkegaard was a student and within six months of his mother's death) is a rather unpleasant – and extremely sarcastic – article entitled 'Another Defence of Woman's Great Abilities'. In this chapter, however, I will focus primarily on two of the main texts that belong to the first period of Kierkegaard's authorship proper, and that belong with the pseudonymous – so-called 'aesthetic' – writings. It is in part 1 of *Either/Or* (1843a), henceforth referred to as *Either*) and in '*In Vino Veritas*', the opening dialogue of Kierkegaard's *Stages on Life's Way* (1845), that the topic of woman is most explicitly addressed. In *Stages* we meet characters who were introduced for the first time in a series of books published in 1843: *Either/Or*, *Fear and Trembling* and *Repetition*. These characters debate 'woman' in a deliberate restaging of Plato's *Symposium* (*c*.385 BC) in which the disputation was about 'love'. Two years previously in *Either* Kierkegaard had also modernized the Greeks, by rewriting Sophocles' *Antigone* in a chapter called 'The Tragic in Ancient Drama reflected in the Tragic in Modern Drama'.

Kierkegaard's reworking of *Antigone* is not done in his own voice, but is ascribed to the papers of the anonymous 'A', who writes (and exists) only in fragments. Nor does the rewrite take the form of dramatic poetry; instead it involves a short prose restructuring of the Sophoclean myth, with two major changes. The first change is that Antigone is presented primarily as Oedipus's daughter, rather than as the sister of Polynices. It is not in the brother/sister relationship that 'woman' is represented in her purest form (as in Hegel). Rather 'woman'/Antigone becomes a means for thinking the father/daughter relationship, so that the shape, potentialities and even the very existence of Antigone's life is, 'as it were, the afterpains' of that of a previous generation: 'Antigone's sad fate is like the echo of her father's, an intensified sorrow' (1843a, p. 156).

This is a significant comment, given Kierkegaard's description of echo as the 'grand-master of irony' in his *Journals* (1829–48, 5186).[4] Kierkegaard's rewriting of *Antigone* is self-consciously coded with references to Hegel. As we saw in chapter 6, for Hegel Antigone represented 'woman' in her purest form and was characterized as the 'everlasting irony in [the life of] the community'. (See Hegel, 1807, § 475, p. 288.) However, for Kierkegaard 'irony' is a transitional moment in the life of a single identity. In ways that should remind us of Irigaray, Kierkegaard's 'woman' becomes not only 'the irony in the community' but also 'the irony in the self'.

As Kierkegaard's *The Concept of Irony* (1841) makes clear, irony is interpreted as transitional: as a mode of existence that hovers between the positive and the negative.

> it is essential for the ironist never to articulate the idea as such but only casually to suggest it, to give with the one hand and take away with the other. . . . In this manner there quietly develops in the individual the disease that is just as ironic as any other wasting disease and allows the individual to feel best when he is closest to disintegration. The ironist is the vampire who has sucked the blood of the lover and while doing so has fanned him cool, lulled him to sleep, and tormented him with troubled dreams. (p. 49)

If 'woman' is linked with irony on this new model, 'woman' will also be associated with that which is somehow between the positive (full individuality) and negativity (lack of selfhood). Despite the comparison between the ironist and the vampire, however, it should not be supposed that Kierkegaard understands this state of transition in merely negative terms:

no genuinely human life is possible without irony. . . . Irony limits, finitizes, and circumscribes and thereby yields truth, actuality, content; it disciplines and punishes and thereby yields balance and consistency. Irony is a disciplinarian feared only by those who do not know it but loved by those who do. Anyone who does not understand irony at all, who has no ear for its whispering, lacks *eo ipso* [precisely thereby] what could be called the absolute beginning of personal life. . . . (p. 326)

'Woman' as the transitional state between individualized self and lack of self provides – like irony – a resource that disintegrates the individual, but that also moves Kierkegaard on to another, richer understanding of the 'genuinely human life'.

The second change that Kierkegaard effects in the classical story of *Antigone* in *Either* is even more substantial. Oedipus has killed the Sphinx; married his mother; and has produced Antigone as the offspring of his marriage. However, the tragic family fate is hidden from all – except Antigone herself, who carries this secret within herself, discussing it with nobody (not even her father). Since Oedipus, her father, is universally admired, Antigone is racked by uncertainty about whether or not he had ever known his guilt and his fate. After Oedipus dies, Antigone has lost all opportunity to ask him this question, and the torment increases. She is 'hurled' by her discovery of his secret 'into the arms of anxiety' (1843a, p. 154).

Although woman is presented in this prose sketch as fulfilling her destiny only when she becomes a bride, when Kierkegaard's Antigone falls in love she feels unable to enter into the marriage relationship (1843a, p. 157). This is because she believes it impossible to conceal this secret from the one with whom she is in love. Love for her intended and love for her father struggle within Antigone with such intensity that only at the moment she dies can she tell her beloved the reason for refusing marriage. Indeed, telling her secret is enough to cause her death, since it is her relationship with this secret (her family past) that comes to be the very essence of herself. Thus, 'the cause of her death is the recollection of her father', but this recollection is caused 'at the hand of one living' in so far as it is caused by her unhappy love (p. 164).

Kierkegaard's own *Journals* show that this reworked Antigone is his own *alter ego*. Kierkegaard's life was also marked by a (never disclosed) secret that related to his father, and an 'earthquake' of discovery that hurled him into anxiety – and that prevented him marrying Regine, the woman he loved (see 1829–48, 5430). In his notebooks, Kierkegaard plays with the figure of Antigone in ways that substitute the outlines of his own tragic story for hers:

No doubt I could bring my Antigone to an end if I let her be a man. He
forsook his beloved because he could not keep her together with his
private agony. In order to do it right, he had to turn his whole love into
a deception against her. . . . (1829–48, 5569)

However, in *Either* Kierkegaard's point is precisely that it is a woman
who is most able to represent the singular individual that falls outside
the norms of individuality and morality as represented by philosophy.

In order to establish this conclusion, Kierkegaard distinguishes
between classic Greek tragedy and modern tragedy. Greek tragedy is
characterized by sorrow: 'The greater the guiltlessness, the greater the
sorrow' (1843a, p. 149). Greek characters are not individualized, but
are representative figures: of family, country, state or social role. Their
destiny is a matter of inheritance, decreed by the gods or by fate. In
modern tragedy, by contrast, what marks man for a tragic destiny is his
own guilt, which presupposes full individuality. As such, the (guilty)
individual experiences tragedy as pain, not as sorrow. Kierkegaard says
that he is using a female character because he believes that 'a female
nature will be best suited to show the difference' between the Greeks
and the moderns (p. 153). Kierkegaard's 'woman' is transitional: she
is not Greek, but she also falls outside the norms of individuality on
both the Kantian and Hegelian models.

As a woman, [Antigone] will have enough substantiality for the sorrow to
manifest itself, but as one belonging to a reflective world she will have
sufficient reflection to experience the pain. (pp. 153–4)

Antigone (as woman) stands between full individuality (guilt) and
complete lack of individuality (sorrow). She is outside the conventions
of the modern and the ancient.

Guilt is possible only for those to whom full individuality is granted.
Kierkegaard's modernized Antigone is neither 'modern' nor 'ancient'.
Her destiny is not just a matter of fate; her feelings are not just ones
of 'sorrow'. But she feels pain for something that is not her own fault
as she tries to take responsibility for the 'sins of the father'. As such,
Antigone is singular: both inside and outside the norms of full personhood which are characteristic of modernity. Her tragedy is determined
by her relationship to a past – a past that is taken up into her own
life, so that it comes to constitute her very individuality. Indeed, it
is 'anxiety' – a temporal relationship that binds future to present and
that endlessly reworks the past – that becomes the mark of Antigone's
own singularity. Her pain is within her (hidden from public view) and
created by her own ambiguous relationship to a past that she cannot

change, yet which also escapes her in that she remains constantly tormented by uncertainty about her father's self-knowledge.

For Kierkegaard's modernized Antigone, there is no appeal to a pair of contrasting universals (as for Hegel's Greek Antigone). Nor is it the case (as in Hegel) that the male is bonded to the universals of the city, whilst woman is bonded to the universals of blood/nature in ways that provide openings onto logical and historical progressions in the overall development of spirituality. Rather, Kierkegaard's Antigone belongs to the modern world: the world of individualized selves. And it is precisely Antigone's failure to fit within any universals that marks her out.

Kierkegaard's Antigone falls outside the universals of both the 'moderns' and the ancient Greeks. However, Kierkegaard does not represent her singularity only in negative terms. Indeed, his own *Journals* show that he used the figure of Antigone productively: to represent the atypical – and, in particular, his own life, which developed out of an obsession with the 'secret' of his autocratic father. Thus, with respect to his own life, Kierkegaard comments in the *Journals*,

> I do not claim and never have claimed that I did not get married because doing so was contrary to Christianity, as if my being unmarried were, from a Christian point of view, a perfection in me. Far from it. Had I been an ordinary human being, the danger for me no doubt would have been something else, that of being taken up too much with women, and I possibly could have been a seducer. (1848–55, 6500)[5]

'Had I been an ordinary human being . . .'. Woman's singularity opens up a way for Kierkegaard to think that he also is not an ordinary human being in the modern sense. Kierkegaard regards himself as falling outside the norms of individuality and the ethics of personhood. But he does not fall into nothingness. Instead, he uses the concept of 'woman' to open up a new subject-position: one that can never be brought simply within a 'new' universal model of the self, abstractly considered.

In Kierkegaard's texts, woman is presented not simply as a logical particular that might (or might not) be brought under a rule; nor as a paradigm individual (who is simply chosen as the representative of a rule). Instead, woman is 'singular'; she brings with herself reference to a rule and her status as an exception to that rule. Woman is always at the margins of a sphere of discourse. Or, rather, woman is always hybrid, in that what makes her special is precisely the way she is awkwardly positioned *vis-à-vis* the conflicting models of self-in-society. As such, the essence of this subject-position is the unique – and historically changing – set of relations that constitute the self in its intimate bond with otherness.

A Singular Subject: The Young Man

In order to understand more about woman's singularity, it will be helpful to turn to the opening dialogue from *Stages on Life's Way* in which Kierkegaard pursues the theme of 'woman' as he reworks Plato's *Symposium* from a heterosexual perspective. Here, as in all the pseudonymous works, Kierkegaard offers his views only via a series of embedded pseudonyms and characters. However, although the characters within '*In Vino Veritas*' argue at some length about erotic love and 'woman', there is no fundamental disagreement between them as to the fact that the concept of woman threatens man's capacities for conceptual understanding. Woman is paradoxical, but nevertheless real; impossible, but nevertheless necessary; relational, but nevertheless existent. Furthermore, as the dialogue unfolds we discover that this incomplete and transitional being is more perfect than man.

It is the character of the 'Young Man' who starts off the discussion about 'woman' in the '*In Vino Veritas*' section that opens *Stages on Life's Way*. The crux of his speech is that in his love for woman 'man' is shown to be comic; and in ways that are not captured by Aristophanes' humorous account of the origins of erotic desire in Plato's *Symposium* (*c.*385 BC, 188e–193e). According to Aristophanes in that dialogue, the gods first created self-sufficient and rounded beings: each had two faces, facing in opposite directions upon a circular neck. Each being also had four legs and arms and two sets of genital organs. Jealous of their completeness, the gods decided to cut these beings in two; but the result of that 'cut' was love, since erotic desire simply is the search for one's lost other half. Kierkegaard's 'Young Man' – who has not yet been 'in love' – objects that Aristophanes has missed the true humour of the myth, despite his reputation as a comic dramatist. The Young Man argues that there is nothing very humorous about such a scenario: about simply being one half of a whole. Instead, what would be more amusing would be if one of the halves thought it was a whole, and still went round locked in an unconscious quest for its lost other half.

If a woman were really only a half-person (as is commonly suggested), there would be nothing comic about love, says the Young Man. What makes love comic is that a male – who is esteemed 'a whole man' – suddenly acts so that it becomes apparent that he is 'but a half person'. The self-dignity and autonomy of that man suddenly collapses as he is taken over by a force that renders him no more than a puppet, and that defies understanding. Any attempt at rationalization is just that – and merely increases the comic:

The more one thinks about it, the more ludicrous it becomes, for if the man actually is a whole, then he certainly does not become a whole in erotic love, but he and the woman become one and a half. No wonder the gods laugh, and especially at the man. (1845, p. 43)

Here it is not the half-personhood of woman that is questioned, but rather the fact that the male supposes himself a whole person in the Kantian sense of a self-legislating, free being.

Woman as Embryonic: Constantin Constantius

Constantin Constantius is the next character to speak. However, since Constantin is older (and has already been in love), he has to work harder to confine woman to the category of jest. Constantin is Kantian in his refusal to question the male's position as the paradigm ethical (and rational) individual. However, he does allow woman a transitional place between the ethical and the merely aesthetical, positioning her as 'not an aesthetic but an embryonic ethical category' (p. 48). As we saw in chapter 4, for Kant it was the 'sublime' that constituted the 'embryonic ethical category'; and a man (a male) proved his superior moral excellence (his 'personhood') by his ability to transcend fear and the potential annihilation of the 'I' that is integral to the experience of the dynamic sublime. For Constantin, the ideal woman is not a person. She should ideally be beautiful, not 'sublime'. She should not have the autonomy, rationality and the self-determining will that personhood entails. For Constantin, the failure of the ethical category to encompass woman is located in her lack: in the fact that she seems like a male, but is also seen to lack the reflection and rationality of the male:

Beautiful is she and lovely when she is viewed esthetically – no one can deny it. But as is said so often, so I, too, will say: One should not stop with that but should go further. Look at her ethically; just start doing that, and you have the jest. (p. 55)

Since woman is not a full person (and not capable of sublimity), she can feature only in comedy, Constantin claims, not in tragedy. Indeed, woman belongs in a transitional category, farce, which only works as comedy because we do not take the characters seriously as persons. In positioning woman as a farcical jest, Constantin is deliberately seeking to block off the power to disturb that she would have if she was conceived of as equal in status and value to the male (pp. 49ff). According to Constantin, it is the male's function to be absolute. Woman exists only in the relational – as transitional between full individuality and lack of individuality (p. 55). As such, no real relationship can exist between the two sexes. Furthermore, this misrelation must be maintained, otherwise man will become no longer an absolute, but a half-man; and woman too will become a half-man (p. 48).

Woman 'wants to be emancipated – she is man enough to say that. If that happens, the jest will exceed all bounds' (p. 56). With his knowing analysis, Constantin seeks to cover over the disruptive power that the concept of woman poses to Enlightenment political ideals of freedom, egality and fraternity. There is no room in Constantin's world for any bonds except those linking autonomous and rational male subjects: Kantian 'persons'. But woman is 'an incomplete form' who might in some better existence be 'led back to the male form' (p. 55). Woman is neither a fully ethical entity (a person), nor simply a beautiful object (the aesthetic). Thus, Constantin's cynical words reveal that he is aware of the reality of woman's threat and her potential for tragedy:

> Here lies her pathos, for woman is man; at least she is man enough to say what hardly any man is man enough to do. Man she is. In saying this, I have viewed her ethically. (p. 54)

Woman and Time: Victor Eremita

For Constantin woman is (almost) a 'person', (almost) capable of agency, (almost) sublime, (almost) ethical; but it is these 'almosts' that make her farcical – a parodic copy of the dignity of the male. By contrast, Kierkegaard's next character, Victor Eremita, finds woman not simply comic, but tragic, and in ways that threaten the male imaginary:

> If I had become a woman and could understand what I now understand – how terrible! If I had become a woman and consequently could not even understand that – how much more terrible! (p. 62)

Woman's misfortune is not simply that she is not treated as equal before the law; it is rather that the concept of woman has come to represent both excess and lack:

> To be a woman is something so special, so mixed, so compounded that there are no predicates to describe it, and the many predicates, if they were used, contradict one another in a manner only a woman can

tolerate, indeed, even worse, can relish. . . . [H]er life in the romantic consciousness has become meaningless. Thus, one moment she means everything, nothing at all in the next, yet without ever finding out what significance she actually does have, and still this is not the misfortune – it is mainly that she cannot come to know it, because she is woman. (p. 56)

Victor would seem to agree with those postmodern feminists who argue that the Enlightenment concept of the self cannot simply be broadened out in such a way as to include women within its boundaries. What woman lacks, according to Victor, is not only reflective consciousness, but the type of self-identity which can persist and develop through time. Woman is understood to be – and, indeed, is educated into being – no more than a series of unrelated personae. Thus, as Victor says, the young girl first experiences herself as worthless; then follows an ambiguous period in which her worth fluctuates; then a 'marriageable' period in which she is courted, flattered, praised, and treated as all-important and powerful; then, finally, there is the period of being married and middle-aged during which woman retreats back into insignificance (p. 58). As such, there is no model of personal development or moral maturation that can encompass her life. Woman does not mature; but suddenly ripens, and then is over-ripe. More like a beautiful fruit than a man, she is provided with no stable standards of ethical (or monetary) value.

For Victor the best relationship with a woman would be one charac-terized by negativity and unobtainability. Woman should remain an inspiration and a muse, not a wife or an actual lover. Woman's highest possible role is not the ethical role, since she falls outside the ethical. Rather, her function is fulfilled in awakening in the male the conscious-ness of immortality: making him a saint, a hero, a genius, a poet or some other exceptional figure (p. 60). Thus, for Victor woman's highest function is that of using her aesthetic power to project a man towards the sublime. As Victor sees it, woman exists outside time: as man's dream of sensuous perfection and sensual corruption. Woman has to live this dream: 'Woman's entire meaning is negative; her positive mean-ing is nothing in comparison – indeed, it probably is even corruptive' (p. 61). Woman is supposed to be – and is corruptively educated into being – intuitive, sensuous, the ideal creature of man's desire. Ironic-ally, however, this sensuous creature has the capacity to catapult man outside time and towards an encounter with an infinity that eludes the conceptual understanding – and threatens man's status as a free, reflec-tive, conscious and autonomous 'person'. Victor registers this possibil-ity from an abstract point of view; but lives in dread of it happening to him.

Woman represents temporal and conceptual dislocation – as well as a breakdown in sensible standards of evaluation. Victor, the rational man, is so horrified at this that he claims:

> if I were a woman, I would rather be one in the Orient, where I would be a slave, for to be a slave – either more nor less – is still always something compared with being 'hurrah' [i.e. everything] and nothing. (p. 56)

On the other hand, he also suggests that during the period of seduction, it is 'woman' who exercises her power over the man. In the seducer/seduced relationship, the seducer feels himself to be in control, but his whole activity reveals his dependence on the woman whom he seduces (p. 64).

Here again Kierkegaard's text is coded with unstated references to Hegel, since there are clear analogies between what Hegel says about the master/slave relationship in his *Phenomenology* and what Victor claims about the seducer/seduced relationship in *Stages*. Thus, for Hegel, the master's apparent freedom is dependent on the slave who recognizes him as 'master' (1807, §§ 178ff, pp. 111ff). However, Victor's explicit antithesis between the plight of the Oriental slave-woman and the modern Danish woman also emphasizes the divergences between seduction and slavery. The slave's value is historically fixed: he has no personhood, and has merely instrumental value. But this apparent disadvantage in the slave's situation is also a kind of advantage. The slave is locked into a process of historical development that will dissolve the master/slave relationship into new social and ideational structures. In the seducer/seduced relationship, by contrast, there is no historical resolution – and this is because patriarchy has denied woman any existence in a finite, developmental sense.

Fake of a Fake: The Fashion Designer

Kierkegaard's next speaker, the 'Fashion Designer', is presented as having access to the mysteries of womanhood. But he is also presented (humorously) as feminized – and as lacking male rationality – by his knowledge of the secrets that women disclose only to each other in fashion boutiques and other 'all female' spaces:

> I am a madman, and a madman one must be in order to understand her, and if one was not that before, one becomes mad once one has understood her. (pp. 65–6)

The Fashion Designer claims to know woman from her weak side: as fickle, nonsensical and characterized by fashion. As such, woman is ateleological, with only one end: to become more and more mad. The Fashion Designer exploits the contradiction as he mimes woman's hysteria and the craziness of her purposive purposelessness.

Thus, according to the Fashion Designer, woman does have spirit, but it is of a prodigal kind. She is also reflective; but her reflection is directed upon her own image. For the Fashion Designer, the reality of woman – her 'a priori' and her 'a posteriori' – is constructed in the mirror of the male gaze. Like many recent psychoanalytic feminists, the Fashion Designer claims that woman is trapped within the mirror of male desire. Even when alone and apparently careless of her appearance, she constructs herself via this internalized male gaze (pp. 67–8). However, woman does not belong to any man: 'she belongs to that phantom produced by feminine reflection's unnatural intercourse with feminine reflection: fashion' (p. 69).

The Fashion Designer claims that women live in a fake reality. But so does he, and the 'truth' that he offers about woman is offered from the perspective of one who has surrendered the stable identity and autonomy that is supposed to characterize males. He is a fake of a fake. With the Fashion Designer we have a preview of that form of postmodernism in which all reality is only simulation and a play of ever-changing surfaces – except that the Fashion Designer retains a (parodic) belief in God. Incapable himself of attaining truth (since truth does not exist), the Fashion Designer sets himself to help 'that sublime genius who likes to laugh at the most ludicrous of all animals' (p. 71).

Infinitude of Finitudes: Johannes the Seducer

From the Fashion Designer we move on to the character of Johannes the Seducer. As Socrates in Plato's *Symposium* claims to have learnt the truth about love from the priestess Diotima, so Johannes claims to have learnt the ultimate truth from a woman – or, rather, from the collectivity of his female victims. Reworking the myths of origin from the Platonic text, Johannes the Seducer declares that at the beginning there was only one sex: that of the male. Jealous of the dynamic force of the being they had created, and fearful that man was out of their control, the gods would have liked to rub him out. But man was not an invention which could simply be 'retracted as a poet retracts his thought'; nor could the gods simply compel man to obey them in a direct way (p. 74). Instead, man 'had to be taken captive and compelled by a force that was weaker than his own and yet stronger – and strong enough to compel'. That force was woman: an enchantress, 'full of deceit' who 'cast her spell on man', making him 'a prisoner of all the proxilities of finitude' (p. 75). Woman traps man in the realm of the phenomenal.

According to Johannes, woman is the most seductive thing in heaven and earth. However, in each age there are individual men (the male seducers) who become aware of the deception and manage to 'eat only the bait'. They are never trapped by merely sensual pleasure. Throughout his recasting of the myth of origin, Johannes's language has strong philosophical connotations since he describes this bait-food as analogous to nectar, which – in Plato's account of erotic love in *Phaedrus* (*c.*370 BC) – was the food of the gods (the food of being) on which philosophers and lovers of beauty feed, before re-entering the mortal frame as new-born infants (247c–e). However, woman is linked by Johannes with finitude, deceit and the phenomenal. She is the nectar of becoming, not the food of being.

In both Greek and Judaeo-Christian myth, woman represents the finite. Created out of man's body, she illustrates a type of perfection that does not imply completeness. Picking up the theme of the contradictory nature of the concept of woman, Johannes now presents the nature of that contradiction in a more favourable light, as he suggests that change and existential dependence is better than being, self-sufficiency and completeness. Man pretends to himself that he is free; that he is autonomous; a legislating subject. Woman, however, is more perfect in that she exists only as incomplete being: 'She is not *ebenbürtig* [of equal birth] with man, but subsequent, a part of man and yet more perfect than he' (p. 76).

Johannes employs classical philosophical resonances that link woman to the temporal world of becoming, not to the fixed and unchanging world of being. However, Johannes reverses the values of the Platonic texts, allowing infinity (being) to emerge from change and from continual motion, and from that which simply seems to exist:

> woman cannot be exhausted in any formula but is an infinitude of finitudes. Trying to conceive the idea of woman is like gazing into a sea of misty shapes continually forming and reforming, or like becoming unhinged by looking at the waves and the foam maidens who continually play tricks, because the idea of woman is only a workshop of possibilities. . . . (p. 76)

The metaphors of infinity and water that Johannes uses here ally woman with the sublime, and with that which overspills the orderly concepts that are used to construct the Kantian space-time world. But

Kierkegaard's infinity does not stand over against the 'I' in ways that threaten that 'I', in the manner of the Kantian (and Lacanian) 'sublime'. Instead, Johannes the Seducer uses 'woman' to make us think finitude differently, so that the noumenal or 'absolute truth' is not cut off from the phenomenal, but involves a transition that occurs within the phenomenal.

Johannes uses the metaphor of a 'display fruit': one of those artificially ripe, polished fruits in a greengrocer's window that will never be eaten, but is there to tempt the passer-by inside to buy something more real:

> woman is a display fruit; the gods knew of nothing to compare with her. She is, she is right here, present, close to us, and yet she is infinitely far away, concealed in modesty until she herself betrays her hiding place – how, she does not know; it is not she, it is life itself that is the cunning informer. (p. 78)

Woman, the most sensuous and most finite being, is also nearest the infinite. Woman is a 'play of forces' that are 'unified in the invisible center of a negative relationship in which she relates herself to herself' (p. 77). Woman is a fiction: an idealized figure who 'bears a world of desire within her' (p. 77). However, woman is not *just* a fiction for Johannes; she is also real:

> Woman, even less than the god, is a whim from a man's brain, a daydream, something one hits upon all by oneself and argues about *pro et contra*. No, only from herself does one learn to talk about her. (p. 73)

Johannes thus indicates that by talking with (and seducing) 'woman' one can find a new form of being – one that exists in the phenomenal, but that escapes from the phenomenal. The idea of woman as 'only a workshop of possibilities' contains within it possibilities for other modes of being.

In the dialogue as a whole, the workshop of possibilities relating to woman is linked with two factors. Firstly, woman is not a full individual: a free, rational and autonomous 'person'. Instead, woman is a 'transitional' being: positioned somewhere between full Kantian subjecthood and lack of individuality. She belongs in an 'embryonic ethical category'. Thus, in the case of woman, action emerges not out of autonomy, but out of an acceptance of dependence and being bound to the other. The second feature of woman's predicament that the dialogue emphasizes is that a woman is not allowed to develop as a personality in time. She is educated into absurdity: into the kind of relationship with history that makes the leap into a different kind of freedom possible:

> For what else is woman but a dream, and yet the highest reality. This is how the devotee of erotic love sees her and in the moment of seduction leads her and is led by her outside of time, where as an illusion she belongs. With a husband she becomes temporal, and he through her. (p. 80)

If woman steps into the everyday – if she marries, develops, has children – the leap into infinitude will no longer be possible. To maintain her status as woman, she has to remain the play of forces of man's desire: unattainable, a fiction, but also real in her fluidity.

Seducer and Seduced

Although it is not with Johannes's words that *Stages on Life's Way* ends, nowhere in the dialogue is there an effective counter to the view of woman that puts her outside history and outside full individuality. Thus although '*In Vino Veritas*' is followed by some 'Reflections on Marriage' by Judge William, the latter also accepts that 'A feminine soul does not have and should not have reflection the way a man does' (p. 166). The Judge links woman with the pre-reflective, the intuitive, the immediate. He believes that 'a woman in understanding is not a man in understanding'. She is incapable of conceptual thought, thus 'The highest understanding a woman has – and has it with honour and with beauty – is a religious immediacy.' The Judge has an unpleasant way of reducing back into banality the sexual clichés that Johannes managed to use as a lever to attack male certainties. But there is, nevertheless, an essential agreement between him and Johannes as the Judge remarks: 'In her immediacy, woman is essentially esthetic, but precisely because she is that essentially the transition to the religious is also close by' (pp. 166–7). For woman – but not for man – the Judge will valorize a swooning, passive, non-autonomous attitude of mind. In ecstasy, 'she is transferred from the immediacy of erotic love into that of the religious' (p. 167).

In Kierkegaard's texts the characters and identities move in and out of each other. They function, as the internal (pseudonymous) editor of '*In Vino Veritas*' remarks, in a way that is '*unheimlich*' (uncanny): as ghosts fading and vanishing, 'surprised by dawn', and as 'subterranean creatures' which appear and disappear into fissures that can be found only in the dark (p. 82).[6] Thus, the voices act together to construct a subject-position; but this position is not that of an autonomous agent. Rather, all of the voices exist within a single (fragmented) self which is presented as lacking access to its own pre-conscious memories and desires. Breaking down the freedom/passivity antinomy, Kierkegaard addresses an actual and hypothetical *female* reader; one whom he seeks to leave free, yet dependent on him for her moment of ripening. As such, he aims at not only a different self/other relationship, but also a different author/reader relationship. Kierkegaard does not pretend to be a woman; but as an author he operates as a seducer, and it is the seducer who positions himself as dependent on woman/his victim/the reader.

For Johannes it was only via the act of seduction that a male could escape being trapped (by the delights of the senses) on the plane of phenomenal reality. There is evident irony in this; but what is important to bear in mind here is Victor's claim that although it seems to be the seducer who has power in the seducer/seduced relationship, the seducer's whole activity reveals his dependence on the woman whom he seduces. Again, this is analogous to the privileging of the slave's consciousness in Hegel's account of the master/slave relationship in the *Phenomenology*, but again also it is different in that it is via work that Hegel says that the slave receives the recognition from others that is necessary to make him free (§ 195, p. 118). Woman/the seduced is, by contrast, tricked by the seducer to think that she has freely given her virginity. And the seducer also tricks himself if he thinks that it is he who is free and in control. Neither male nor female (seducer nor seduced) is privileged, despite Jean Baudrillard's claims to the contrary in *Seduction* (1979), in which he uses Kierkegaard for his own (anti-feminist and) postmodern ends.

For Baudrillard all that there is to reality is simulation. We now live in the age of seduction/simulacrum in which there is no 'hidden' reality behind the image. This is the postmodern 'real': a reality that is represented by 'woman' as surface, but which is also profoundly anti-female. Criticizing psychoanalysis for its structures of the self and desire – and criticizing feminism for seeking either to reverse or appropriate these structures – Baudrillard posits another model for thinking identity. Here meaning/self is not created (as in Lacan) by the blanking out of Otherness. Lacan had used Plato, Kierkegaard and Aristophanes' myth of a primary 'cut' from the Other/the mother in the narrative that he provided about the origins of ego.[7] According to this narrative, the 'real' is unobtainable and falls outside language which establishes the fictions that are necessary if we are to remain sane. However, Baudrillard also employs Kierkegaard in his undoing of Lacan. For Baudrillard the feminine is not that nostalgia for an Otherness that forever eludes the masculinized self; it is instead 'what seduces the masculine' – and the 'strength of the feminine is that of seduction' (1979, p. 7).

> In seduction the feminine is neither a marked nor an unmarked term. It
> does not mask the 'autonomy' of desire, pleasure or the body, or of a
> speech or writing that it has supposedly lost (?). Nor does it claim to
> some truth of its own. It seduces. (p. 7)

Moving (as I also would wish to move) beyond the Lacanian frame
in which femininity is equated with that which is pushed 'beyond' self,
Baudrillard makes a further move that I would wish to resist. He equates
reality with femininity – and with a seductive surface in which there is
neither a 'beyond' nor depth. For Baudrillard reality *is* appearance; it
is the realm of symbolic play that is set up by the relation of synchronic
signifiers:

> What does the women's movement oppose to the phallocratic structure?
> Autonomy, difference, a specificity of desire and pleasure, a different rela-
> tion to the female body, a speech, a writing – *but never seduction.* They are
> ashamed of seduction, as implying an artificial presentation of the body,
> or a life of vassalage and prostitution. They do not understand *that seduc-
> tion represents mastery over the symbolic universe, while power represents only
> mastery over the real universe.* The sovereignty of seduction is incommen-
> surable with the possession of political or sexual power. (p. 8)

Baudrillard estimates the power of the feminine in the symbolic universe as incommensurable with the power of the masculine in the 'real
universe', because, for him, there *is* only the symbolic universe – only
appearance; only ludic surfaces, inscribed by symbolic codes.

Baudrillard's comments reveal ignorance of feminist debates. But dis-
regarding these political objections to his procedures, we can see what
has gone wrong with Baudrillard's ontology by looking at the comments
that he makes about Kierkegaard, who is interpreted as establishing the
priority of the feminine/the phenomenal. Using as his example 'The
Seducer's Diary' from *Either*, in which the character of Johannes the
Seducer made his first appearance in Kierkegaard's pseudonymous works,
Baudrillard identifies Cordelia – Johannes's victim – with 'a seductive,
that is, dangerous, power'. Baudrillard goes on:

> The seducer by himself is nothing; the seduction originates entirely with
> the girl. This is why Johannes can claim to have learned everything from
> Cordelia. He is not being hypocritical. The calculated seduction mirrors
> the natural seduction, drawing from the latter as from its source, but all
> the better to eliminate it.
>
> This is why he does not leave anything to chance, the girl being
> deprived of initiative, a seemingly defenceless object in the game of seduc-
> tion. She has already played her hand *before* the seducer begins to play his.
> Everything has already taken place; the seduction simply rights a natural

imbalance by taking up the pre-existing challenge constituted by the girl's natural beauty and grace. (p. 99)

In Baudrillard's model, the only 'game' for the female is a game of 'nature' – of 'natural beauty and grace'. She is appropriately seduced because 'nature' has coded her seductive – and 'dangerous'. But this does not fit Kierkegaard's account of the seduction by Johannes in *Either*, in which Johannes's 'Diary' and letters are positioned after various female voices – and 'Silhouettes' – which retell the story of a seduction from the perspective of a victim. Kierkegaard's authorial strategy never allows us to leave Johannes's words unquestioned. Kierkegaard shows that Johannes aims to leave the girl 'free' to choose her seduction; but he does not let us forget that the choice is effected in ways that make it impossible for the reader to distinguish compulsion (rape) from freely given assent (seduction). The first sentence of this Baudrillard passage is correct: the seducer by himself *is* nothing. But Kierkegaard does not represent the self/other relationship in the agonistic terms used by Baudrillard in this passage. Just because the seducer by himself is nothing, it does not follow that the only agency is that of the seduced (raped?) victim.

According to Baudrillard, Kierkegaard's character Johannes the Seducer leads away from the self/other model of identity into an account of reality in which there is only surface. But within *Stages on Life's Way*, Johannes the Seducer suggests a different move. 'In the moment of seduction' the seducer leads woman 'and is led by her outside time'. The move 'outside time' does not take us into a 'beyond'; it does not take us into a Kantian realm of the noumenal. Instead, it takes us towards a different ordering of phenomena; in which depth is given to surfaces by temporal folds which are established via the jostling of competing narratives. 'Reality' becomes a multifaceted folding of surfaces. There is no 'beyond'; but there is more than a synchronic play of surface appearances.

Baudrillard insists that there is only surface; only simulacrum. But in order to reach this conclusion Baudrillard acts as an ontological rapist: holding down the appearance of things into a unidimensionality that can only ever be oppositional to 'reality' as conceived by the philosophers. For Kierkegaard, by contrast, 'reality' is an interpenetration of the merely finite and the infinite; the phenomenal and the noumenal; with actuality emerging from complex potentialities patterned by power. Within the Kierkegaardian texts, both seducer and seduced are locked into a relationship of mutual dependence, within which each believes her/himself free; but in which what freedom there is is controlled and dependent on the gift/existence of the other. 'Reality' is constructed by the interrelationship of seducer and seduced, and in networks of mutual dependency. 'Reality' is not just 'surface' and a play of ludic appearances, but emerges from the tensions between self and symbiotic other – and from a jostling of actual and potential identities.

In this respect, it is interesting to compare the opening to *The Concept of Irony* (1841). Here Kierkegaard notes that the phenomenon is always '*foeminini generis* [of the feminine gender]' and complains about the 'jingling of spurs and the voice of the master' adopted by the 'philosophical knight' (p. 9). However, instead of using this metaphorics to deconstruct truth in the manner of Derrida, who uses remarkably similar imagery in *Spurs* (1978), Kierkegaard uses it to appeal for a symbiotic relationship between the 'feminine' phenomenon and (masculine) philosopher. Even if the philosopher does bring with him the concepts (the rules) that he uses to order appearances, 'it is still of great importance that the phenomenon remain inviolate and that the concept be seen as coming into existence through the phenomenon' (p. 9). Seducer (philosopher/master/self) and seduced (appearance/the other/female) have to function together.

Kierkegaard is unlike Derrida, who seeks to destabilize the relationship between 'phenomena' and concepts for epistemological (sceptical) ends. However, he is also unlike Baudrillard, who uses surfaces and simulacra to displace the philosophers' 'real'. Of the characters in *Stages*, Baudrillard most resembles 'The Fashion Designer' – not the multiplicity of personae that mark out Kierkegaard's own authorial position. Kierkegaard radicalizes philosophy not by giving up on 'truth' or 'the real', but by developing an alternative ontology in which 'reality' is born from multiple possibilities, and in which 'self' and 'other' emerge together through repeated movements that never simply reproduce a 'given' that remains 'the same'. For this emergence the competing narratives and ironic voices are integral: they 'help the phenomenon to obtain its full disclosure' (1841, p. 9).

Of Echoes and Depths

In *Fear and Trembling* (1843b) – a work of philosophy that Kierkegaard claims in his *Journals* 'actually reproduced my own life' (1848–55, 6491) – we are asked to think the relationship between a son (Isaac) and his murderous father (Abraham, the 'father' of Old Testament faith) who takes him up a mountain in order to kill him. Kierkegaard's pseudonymous author tells and retells the story; but alters details so that throughout the reader (and narrator) is left with an ambiguous past. Far from being just surface, we are presented with alternative Abrahams; alternative 'facts'; alternative realities; alternative narratives in which we could fit this singular event. And these 'repetitions' of the story mean that we are left neither with the 'true' underlying meaning of the story, nor with a single 'surface' of unilinear 'events'.

The identities of Abraham and Isaac are given resonance and temporal depth in much the same way that Kierkegaard's modernized Antigone works and reworks her relationship with the past in *Either*. As we have seen, in Kierkegaard's version of the Greek myth, the father/child relationship is central, so that Antigone's 'sad fate is like the echo of her father's' (1843a, p. 156). However, that echo is a form of repetition that transforms the present; it does not simply repeat a past or a destiny that is fixed (fated) in the manner of the Greek tragedies. The past is taken up into Antigone's identity via an anxiety about a hidden (and necessarily unobtainable) 'secret' about her father that can give her no rest.

Kierkegaard's own identity was as constituted through anxiety as that of Antigone, his female *alter ego*. As he notes in retelling the story of Solomon and David in a 'psychological development' that is explicitly linked in his *Journals* with the Antigone plot:

> If there is any agony of sympathy, it is to have to be ashamed of one's father, of the person one loves the most and to whom one owes the most, to have to approach him backward, with face averted, in order not to see his disgrace. (1845, pp. 250–1)[8]

In the 'agony of sympathy' between the guilty father and his daughter (or son), the very boundaries of the self/other relation break down. As Kierkegaard says of David's son: 'there was a split in his being, and Solomon was like the invalid who cannot carry his own body' (p. 252).

If we look at Sylvia Fraser's autobiographical memoir of incest, *My Father's House* (1987), the terrifying self-quake of memory of rape by her father is triggered by an interlocutor who suggests (like Baudrillard) that '*For such a sexual assault to take place, we must look to the conduct of the child. Some little girls can be seductive at an early age*' (p. 219). Here in Sylvia Fraser's memoir, a Baudrillardian voice intervenes to represent a seducer as passive and the raped child as active. For Baudrillard, what seduces has power; what seems and what is real collapse into each other with the logic of the self-deceiving rapist. For Sylvia Fraser, by contrast, there was an 'absolute' truth that she discovered – a 'true' self and 'actual' past to be revealed – a past confirmed as true by the corroboration of her sister and others around her.

But the move Kierkegaard makes is different from that suggested by either Baudrillard or Fraser. What is real emerges without an appeal to consensus or coherence. It is formed in what seems like an isolated relationship between the self and the 'secrets' of her/his family and her/his past. Except that the self is not fixed; but is itself only configured by a play of echoes; by patterns of relations; as a kind of harmonic or vibration produced by the intersection of present, future and past. There are no 'ultimates' or 'absolutes' – experience itself is suspect – but there is nevertheless a (fluid, shifting, uncertain) 'real' that is composed by the way the self is positioned in the complex dynamics of multiple self/other relationships.

Like the sexually abused child in Sylvia Fraser's memoir, the 'self' that emerges in Kierkegaard's philosophical fictions is divided into fragmented personae, none of which has access to its other 'selves' – none of which has privileged knowledge of the father's guilt. In the face of the (unbearable) guilt of the (loved) father, the boundaries of self fragment to produce 'others' within. These personae enter into an obsessive dialogue with the past as they struggle to decide between whether the father (and hence also the child) was passively fated or wilfully guilty; simply responding to the mechanisms of desire, or sinful with the full autonomy of individuality.

Either/Or . . . neither/nor. In Kierkegaard's texts, the figure of the victimized child comes to stand alongside that of the woman as the signifier of the breakdown in the Kantian model of personhood. Thus, in the oldest journal – the one Kierkegaard says gives the clearest hints about the autobiographical content of *Fear and Trembling* – the story of Abraham and Isaac is presented as follows:

> He grabbed Isaac by the chest, drew his knife, and said, 'You thought I was going to do this because of God, but you are wrong, I am an idolater, and this passion has again stirred my soul – I want to murder you, this is my desire; I am worse than a cannibal. Despair, you foolish boy who fancied that I was your father; I am your murderer, and this is my desire.' . . . But then Abraham whispered softly to himself, 'So must it be, for it is better that he believes I am a monster . . . than that he should know it was God who imposed the test. . . .' (1829–48, 5640)

Like Antigone, Kierkegaard's pseudonymous voices construct a reality and identity through an engagement with a 'truth' that forever hovers out of reach. For Baudrillard there can be no 'secret' about the past – whether we understand that past to be that of Antigone, Solomon, Isaac or Kierkegaard himself. For Kierkegaard, as for Fraser, the 'secret' is real; indeed it is his relationship to this secret that characterizes his identity. There is not just a play of surfaces; selves are split open by (never-to-be-revealed) secrets and terrifying depths. But in Kierkegaard (unlike Fraser) there is also no privileged access to that depth via the mechanisms of memory. There is only a temporally enfolded complex of symbols, traces, feelings, moods that invite us to confront the 'givens' that are made mysterious via encodement with the multiplicity of paths that might have led from the past.

The analogies between Kierkegaard's writings and those of the adult who was once a sexually abused child are not presented as the 'solution' to the great mystery of Kierkegaard studies – namely as to the nature of the 'earthquake' of discovery that changed Kierkegaard's life, and the 'secret' about his father he could never reveal. Kierkegaard's ontology means that there is no such 'objective' truth. Reality exists, but there are a multiplicity of possible 'truths' as self and other emerge together within the force-fields of power. Thus, the point I am making here is not to offer a truth about Kierkegaard's life, but to see the strengths and the weaknesses of the position he offers. Thinking of Kierkegaard as providing a model of identity that is appropriate to that of the seduced boy/woman makes us see how it might be necessary in the end to draw back from some aspects of the Kierkegaardian solution. It warns us that what Kierkegaard ends by providing is a framework within which the victim could rationalize her or his victimization; but without satisfactorily addressing the question of an ethics relating to the abuse of power.

Famously, what Kierkegaard was doing with the Abraham/Isaac parable in *Fear and Trembling* was trying to tempt the reader into judging Abraham neither ethically (condemning him as a murderer) nor aesthetically (seeing him as a hero), but in terms of the category of the 'religious' that involves a 'leap into faith' based on the absurd. I would suggest that the danger in the Kierkegaardian position comes from this later 'religious' move; from the leap into the 'absurd' in which it becomes necessary to trust in otherness – and to forgive one's father/ one's god, even if he is a rapist or a murderer. To reject this part of Kierkegaard does not entail having to reject his use of 'woman' and victimized 'child' as a way of displacing a conception of the subject as autonomous and always in control of his own fate and individuality.

Recollecting Forwards

For Kant, it will be recalled, phenomenal reality is constructed by a sharp cut between self and other: the transcendental ego and the transcendental object. Although phenomenal reality is constructed by the mind pursuing an infinity (the sublime) that escapes conceptual understanding, it is nevertheless constructed as conceptually ordered along a single axis of space/time linearity. The mind imposes space/time form on the multiplicity of sensations. This multiplicity is situated in a single, serial order of moments via three modes of time: duration (or persistence), causal sequence and coexistence (simultaneity). Indeed, these three time modes can only be distinguished one from the other by supposing a backdrop of substances or permanent bodies in space. Thus, (if it exists at all) the noumenal for Kant is the absolute reality (hypothetically) covered over by the merely finite order of space/time phenomenality. The noumenal would exist on a different plane from the merely phenomenally real.

Although Kierkegaard's voices link woman with that which is excessive to the Kantian reality, it is not the Kantian sublime or an unchanging, noumenal reality cut off from phenomenality that is opened up by this move. Kierkegaard's characters suggest that woman is a fiction; but also real. More significantly, they also suggest that the finite and the infinite – the phenomenal and the noumenal – do not exist on different levels of existence. Access to the noumenal and the infinite comes, instead, from a different relation to time. 'Woman' gives man/males access to infinity precisely by being excluded from Kantian serialized time – and also by being excluded from the onwards march of Hegelian history.

To think time in a non-idealist mode, Kierkegaard reverses Plato, who claimed that all knowledge is recollection, and who suggested that behind this world of mere phenomena is an eternal time order in which everything that happens is already present, there in eternity. For Plato there is no novelty. Being is truth. Becoming is a form of illusion. Even birth itself is portrayed as a recycling of being as the soul (temporarily) falls into the prison of the body. Kierkegaard's reversal of this move means that being is birthed by becoming. As the character of Constantin Constantius put it in *Repetition*, which is where he first appeared in Kierkegaard's corpus:

> *repetition* is a crucial expression for what 'recollection' was to the Greeks. Just as they taught that all knowing is recollecting, modern philosophy will teach that all life is a repetition. The only modern philosopher who has had an intimation of this is Leibniz. Repetition and recollection are the same movement, except in opposite directions, for what is recollected has been, is repeated backward, whereas genuine repetition is recollected forward. (1843c, p. 131)[9]

Constantin asks us to think a mode of time which would proceed via echo – and repetition – and which is non-linear in the Kantian sense. But what he is suggesting is also not just the eternal repetition of the same. Instead, 'sameness' itself is constructed by seeing the present in terms of a not-yet-actual ideal. The point that is made about repetition here is the same point that is made about woman in *Stages*. It is woman/ repetition that brings the ideal in contact with the real so that what is created is a kind of double existence: outside the moment (the merely finite) and outside history considered as a succession of moments.

Identity is not created by mirroring a pre-existent reality (as in Plato); but neither is it simply constructed by living through a succession of finite moments. Instead, identity depends on a repetition that brings into existence (births) an order of events that was already potentially there in the past; but that is brought into existence in the 'nook' of the moment. The 'now' is constituted by the relation between the multiplicity of possible paths that emerge out of the past and the multiplicity of possible directions that stretch out towards the future. Repetition operates through a kind of double consciousness that relates that which is fixed (ideality) to that which is merely possible:

> When ideality and reality touch each other, then repetition occurs. When, for example, I see something in the moment, ideality enters in and will explain that it is a repetition. . . . Ideality and reality therefore collide – in what medium? In time? That is indeed an impossibility. In what, then? In eternity? That is indeed an impossibility. In what, then? In consciousness – there is the contradiction.[10]

Consciousness/the self is what constructs this double movement – but it is also itself constructed by the movement: 'Consciousness, then, is the relation, a relation whose form is contradiction.'[11] The past is reworked by the individual's consciousness, but this consciousness is itself dependent on an otherness that preceded it. The self is a form of double-coding – of echo, that 'master of irony' – that acts as the 'nook' in the multiplicitous paths whereby the future and the present emerge from the past. In *Stages on Life's Way* this 'nook' of eight intersecting paths is explicitly linked to a place in the forest that is both 'Out-of-the-way, hidden, and secret' and a meeting point of different directions and possibilities (1845, p. 16). This 'nook' is also explicitly linked to echo; to the 'birth' of recollection, and to the position of the seduced woman who is left alone (p. 19). Woman/the seduced victim is both individual and marked as singular by her hybridity.

For Kierkegaard it is woman who gives us a model for the singular individual: as being something other than just a particular instantiation of a universal or some kind of monster or freak. The fact that there are no predicates adequate to define 'woman' – or even 'women' – does not entail that there is nothing that woman represents. Nor does it entail a reality that is mere appearance; mere surface, inscribed with significance only by being positioned synchronically within a play of symbolic codes. On the contrary, what woman represents is an ideal of identity without closure that is ontologically bound up with otherness, inheritance and an (ambiguous) past. Kierkegaard's 'woman' is 'mere' appearance, but an appearance extraordinary and singular enough to bring into question the appearance/reality divide. She is 'phenomenal' in the double sense of the definitions cited at the opening of chapter 1 of this book. As such, Kierkegaard's writings release philosophy from the constraints of a Kantianism that regards 'phenomena' and 'noumena' as opposed.

Was Cordelia 'seduced' in *Either/Or*? Or was she 'raped' by Johannes? In the reworked story of Antigone, was her father (Oedipus) aware of the incestuous nature of his marriage? Was he guilty? Or was his tragic destiny merely fate? Was the character of Abraham in *Fear and Trembling* a murderer? Or does the fact that it was God who ordered him to kill his son Isaac mean that he transcends such merely ethical categories? Analogously, what was the 'secret' that provides the logic for Kierkegaard's own philosophical development?

Kierkegaardian selves are locked in relationships of power and interdependency that are ambiguous, relational and non-Cartesian. But the Kierkegaardian self does not disappear, even though it falls outside the horizons of 'certain' knowledge. Instead, identity becomes a form of patterning that exists always only in dialectical relationship to a range of open possibilities: possibilities that are perhaps most easily grasped as parallel Kantian spatio-temporal 'realities', but that Kierkegaard himself explains as a mode of 'repetition' whereby time and identity themselves are birthed. And, indeed, simply multiplying Kantian space-time realities does not sufficiently capture the Kierkegaardian moves, since his voices suggest pasts, presents and futures that are neither causally determined nor a product of Kantian freedoms.

In Kierkegaard's 'aesthetic' works the self cannot be fitted within categories that position it as autonomous and as responsible for its own agency. Neither is it Kant's 'transcendental object' – the embodied, permanent and spatially located 'not-self' – that acts as a stable reference point for a unified and homogeneous 'I'. But the self does not disappear. Instead, it emerges in a 'workshop of possibilities': a workshop in which echo and feedback-loops link an (uncertain) past to an (undetermined) future. As we will see in more detail in the next chapter, the Kierkegaardian self is constituted by patterns of movement. It is the overlapping and incongruent horizons of a multiplicity of space-time 'worlds' that keeps the boundary between 'I' and 'not-I' fluid – and opens the Kierkegaardian 'I' to possible others within. As such, Kierkegaard's aesthetic writings offer a radical subversion of the concepts of autonomy, selfhood, rational personhood and masculinity – using 'woman' as a productive point of departure.

9
Scoring the Subject of Feminist Theory: Kierkegaard and Deleuze

As a philosophical author concerned with breaking apart the notion of discrete and autonomous selves, Kierkegaard made extensive use of the notion of 'echo'. He also employed other metaphors relating to music and to sound for his ontology of becoming, in which novelty is the norm and in which identity is birthed out of repetition. Analogously, in *A Thousand Plateaus* (1980) Gilles Deleuze and Félix Guattari offer the *'ritournelle'* (refrain, repeated chorus, 'riff' or musical phrase) as one of a number of concepts that can be used philosophically to provide continuity and coherence within a frame that privileges 'becoming' – and thus undermines 'being'. In effect, Deleuze employs aural repetition as a counter to Kant's schematism of the imagination, and to substitute for Kant's 'permanent' objects that are linked linearly in a unified and homogenized space-time.

Since it is these objects that ground (and provide the necessary counter-pole to) the transcendental self in the Kantian scheme, the Deleuzian move is part of a reconceptualization not only of identity, but also in effect of the self itself. Furthermore, since Deleuze is currently an important influence on postmodern feminist theory, I wish to examine his metaphysics of music and his account of 'the girl' in *A Thousand Plateaus* – and compare it with that of Kierkegaard's analogous strategies in his aesthetic writings. I will argue that Deleuze is less politically useful for feminist theory than is Kierkegaard's analysis of both the 'self' and the 'girl'. But first I need to make some more general comments on the relationship between identification and reidentification of particulars in the case of sound and in the case of sight.

It is known that those born blind and suddenly able to 'see' can barely manage to schematize 'objects' from the apparent chaos of visual data that present themselves to the senses (Sacks, 1995, pp. 102–44). These newly seeing subjects have not learnt the techniques for ordering visual data and bringing them under concepts, or for correlating these data with the inputs provided by other senses, such as touch and sound. But although Sacks has hypothesized that these previously blind subjects experience difficulty because vision gives access to a 'simultaneous perception of objects', whereas sound and touch involve building worlds out of slow 'sequences of impressions' (p. 117), this seems both philosophically puzzling and scientifically contentious. More plausible is the neurobiological claim that without habitual patterns of usage the potential cortical linkages for mapping visual data remain unestablished, and the brain develops an alternative dynamics for coherently responding to – and topographically mapping – input received from the sensory organs of sound and touch (Edelman, 1992, pp. 86ff). Such a newly seeing subject would also have failed to have developed 'maps that map the types of activity occurring in other cortical maps' (p. 109), and thus could not easily bring the sensory input together with concepts.

Sight and sound also represent the relationship between 'self' and 'other' in accordance with a different logic of sameness and difference – and in ways that cannot simply be explained in terms of the 'speed' of impressions. Thus, for example, the field of vision has a focal point, and edges defined as such in reference to the gaze. Even more significant is the fact that we can exercise conscious control over what we see. Thus, we close our eyes when we would go to sleep, or wish to exclude images that would give us pain. Perhaps even more than the hand that wilfully touches (as opposed to simply being touched), sight contributes to our sense of agency, of 'mastery' of the world. As such, sight seems teleological: directed by the ends and the desires of the 'I'. The fact that we focus our eyes on what is ahead of us – and that we can move our heads easily – means that for the subject trained from childhood to orient himself via sight, the data yielded by vision seem to come in discontinuous and manageable bundles. For the most part we never even notice the crowding in of simultaneous visual data that requires the 'forgetting' of visual irrelevancies that Nietzsche described in his 1873 account of seeing a 'leaf'. (See chapter 7 above.)

The perceptual model yielded by sound is not ateleogical; but nevertheless it works 'backwards' if we take the directedness of vision as the perceptual norm. We cannot so easily exercise conscious control over what we hear. In so far as we focus our ears and decide to listen, we tune out and render innocuous that which is superfluous to our needs, expectations or desires. But our ears are not neutral 'filters', and have evolved in ways that favour the patterns and tonalities of speech. Pulse, rhythm, melodic narrative or the tonalities of voice act as mnemonics, and provide us with means of holding on to a past – or grasping towards an ending that has yet to be stated (or may be left open). As such, sound relies not on linear temporalities, but on memories, echoes, anticipations of danger, emphases, phases, transitions: interruptions to established continuities. Even the notion of a single unit or 'datum' of sound is problematic.

When we go to sleep our ears remain active, and keep us in continuous dynamic relationship with an environment which is indefinite and outside the circle of vision, surrounding us on all sides. There are no easily recognizable edges or centres to the sounds that come at us. Hearing favours the ever-present, the unavoidable and the continuously evolving; we have to be trained to artificially divide this potential infinity into 'moments' or 'sound-bites'. Thus, hearing suggests a model of identity that does not operate in terms of discrete units. Our ears let the outside world (the 'other') inside the screen of the 'I', whilst filtering into background 'noise' and rendering inconspicuous that part of 'otherness' that cannot also be used by the 'I'. If we want to rethink identity in ways that do not rest upon an oppositional relation between self and 'other', then it is useful to think more about the way identity is established and maintained in the aural field. Lacan tells us that his own account of the ego cannot be understood without reference to optics and to the mechanisms of vision and the gaze (1964, pp. 71–89). Analogously, an emphasis on music and sound opens up possibilities for thinking the self as maintaining direction and control without the 'cut' from the Other that is foundational to Lacanian psychoanalysis.

Kantian Sounds/Kantian Sight

The predominant model of 'reality' in western philosophical discourse is that of a temporally linear world that moves steadily from past through present to future, through a linked series of static frames that constitute the 'moment' or the 'now'. Even before the invention of the camera, it was tempting to explain motion as illusory – as no more than the sum of discrete and discontinuous states – despite the celebrated paradoxes (such as those of Zeno) which result from such a model. The fact that sight has been privileged over the other senses has a bearing on such a conception of the 'real'. An emphasis on vision also seems to have contributed to the long-standing appeal of the notion that the mind perceives and thinks by 'bundling' diverse and discontinuous images under concepts. It is interesting in this respect that those philosophers who have wanted to concentrate instead on the 'flow' of time have frequently chosen sound as their primary object of analysis. One celebrated example is Edmund Husserl's *On the Phenomenology of the Consciousness of Internal Time* (1893–1917). Husserl's analysis does, however, differ substantially from the one given here since he normalizes natural perception, and treats the experience of sound in terms that reduce movement itself to a series of curiously static 'poses' that 'waxify' temporal duration, in much the same way that Adorno claimed Husserl's account of nature 'waxified' flesh. (See chapter 7, above.)

Thus, Husserl's analysis of temporal flows proceeds through such examples as listening to a single tone that is 'given' to hearing with a temporal duration (pp. 26ff). One instance is his attempt to understand what is involved in the perception of the tone 'line' of a steam whistle 'or, rather, of the whistling of the whistle' (p. 117). As such, not only does Husserl presuppose an already constituted 'I', but this 'I' is placed in relation to an already constituted 'unit' of sound such as 'the whistling of the whistle'. He is less interested in the question of how a single 'object' or 'tone' is differentiated as the 'same' from amongst the simultaneity of sounds presented to the senses. Indeed, Husserl's analysis starts from – but also adapts – a notion of the phenomenal that derives from Kantianism, and in ways that should again remind us of Adorno's claim that 'It is impossible to correct a mistake of idealistic epistemology without necessarily producing another error' (Adorno, 1956, p. 211). By contrast, I am concerned with the logic of 'hearing' (not 'listening') in terms of charting the ways in which a pattern of persistent 'objects' and 'subjects' might emerge out of flow.

Amongst the senses, human vision is distinctive; but it is taken as the norm, so that the perceiving self is presented as an active agent that synthesizes the 'bundles' of otherwise discontinuous data. Kant's world is above all a *visual* world. In the three stages of synthesis that comprise his account of the transcendental self, first come the preconceptual moments or time-slices in which sense data are presented to the 'I'. Then come the procedures of active synthesis, in which the 'I' groups the data into homogeneous sets and locates them in terms of an object (the not-I or 'transcendental object'): a process which requires a counter-synthesis which brings the multiplicity of sensations under concepts in a unity of experience. From these three stages of synthesis in the so-called 'subjective deduction' of Kant's first *Critique* comes the temporal

continuity of the 'I' and the spatial stability of the 'not-I'. (See 1781/
7, A98–110.)

If Kant had concentrated on sound, he would have devised a different model. Not only are we more passive with respect to sound, but
even the notion of a multiplicity of distinct sensations that needs to be
bundled is a curious starting point for a mode of experience which is
not episodic, but continuous. Sound is there in an infinite and continuously evolving flow, with noises that can blend and blur without there
being an agent that 'bundles' them. Hearing itself is a disentangling and
filtering process: one that involves a gradual decipherment or imposition of patterns onto an impermanent and continuously changing plane
of sound. As Robin Maconie puts it:

> The converse of music is noise. A scientific description of noise is 'undif-
> ferentiated sound'. In order to discern noise it is necessary to determine
> either that the sound in question is acoustically 'without form', or else
> that it is incapable of signifying anything useful, 'unintelligible' to human
> ears. The term 'noise' can only ever express a provisional judgement.
> (1990, p. 13)

This judgement involves recollection – and also anticipations of order
and change.

Where one sound wave meets another, there is not a sharpening of
definition, but indistinctness – out of which new identities might gradually emerge. To hear something involves not recognition of 'the same',
but the openness to difference, the indefinite and the indistinct. 'Sameness', however, is also presupposed, since hearing presupposes that we
are 'attuned' to the normal everyday sounds of our environment and
also to the patterns of our 'mother tongue'. Hearing involves a dynamic
response to novelty in a non-episodic continuum. Indeed, the 'I' constitutes itself through taking the 'other' within the self. Furthermore,
what is present to the senses is not a blur or a blend of discrete entities (sound qualia), but a range of patterns, rhythms and coded orders
that can suddenly emerge from the indefinite possibilities of 'noise' in
accordance with the memories, expectations or bodily habits of the
listener.

Kant himself was dismissive of the world of sound. There was not
only his celebrated impatience with the hymn-singing from the nearby
prison that interrupted his thought. (See Kant, 1790, § 53, p. 200fns.)
He was also aware that sound fell outside his system since it involved
a *bodily* response – and not simply a judgemental response – to the
physical environment. Music, he claimed in the *Critique of Judgment*,
involves a 'quickening' that 'is merely bodily' (§ 54, p. 202). It involves

a 'play' from bodily sensations to aesthetic ideas, but the pleasure in this 'play' comes from the fact that aesthetic ideas double back onto the body with 'concentrated (*vereinigt* – also "unified")' force. Thus the 'unity' of music is primarily bodily, and not imposed by the mind in the manner of the 'syntheses' of sight. Music involves 'the furtherance of the vital processes in the body': it is an 'affect that agitates the intestines and the diaphragm' (§ 54, p. 203). As such, music is agreeable, and properly described as neither beautiful nor sublime. Kant compares it instead to 'the feeling of health that is produced by an intestinal agitation' (§ 54, pp. 202–3).

Productive Echoes

What Kant saw as a disadvantage to music, others have regarded as its distinctive virtue. As Susan McClary puts it in her book on feminist music aesthetics: 'By far the most difficult aspect of music to explain is its uncanny ability to make us experience our bodies in accordance with its gestures and rhythms' (1991, p. 23). In the case of sound, the 'I' intervenes; but this 'I' is not simply the *cogito*. It is embodied. In the 'intestinal' response to music, it is not the case that the 'I' disappears into the background noise of the world. Instead, identity is maintained by the way the embodied 'I' responds to that which seeps into it from outside and the way it focuses on rhythms, harmonies, dissonances, resonances and other vibrations that sound patterns produce. The tension between memory, anticipation, habit and desire that enables us to distinguish music from that which simply recedes into background noise also involves bodily habits and expectations, as well as the *cogito* itself.

As Oliver Sacks shows in the first case study in *The Man Who Mistook His Wife for a Hat* (1985), continuity of self can be maintained musically – by singing to oneself – when the ability to fit images to concepts (Kant's schematism of the imagination) has been lost. Sacks's 'Dr P.' can see a glove; can describe it spatially as a 'continuous surface' that is 'infolded on itself', with 'five outpouchings' (p. 13). He can, however, no longer bring it under the concept of 'glove', or imagine how such a remarkable object might be used. Dr P. cannot recognize everyday objects: not even his own face in the mirror. On the other hand, he can dress as long as there is no sudden interruption that breaks the pattern of music that gives continuity to his days. Thus, Dr P.'s wife says:

> he dresses without difficulty, singing to himself. He does everything sing-
> ing to himself. But if he is interrupted and loses the thread, he comes to

a complete stop, doesn't know his own clothes – or his own body. He sings all the time – eating songs, dressing songs, bathing songs, everything. He can't do anything unless he makes a song. (pp. 15–16)

Music figures in several of Sacks's other case reports, and is discussed at length in 'Reminiscence': his analysis of various cases of 'musical epilepsy' in which an electrical disturbance of the brain seems to directly trigger 'hearing' a concert of fixed, stereotyped and repetitive tunes at a maddeningly loud volume (1985, pp. 125–42). The fact that epileptic stimulation of the cortex seems to generate the hearing of music in a substantial number of cases (perhaps three per cent) is explained by Sacks with reference to the role that memory plays in both epilepsy and musical recall. Thus, epileptic hallucinations are described as always involving 'memories of the most precise and vivid kind, accompanied by the emotions which accompanied the original experience' (p. 130).

Sacks uses Bergson and Kierkegaard to understand what he is finding, and to argue that the lives of these patients still possess a continuity and an integrity that means that it is a mistake to present them as no-longer-persons and simply as neurological machines.[1] However, Sacks's reports also make it clear that it is also a mistake to regard the self as an autonomous agent. For Sacks the self is comprised by neural pathways that are 'scored' by memory; but this 'scoring' has phenomenological depth – a depth that is provided by the echo of experience. Thus, for example, Sacks uses his observations on musical epilepsy to argue for there being patterns of meaning 'scored' or 'scripted' on to the mind, so that the mind itself is 'an enchanted loom' that weaves ever-changing patterns of meaning that 'transcend purely formal or computational programmes or patterns' (1985, pp. 140–1). In discussing the case of 'Mrs O'M.', one of the subjects with musical epilepsy, he comments:

> Personal patterns, patterns for the individual, would have to take the form of scripts or scores – as abstract patterns, patterns for a computer, must take the form of schemata or programmes. Thus, above the level of cerebral programmes, we must conceive a level of cerebral scripts or scores.
> The score of [the tune] 'Easter Parade' . . . is indelibly inscribed in Mrs O'M's brain – the score, *her* score, of all she heard and felt at the original moment and imprinting of the experience. (p. 141)

For Kierkegaard, the self is shaped in analogous temporal loops, harmonies and 'scores'; but it is not simply shaped by the past. Indeed, the past itself is experienced only through the harmonics – as an elusive precursor of present and future desires. In a sense, the self shapes itself;

but there is no sharp divide between self and not-self. Instead, the self/ other divide is established relationally – via repetitive iterations that mark out time. Kierkegaard provides us with a model of the self that can allow self-shaping, whilst also limiting the power of the subject, and positing a self that is shaped by forces outside it. Kierkegaard shows that musical repetition can mark out depths, as well as surfaces. Like an echo machine in a recording studio, Kierkegaard's recollection – and time itself – loops round on itself, and in ways that allow new patternings and novelty to emerge from the thematic resonances and auditory 'fuzz'.

Thus, in his short narrative *Repetition*, Kierkegaard's character Constantin Constantius sets up a distinction between structured novelty and 'noise'. 'Repetition' does not simply involve the recurrence of the same: it is not a mere 're-take' of the past:

> The dialectic of repetition is easy, for that which is repeated has been – otherwise it could not be repeated – but the very fact that it has been makes the existence into something new. When the Greeks said that all knowing is recollecting, they said that all existence, which is, has been; when one says that life is a repetition, one says: actuality, which has been, now comes into existence. If one does not have the category of recollection or repetition, all life dissolves into an empty, meaningless noise. (1843c, p. 149)

'Noise' is sound that has not passed the screen of the embodied *cogito* and been filtered into music, rhythms, the patternings of code or speech. Finding 'repetition' – screening out the infinite possibilities and finding pattern – is for Kierkegaard the process whereby the 'I' shapes the past and the future into actuality, and in the process also takes shape itself.

As we saw in the last chapter, Kierkegaard insists in *Repetition* that 'Repetition and recollection are the same movement, except in opposite directions', and that 'genuine repetition is recollected forward'(p. 131). What is posited here is a mode of time which would proceed via echo – and repetition – and which is non-linear in the Kantian sense. Kierkegaard is also asking us to think individuality as that which is brought into existence along with an order of events that was already potentially there in the past:

> the individual is not an actual shape but a shadow, or, more correctly, the actual shape is invisibly present and therefore is not satisfied to cast one shadow, but the individual has a variety of shadows, all of which resemble him and which momentarily have equal status as being himself. As yet the personality is not discerned, and its energy is betokened only in the passion of possibility, for the same thing happens in the spiritual life as with many plants – the main shoot comes last. (1843c, p. 154)

Kierkegaard goes on to compare each of the possibilities of the individual to 'an audible shadow' (p. 155). Self-shaping (or becoming an individual) is like an alien wind that gradually takes on a regular pattern as it blows across a unfamiliar landscape. This wind

> produced now a shriek almost startling to itself, then a hollow roar from which it itself fled, then a moan, the source of which it itself did not know, then from the abyss of anxiety a sigh so deep that the wind itself grew frightened. . . . (p. 155)

Although in the end, a pattern emerges and the wind plays a melody that remains 'unaltered day after day', this sequence only emerges slowly. The individual is *like* a new wind, Kierkegaard's character Constantin Constantius says; but (s)he is not *just* a wind, since the 'I' does not just want to be heard, it is also '*gestaltende* (shaping or configuring) and therefore wants to be visible at the same time' (p. 155).

Kierkegaard's 'I' is 'birthed' by the patterns of repetition; but (s)he also brings those patterns into existence. The 'I' finds its melody or shape through a process of screening out sudden and indefinite noises into patterns. But as in the case of the perception of sound, the patterning could not come except by absorbing that which comes from outside. And it is mood – and the repetitions and rhythms of the embodied self – which establish patterns of resonance within this absorbed 'otherness'. That which is the self's 'essence' or identity emerges through patterns of flow, and cannot simply be ascribed to the *cogito*'s conscious decision or 'will' to produce itself. To return to Sacks's hypothesis of a brain that is 'scored', the Kierkegaardian model would mean that the way in which this score is interpreted is not fixed in advance – nor is it laid down simply by external factors. Neither fully autonomous nor completely determined, the self is produced relationally: in the resonances between self and other; in a 'present' that is a generative caesura between future and past.

Metaphysics in Movement

Deleuze and Guattari reference Kierkegaard at several pivotal moments in *A Thousand Plateaus* (1980). In particular, they quote Kierkegaard's phrase 'I look only at the movements'.[2] And this could indeed stand as the motto for Deleuze's own philosophical *oeuvre*, both in his more orthodox works on the history of philosophy, and also in the more experimental works co-authored with Guattari. For Deleuze and Guattari the key thing about the musical 'refrain' – and why they employ it as a counter to a metaphysics of substance in this second volume of *Capitalism and Schizophrenia* – is that within music there is progress and continuity that does not proceed linearly via a linking of 'points' or individualized notes (1980, pp. 294ff). Music is multilinear, they claim: 'everything happens at once' (p. 297), and this means that music involves a 'becoming' that does not link past to present in a linear way (pp. 294–5). In music, there is neither beginning nor end: always only an 'in between'. Music works in terms of 'blocks' of sound (not points); and a sound block 'is always and already in the middle of the line' (p. 296). Their claim is not that music has its origin in the *ritournelle*: the repeated musical phrase, chorus, refrain or musical 'riff'. But rather that without such 'riffs' music could not occur (p. 300).

Although Kant himself is not mentioned in the two chapters in *A Thousand Plateaus* on music, it is Kantian metaphysics that is being negated throughout. Music – and repeated blocks of sound – is used to represent an alternative mode of 'belonging together' that is secured materially, and not just by the 'syntheses' of the imagination. Repeated musical phrases can order the 'chaos' of sensations in ways that do not involve representing identities as closed 'unities' that are 'formed' by the imposition of linear space-time grids onto a material world. Thus, we are told that the song is a simultaneously calming and stabilizing place within a chaotic system (p. 311), and the beginnings of an order that develops from within chaos – what Deleuze and Guattari term a '*chaosmos*' (p. 313). The refrain is a means of marking territory; but a means that links space not linearly through 'points' (in Kantian fashion), but in terms of milieus or blocks. And it is rhythm that provides the key linking mode: a rhythm that also does not work simply sequentially, but via heterogeneous blocks (pp. 312–13). Thus, Deleuze and Guattari represent music in terms of coded signals – expressiveness – that are not 'things', but functional and transitory actions that have enough temporal constancy to mark out a spatial range (pp. 314ff).

In chapter 2 of *Individuals* (1959), P. F. Strawson provided an analogous (but much more literal) reworking of Kantianism as he substituted aural sensations for visual sense data within the context of a Kantian frame. Asking under what conditions it would be possible to identify and reidentify particulars if a subject only received sensations that were ones of sound, Strawson argued that a subject would need a conceptual equivalent of space in order to have a workable concept of self and 'not-self'. He also insisted that such an equivalence could only be obtained by plotting the aural sensations against a 'master sound' that provided a continuity of tone in terms of loudness, pitch and timbre. According to Strawson, 'sound particulars' have to be treated as the equivalents of material objects, and have to be represented in terms of a unified space and a single time-frame. However, even such a plotting would not be sufficient for the auditory observer to escape solipsism, and to adequately distinguish between veridical and illusory knowledge: between 'subjective' and 'objective' modes of thought.

It is useful to compare Strawson's *Individuals* with *A Thousand Plateaus*, since this juxtaposition emphasizes what is distinctive about the two approaches. Strawson's book – subtitled *An Essay in Descriptive Metaphysics* – purports to show that the categories of both 'material objects' and 'persons' are basic to our conceptual scheme (p. 246). Strawson thus, in effect, offers a revision of Kantianism, arguing that we need to add to the categorial framework if we are to adequately distinguish 'self' from 'not-self'. By contrast, Deleuze and Guattari are offering not a descriptive metaphysics, but what is, in effect, a revisionary materialist metaphysics. Much of Deleuze and Guattari's 'evidence' for alternative models for thinking 'belonging together' is taken from the study of animals, birds and insects, as well as anthropology. Deleuze and Guattari thus succeed in showing that our 'common sense' modes of thinking identity in terms of stable substances and space-time objects are limited.

Although the notions of 'material object' and 'person' might ground the dominant metaphysics of the west (as Strawson would claim), Deleuze and Guattari's observations on *ritournelle* allow us to see that other conceptual schemes are available to us. Patterns of repeated sound – and not only (as Strawson would have it) a single 'master sound' – provide enough coherence for there to be alternative modes of 'belonging together' that are neither 'subjects' nor 'objects'. The Deleuzian *ritournelle* is neither a single unit, nor a collection of units. One refrain merges into other refrains not by processes of antagonism or opposition (whereby the identity of the refrain is only ever established in reference to what is not the refrain). Instead, the identity of the repeated chorus, phrase or riff is only ever established gradually, by a process of temporal development – or what Deleuze and Guattari term 'the *labour of the refrain*' (p. 302). However, order (and hence selves and objects) does not disappear, even though it has to re-emerge out of fuzzy conglomerates. It is this notion of temporalized individuation – of *open* identities that can include 'otherness' within – that offers rich possibilities for rethinking the self.

There are, however, puzzles with Deleuze and Guattari's analysis. In particular, they seek to bypass memory in their description of musical repetition. *Ritournelle* is described as *anti-memory*, and instead described in primarily animal, ornithological or 'machinic' terms – as surface codings. Memory, they suppose (why?), operates in terms of linear linkages, and moves kinematically along the horizontal line of the flow of time – from the 'old present' to the 'actual present' – or via 'stratigraphy', which orders time vertically: 'from the present to the past, or to the representation of the old present' (pp. 294–5). What is blocked is the Nietzschean account of the relationship between memory and forgetting that I discussed in relation to Adorno in chapter 7 of this book. On Adorno's model (which is also influenced by Kierkegaard), what is forgotten – the multiplicity of sensations prior to synthesis under concepts – remains within memory like a shadow, and keeps alive the multiplicity of sensation in non-linear modes. Thus, one of the main differences between the account of 'repetition' offered by Kierkegaard and that developed by Deleuze and Guattari lies in the role that is given to 'memory' – and therefore also to feedback-loops, echo and depth. As we will see, this also means that there is a subtle (but important) difference in the role allotted to 'woman' – and, in particular, the 'girl' – in *A Thousand Plateaus* and in Kierkegaard's aesthetic works.

Becoming a Girl

Deleuze and Guattari develop an attack on a metaphysics of substance that uses linear causalities to link together 'molar identities' horizontally in time. The so-called 'molar identities' are groupings of properties or substances that are held together extensively (in space) as unities by 'a succession of framing forms, each of which informs a substance and in turn serves as a substance for another form' (1980, p. 335). Against such a conceptual scheme, the two authors posit less rigid, more 'supple, more molecular, and merely ordered' modes of organization (p. 41). Marking the plateaus of thought, we find the 'refrain', the 'rhizome', 'nomad', 'pack' or 'assemblage', as well as 'becoming-intense', 'becoming-animal', 'becoming-imperceptible' (pp. 232ff). These involve also a 'becoming-woman' and a 'becoming-molecular' that have as a necessary first stage 'becoming a girl' (pp. 272–9).

In their comments on 'becoming-woman' or 'becoming a girl' Deleuze and Guattari make a number of moves familiar to those working in the French poststructuralist tradition. 'Women' are not 'woman'; young females are not 'girls'. Instead, 'becoming a girl' is a state of transition that 'molar identities' must pass through in order to break away from a mode of being in which all change 'happens' – and all attributes 'belong' – to substances. Furthermore, since conceptualizing the self in terms of a unified 'I' typifies the metaphysics of substance, 'man' (a male) 'is the molar identity par excellence' (p. 292). Thus, all breakdown of identity is described by the two authors as a breakdown of masculine identity, and 'becoming-woman' is portrayed as a 'first quantum' in the headlong rush to 'becoming-imperceptible' (p. 279). 'Even women must become-woman' (p. 291). And they do this by themselves becoming girls: 'the girl is the becoming-woman of each sex' (p. 277).

> The girl is certainly not defined by virginity; she is defined by a relation of movement and rest, speed and slowness, by a combination of atoms, an emission of particles: haecceity. . . . She is an abstract line, or a line of flight. The girls do not belong to an age group, sex, order, or kingdom: they slip in everywhere between orders, acts, ages, sexes. . . . (pp. 276–7)

On Deleuze and Guattari's model even the 'becoming-woman' of women is not something that women themselves perform. Instead, the 'becoming-woman' of women results from changes in the organization of social structures of *males*, produced by social transitions within capitalism (pp. 291–2). How advantageous these changes might be for women themselves is dubious, given the fact that D. H. Lawrence, Henry Miller and Henry James are all listed as approximating to the state of 'becoming-woman' through their authorship (pp. 276, 290). Deleuze and Guattari express a degree of sympathy for the women's movement; but the extent of their approbation is strictly limited. Identity politics can only ever be a stage on the way to a more revolutionary form of 'becoming': 'a molecular women's politics that slips into molar confrontation, and passes under or through them' (p. 276). In other words, Deleuze and Guattari demand a move beyond sexual difference; not one that would use the specificity of the female subject-position to mark out a new metaphysics of identity.

'Girls', 'woman' and, indeed, 'women' are not allowed a subject-position of their own; but are instead allowed to occupy only an awkward position between (full) molar identity and the transitional state of becoming molecular. Thus, on the one hand, it is claimed that 'There is no becoming-man' because the male (as molar) is a mode of being, not of becoming (p. 292). On the other hand, Deleuze and Guattari indicate that 'each sex contains the other and must develop the opposite pole in itself' in order to become 'molecular' (p. 276). To 'become-woman' *women* must become masculine; but such a becoming is also impossible since the masculine represents (molar) being, not (molecular) becoming. The privilege given to 'woman' means that flesh-and-blood

'women' remain (once again) a blind spot in the philosophical configurations of 'becoming' and 'being'. With spasmodic references to
Kierkegaard – and even more indirect references to Kierkegaardian
figurations such as 'the knight of faith' or 'the secret' – Deleuze and
Guattari appropriate 'the girl' to indicate a breakdown of the normal
(male) subject-position. However, since there is no attempt to reconstruct
identity based on 'the girl', 'woman' remains man's 'other' – as in the
Hegelian and psychoanalytic models that the two authors oppose.

It might therefore be thought surprising that feminist theorists
should find anything of interest in Deleuze and Guattari's often unwittingly misogynistic prose. There are nevertheless a number of features in
Deleuze's conceptual revisionism that have appealed to feminists searching for alternatives to Lacanian psychoanalysis or Derridean deconstruction. Thus, for example, Deleuze's sustained attack on the notion of dead
'matter' which is shaped into substances by an active 'form' is usable
by feminists, if it can somehow be disentangled from the rhetoric of
'becoming-woman' within which it is framed. In the history of western
philosophy it is 'woman' who has been equated with matter; man with
the shaping formative force. Deleuze's attack on hylomorphism bears
some similarity to analogous moves made by those theorists who are
interested in the position of *women* in the history of the west. Moreover,
Deleuze's *positive* attitude to changing modes of classifying is also attractive to feminists, as we see, for example, in Elizabeth Grosz's *Volatile
Bodies* (1994). Since Deleuze continually plays with alternatives to hylomorphism, his writings escape the metaphysical paralysis which pervades
the tradition of deconstructive theory.

Deleuze and Guattari's response to metaphysics differs sharply from
that of Derrida. Thus, for example, in 'He Stuttered' (1993) Deleuze
uses a language that 'stutters' performatively, so that new possibilities
and a radicalized conception of space-time emerge. Deleuze does not
simply attempt to subvert, parody or ironize a 'phallogocentric' language and metaphysics from within. If 'woman' is (as Kierkegaard's
'Johannes the Seducer' would say) 'only a workshop of possibilities'
(1845, p. 76), then for Deleuze and Guattari this workshop is one in
which real possibilities are forged. We are not dealing here simply with
the logically possible – but unattainable and/or unspeakable – condition
of the Lacanian *féminin*. And neither is 'woman' simply reducible to
concealed absences and tensions (*différance*) within phallogocentrism,
as Derrida would claim.

Oddly, however, in one of the most influential appropriations of Deleuzian philosophy for feminist theory (that of Rosi Braidotti), Deleuze's
position has been combined with an anti-ontological bias that comes

more from the deconstructionist standpoint that would represent all metaphysics as irredeemably 'phallogocentric'. In fact, Braidotti's position is hard to untangle since she seems deeply ambivalent about ontology, which she defines as 'the branch of metaphysics that deals with the structure of that which essentially is' (Braidotti, 1994, p. 177). Thus, on the one hand, she claims within the text of her own *Nomadic Subjects* that sexual difference is ontological: '"being-a-woman" is always already there as the ontological precondition for my existential becoming as a subject' (pp. 187–8). On the other hand, in the 'Introduction' to this same volume of collected essays Braidotti exhorts us all to become 'nomadic feminists' and links such feminism with exposing 'the illusion of ontological foundations' (p. 35).

It is true that Deleuze links metaphysics with a dominant philosophical tradition that thinks identity in terms of essences, form, matter, substances, and a stable self that can be understood only in terms of the not-self or 'object'. However, Deleuze does not give up on the philosophical past; but instead revisits it in order to posit parallel possibilities. Subject and object become a series of flows, assemblages, 'packs' of molecular energies that function effectively together within a certain space-time plane, but that do not comprise an organic unity that is inherently or teleologically united. Braidotti recognizes that Deleuze is making a 'postmetaphysical' move that involves a new 'figuration' of the subject. However, she also represents metaphysics as homogeneous in a way that is at odds with the Deleuzian strategy. Metaphysics is described by Braidotti as necessarily dualist: '*a* political ontology' that is committed to the separation of mind and body, and that offers '*a* theory about their interaction, about how they hang together', and '*a* proposition about how we should go about thinking the fundamental unity of the human being' (p. 108, emphases added).

With such a simplistic definition of metaphysics – a definition at odds with Deleuze's own attention to historical variation – it thus becomes easy for Braidotti to claim that 'the cyborg is a postmetaphysical construct' (p. 108). Donna Haraway's (1984) figure of the machine/human hybrid can count as postmetaphysical in so far as it is post-dualist, and replaces the mind/body split that is (falsely) supposed the distinguishing feature of the metaphysics of western modernity. Like feminist postmodernists mentioned earlier in this book, Rosi Braidotti uses also an *epistemological* definition of modernity that explicitly makes Descartes (and not Kant) central: 'what marks the age of modernity is the emergence of a discourse about what it means to elaborate a discourse' (1994, p. 210). Thus, whereas Deleuze's own 'postmetaphysical' project can best be understood in terms of an extended dialogue with Kant, Braidotti follows the standard feminist postmodern track of placing Descartes – and epistemological issues relating to the adequacy of representation – at the heart of contemporary debate.

Indeed, Braidotti ends by arguing against philosophy in a way very foreign to Deleuze's creative re-imagination of its past and future. Thus, there could be no stronger contrast between Deleuze and Guattari's re-vision of philosophy as 'the discipline that involves *creating* concepts' in *What is Philosophy?* (1991, p. 5), and Braidotti's own anti-philosophical move:

> one of the first targets of the feminist practice of difference should be, in my opinion, to question the very gesture or stance of high theory and especially of philosophy as being representative of the power of/in discourse that we are trying to critique. (1994, p. 211)

Braidotti argues for 'women's studies as a practice of sexual difference in the nomadic mode' as the replacement for feminist philosophy (p. 211). And this need to move beyond philosophy is specifically linked with 'the crisis of metaphysics' that poststructuralism forces on us (p. 210). This so-called 'crisis' is described as 'Nietzschean', but is also seen as coincident with Freud's attack on 'the founding illusion of the Cartesian subject' (p. 211). More specifically, Braidotti claims that it is impossible to think about the origin of philosophy from within philosophy itself. But this is a version of the history of philosophy (and Nietzsche) that Deleuze himself would reject – and, in effect, reworks Heidegger's and Derrida's view of philosophy's past. Instead of radicalizing metaphysics and philosophy in the way effected by Deleuze, Braidotti's own 'nomadic mode' involves a lapse back into deconstruction and an overemphasis on epistemology and the question of representation.

In this respect I have more sympathy with Deleuze's *philosophical* project than with Braidotti's de-philosophizing of feminist theory for supposedly feminist ends. However, I have strong reservations about Deleuze and Guattari's metaphoric language that links 'woman' and the 'feminine' with molecular 'becomings' and 'assemblages', so that any concern with *women* or identity politics is dismissible as masculinist. I also have a concern with the way that Deleuze and Guattari think 'assemblages' only in terms of surface patternings or flows, so that questions of depth fall out of account. A consideration of this last point will lead us back to Kierkegaard – and why the latter's interest in 'the girl' might be considered preferable to that of Deleuze. But, first, it is necessary to look more closely at the current feminist uptake of the Deleuzian figurations of the 'rhizome' and the 'nomad' – and the problem of the nature of 'the manifold' (difference) that this language conceals.

Lines of Flight

A 'rhizome' is a corm or plant (like couch grass) that spreads horizontally, instead of vertically through a generational passing on of seeds.
And it is this figuration of 'belonging together' that feminists like Elizabeth Grosz have found commensurate (if not coincident) with feminist
theory (Grosz, 1993, p. 209). Grosz picks out five features of 'rhizomatics' as both basic for Deleuzianism and attractive for feminists
(pp. 199–200). The first of these features is the claim that the rhizome
involves a bringing together of diverse fragments. The second feature is
that the rhizome is based on heterogeneity: it links together elements
that are diverse and that do not necessarily belong together. Third, as
Deleuze and Guattari put it, the rhizome is 'reducible neither to the
One nor the multiple': it is composed not of individuals or parts of a
whole, but of directions of energy or motion – the so-called 'lines of
flight'.[3] Fourth, the rhizome is subject to ruptures, breaks and discontinuities anywhere within it whilst retaining its structure. Fifth, and
finally, the rhizome is a form of mapping – a cartography – rather than
a 'trace' that points back to an originary root or source.

If 'woman' denoted a relationship that was rhizomatic, it would link
together entities that were not of the same form or essence; but would
instead signify a loose 'assemblage' – a variety of surface relationships
that could be broken apart (and re-joined differently) along a multiplicity of axes. However, even recognizing that Deleuze and Guattari's
figure of the rhizome is supposed to displace Hegel's celebrated modelling of identity as the growth and budding of leaves on a tree (1807,
§ 2, p. 2), there is something extremely odd about the rhizome metaphor. And this is because the structure of the rhizome is maintained by
genetic continuities and origins in ways that bring back in the notion
of a unified identity, or an originary parent or source. Perhaps in recognition of this, in *A Thousand Plateaus* Deleuze and Guattari employ a
variety of different images for the modes of 'belonging together' that substitute for Kantian 'substances' or Aristotelian and Platonic 'forms'. One
of these alternative metaphors is the 'pack' of wolves; another is the band
of 'nomads' that moves across the landscape without fencing the land
(1980, pp. 239ff; 380ff). There are, however, also problems with these
figurations for the Deleuzian project that tries to think 'assemblages'
and groupings that are reducible neither to unities nor to multiplicities.

The wolf 'pack' is a non-stable grouping or assemblage that grows
larger or smaller as individual wolves join it, die or move on alone. The
strength of the 'pack' comes from a combination of forces or energies

that operates effectively in so far as these are (temporarily) directed towards the same ends. In effect, this is a Nietzschean model of identity. (Deleuze wrote on Nietzsche, and continued to use the latter's notion of 'active' and 'reactive' forces throughout his own philosophical *oeuvre*.) But the problem with the 'pack' model is that the pack is also made up out of heterogeneous 'individuals' that all belong to the same species (wolf) and that only count as pack-members in so far as members of the same species are able to join or dissociate themselves from the assemblage. The pack thus also seems to involve a unity (the species) that seems at odds with the ideal, loosely organized grouping that only counts as a unity in terms of its 'lines of flight'.

Of course, Deleuze and Guattari's point in using the figuration of the 'pack' is not that we cannot think it in terms of unity and identity, but that we can use the notion of the pack to think identity otherwise – and consider loose groupings that come together merely as lines of energies or force coincide. But note, however, that this use of the notion of 'pack' now meets a new objection – of bringing together a 'multiplicity' that suggests original heterogeneity: 'bits' or 'fragments' that only come together via a kind of (temporary) 'glue'. This bond is provided not (as in Kant) by the 'syntheses' of the imagination, but by social deformations and 'matter' itself. However, the underpinning metaphor still suggests separate parts that need to be 'bundled' together. And this begs the question of whether this underlying heterogeneity of 'bits' – temporarily united as a 'pack' – might still be taking the male subject as norm.

In both *A Thousand Plateaus* and the earlier *Anti-Oedipus* (1972), Deleuze and Guattari explain the origins of the 'centred' and 'oedipalized' self in terms of the couplings of hands and body organs formed by activity, desire – and the processes of capitalist production. Traditional Marxism opposes the alienated man, dismembered as a self by his relationship to the processes of industrial production, to the utopian, 'integral' man whose body and labour are his own. But Deleuze and Guattari contest the notion of an 'integral' or a 'natural' body that belongs to the species. Bodies, like selves, are envisaged not as a collection of parts, but as a series of bodily states. The so-called 'Body without Organs' is the flow of undifferentiated desire that is then shaped and formed through couplings of voice and hearing; hand and eye; eye and pain. (See Lingis, 1994.) Capitalism links body parts in distinctive ways; but Deleuze and Guattari do not foresee the restitution of a 'natural' man. Instead, they envisage further dismemberment – and new couplings – via the processes of capitalist evolution. New modes of machinics will reconstitute the public/private divide, just as the privatized body is itself a product of capitalist modes of organization.

The historical transformations which constitute and break apart the individualized subject or 'person' are analysed in ways that do not address the specificity of women's relationship to the means of production (and reproduction). Indeed, as in classic Marxism, questions of reproductive relationships continue to be subordinated to relationships of production and capital. Women become simply 'minoritarian' incursions into those patternings of society (and into those configurations of self) which forge all 'humans' into equivalent molar identities. Thus, when Deleuze and Guattari develop the image of the 'Body without Organs' as a counter to the organic model of the (privatized) body and the (centred) self, they present this undifferentiated and 'organless' body as the flow of energies and drives that ontologically precedes the shaping of the individual into an 'organic' whole. This body is presented as if it were prior to difference, including sexual difference.

Although Deleuze and Guattari offer a form of transcendental materialism that counters the emphasis on being and substance in Plato and Kant, their materialism – indeed their emphasis on 'woman' and the 'girl' – nevertheless blanks out material differences between the two sexes. 'Becoming-woman' does not involve the mature (fleshy) female body. The flows and intensities of desire seem gender-unspecific, but assume maleness as the only possible norm for an identity. Deleuze and Guattari emphasize production; what they do not consider is reproduction – or the fact that women (unlike men) have traditionally been treated as flows of pleasure and desire that lack overall coherence or unity (more like a 'Body without Organs' than like a Kantian 'person' or Kant's 'transcendental self'). As Irigaray puts it: for women 'isn't the organless body a historical condition?' (1977, p. 141). Although 'woman' is not simply that which falls outside the horizons of representation (as in more orthodox varieties of poststructuralist thought), and is instead an attainable intensity, there is nevertheless an abstraction from the repetitions and rhythms of embodied (sexually specific) lives.

Furthermore, Deleuze and Guattari do not – cannot – consider the fact that the mother's relationship to her child might produce modes of 'belonging together' that are neither the bonding of two individuals not a temporary grouping of fragments via 'assemblages' or 'packs'. Indeed, there is on Deleuze and Guattari's behalf a refusal to think the mother/child relationship in ways that don't reduce merely to the oedipalized model of father/son relationships or – as the only alternative – to the form of 'belonging together' that is appropriate for the 'nomad', 'assemblage', 'pack' or 'gang'. For Deleuze and Guattari the nomad is distinguished by the way he moves through space: his 'territory' does not enclose a land or function as a line connecting points. Instead, 'points for him are relays along a trajectory' (1980, p. 380).

Explicitly distinguished from the 'migrant' and the 'exile', the nomad is cut off from community as he moves through his 'tactile', 'sonorous' and 'haptic' space. Nomadism is constituted by 'speed', 'rushes', 'becomings', 'absolute movement', involving intensive (not extensive) 'lines of flight' (pp. 380–2). Deleuze and Guattari link American 'Indians without ancestry' to the shifting and displaced frontiers of American rhizomatic travel, and claim that 'everything important that has happened or is happening takes the route of the American rhizome: the beatniks, the underground, bands and gangs' (p. 19). And this is revealing. For the 'nomad' is more like the beatnik in Jack Kerouac's novel *On the Road* (1957) than like the more material modes of becoming that characterize American Indians, gypsies, migrants, aboriginal Australians or Bedouin.

Deleuze and Guattari mention Kerouac by name. But the flights and evasions of *On the Road* are utterly different from accounts of journeys offered by American Indians themselves. In Kerouac's novel there are no children, and the only women are 'chicks': (temporary) sexual partners who approximate male freedoms. The novel starts with the breakdown of the narrator's marriage; and the journey of the two male buddies across America ends when Dean Moriarty leaves the narrator in the lurch, as the latter falls ill with dysentery and fever. There is a willed forgetfulness of relationships of care and community, and a romanticization of flesh that is simultaneously sexual, individualized, yet also abstract. Indeed, Kerouac self-consciously idealizes a world without relationships of dependency, and instead attempts a flight from the 'poor atomistic hulk' of flesh within which the narrator experiences himself as trapped (1957, p. 302).

By contrast, in *Black Elk Speaks* (1932), the Oglala Sioux Holy Man who retells his life-story to John G. Neihardt (Flaming Rainbow) adopts the voice of mythical grandfathers to evoke a number of spiritual roads – and journeys across America – that are to be undertaken by the people together. Here the collectivity of the tribes (which explicitly includes the sick, the old and children) will forge a new relationship to the earth, and to the holy and endless 'hoop' which is 'one power in the people without end' (Neihardt, 1932, p. 35). Deleuze and Guattari's reference to the American Indian cuts him off from community, from relationships of care, and from a deep (non-beatnik/non-alienated) relationship to the land and to others. In effect they treat the American Indian as if he was always young, fit, male, a 'brave': locked into a game of (Americanized) freedom. A game that celebrates 'Red Indians' and demonizes the cowboy 'brother' who would fence in the land.

Through the Loophole

Kierkegaard's writings also explore the loss of bonding, but they do not celebrate it – despite the meditations on 'girls' by 'Johannes the Seducer' in the '*In Vino Veritas*' dialogue, and also by the (male) diarist in ' "Guilty?"/"Not Guilty?" ', also in *Stages on Life's Way*. As we saw in the last chapter, according to Johannes, 'girls' (and not wives) belong in a time order that takes 'man' outside time: 'This is how the devotee of erotic love sèes her and in the moment of seduction leads her and is led by her outside of time, where as an illusion she belongs' (1845, p. 80). The diarist also meditates on 'girls' as a phenomenon capable of releasing the masculine self:

> how strange it must be to be a young girl, to enter into life so briskly. I believed I would be released, that I would be changed, that I would have seen myself in love and by looking in love at her I would see myself saved – then I would have become like her, a bird on a branch, a song of joy in youth. (p. 215)

Kierkegaard's 'girl' escapes the linearities of Kantian history in much the same way as that of Deleuze. But a 'girl' or a 'woman' for Kierkegaard is not just a nomadic line of flight away and on from the paradigmatic molar identity: the oedipalized (masculinized) self. Kierkegaard's pseudonymous voices work rhythmically (and repetitively) to mark out a (multiplicitous) order through temporal flashbacks and competing 'takes' on the relationship between past, present and future. The result is a novel model of temporality and also of self which refuses the Greek notion that all becoming is only a recollection of being, whilst also rejecting the Heraclitean counter-thesis that life is only a stream. Instead, the concept of 'repetition' is employed to open up a third alternative that permits change and novelty – and that allows order to emerge from flux in a way that prioritizes becoming over being.

Kierkegaard sides with Antigone: the daughter and sister of Oedipus who acts as a catalyst in terms of the development of social relationships. Describing 'echo' as that 'master of irony', Kierkegaard makes 'woman' – Hegel's 'everlasting irony (in the life of) the community' – a productive resonance that does not merely mimic or palely shadow male universals. He privileges the ambiguity of Antigone's familial and social position to mark out a new subject-position which is through and through relational, but that cannot simply be reduced to exterior relationships. What characterizes Kierkegaard's reworked Antigone is her relationship to her father's 'secret': to a past that forever escapes her and that must be endlessly reworked. Via loops, auditory feedback, echo and repetition Kierkegaard reconstructs identity in ways that allow us to think self not just as a multiplicity of surfaces or territories, but also in terms of dependency and depth.

For feminists to opt in to the Deleuzian version of this ontology would be to opt for a system in which self is just a surface phenomenon, and hence agency (and also political agency) cannot be thought. It would be also to re-imagine the territories of productive labour, whilst simultaneously forgetting the rhythms of reproductive labour – the *work* involving in caring, protecting and sheltering dependants. Thus, as we saw earlier, for Deleuze women must undergo a 'becoming-woman'; but 'becoming-woman' for women depends in changes in technology and production that operate on the psyches and social structures of males. For Kierkegaard, by contrast, Antigone is a model for a self that is created in the moment: in the 'nook' of present, future and past. This self is not created solely by itself, nor is it a passive victim of circumstance or of the 'system' as a whole. Political agency is possible; but the agent has to live with radical ambiguities; an infinity of potential 'realities'; with power discrepancies; and with relational dependence on others.

Thinking female selves in terms of patterns emerging out of flow and movement does not necessitate giving up a 'depth' model of the self. Neither does talk of such a self entail closing down the possibility of historical and cultural singularities, or of new unthought-of possibilities emerging in the future, the present, or even from the past. The specificity of the female subject-position is neither solely biologically 'determined', nor simply the result of cultural 'construction'. Instead, different temporalities of experience (through repetition and habit) 'score' women's lives, as do also the differential positionings of race, class and community. The female sex 'is not one'; but neither is it entirely without its own distinctive morphology. Like Kierkegaard's 'alien' wind blowing over a strange landscape, the female self is shaped as it negotiates and renegotiates obstacles, and as it registers the resonances and echoes that its repeated movements produce. Neither totally free, nor totally determined, the Kierkegaardian 'woman' opens up a line of flight that escapes the linearities of Hegelian histories and Kantian temporalities – but which also loops in ways that suggest a multiplicity of dimensions that cannot be contained by the thousand temporal territories which mark out the plateaus of thought.

10
Coda

In a recent book, *Substance Among Other Categories* (1994), Joshua Hoffman and Gary S. Rosenkrantz offer 'an exploration of the ontological landscape of ordinary discourse and thought' and claim:

> Most philosophers would concede that there is an ordinary, commonsense, or 'folk' conceptual scheme, and that this scheme has certain ontological presuppositions. Foremost among these is the idea that there are enduring things, or individual substances, continuants such as people, rocks, flowers, and houses. (p. 1)

The two authors then go on to both analyse and defend this 'core' notion of substance, arguing that it is not adequate to regard a substance as that which persists through change (pp. 29–33). Instead, they claim that 'substance' needs to be theorized as 'in some way independent of any other substance' (p. 2). They cite Descartes and Spinoza in support of such a strong account of 'substance', and even argue that although empirical science might seem to have 'rejected the existence of substances, it is questionable whether it has done so justifiably' (p. 6).

Hoffman and Rosenkrantz present themselves (p. 5) as offering a 'descriptive metaphysics' (along with P. F. Strawson), and as avoiding the type of 'revisionary metaphysics' which my last chapter associated with Deleuze and with Kierkegaard – and which this book as a whole has been concerned to explore. These two philosophers are working in the analytic tradition, and thus seem unfamiliar with contemporary attacks on a 'metaphysics of substance' that have been generated from postmodernists, poststructuralists and others who engage with European traditions of philosophy:

While there is a large body of recent work devoted to the production (or destruction) of philosophical analyses of concepts such as knowledge and causation, the concept of substance has been neglected in comparison. (p. 6)

Whereas it is good to see an 'ontological turn' also featuring in analytic philosophy, Hoffman and Rosenkrantz's starting point needs to be questioned. Of course, we all believe in 'continuants such as people, rocks, flowers, and houses'; but are we really committed to a claim about independent 'substances' when we hold such beliefs? At various key points in their argument, Hoffman and Rosenkrantz appeal to an 'intuitive' notion of a substance as a counter to those who do not see 'substance' as an independent entity. (See, for example, pp. 59, 63.) However, as I also suggested in chapter 3, looked at closely 'common sense' can include grossly divergent experiential reports about the relationship between 'self' and 'other', and is not as philosophically homogeneous – or as secure – as it might at first sight seem. Thus, as I outlined in chapter 1, 'common sense' – and the 'folk' conceptual scheme – has difficulties in dealing with birth and growth.

Although I do not want to claim that a more 'fluid' model of identity has now become a new 'common sense', I am convinced that Hoffman and Rosenkrantz are wrong to read a more-or-less universal ontological commitment to 'substances' from the everyday patterns of linguistic referral to 'subjects' and 'objects'. It is interesting in this respect that when they turn to the question of the underlying ontology of the empirical sciences, what they discuss is physics and not the problem of what might count as 'substance' in biology. Nor do they deal with alternative ontological models – such as dissipative systems – that are also now current in physics and in other 'hard' sciences.

'Common sense' changes as the sciences also change. 'Common sense' was never homogeneous, but developments in the last twenty-five years seem to have accelerated the divergences and alterations. Thus, in *Life on the Screen: Identity in the Age of the Internet* (1995), the sociologist Sherry Turkle records a number of conversations with subjects who spend much of their leisure time playing complex multi-user games and engaging in relationships in 'virtual reality' via the Internet. What Turkle's book shows is the complexity of the users' reports about their own adoptive personae that they assume as they enter this world. The 'virtual' and the 'real' frequently intersect in these subjects' lives. 'We live in each other's brains, as voices, images, words on screen', says one character in an on-line discussion about his 'on-screen' role-playing. He goes on: 'We are multiple personalities and we include each other' (1995, p. 257).

Like Emily Martin in her *Flexible Bodies* (1994), discussed in chapter 3, Sherry Turkle confuses the ontology of a 'flexible' subject with an ontology of the 'fluid' (Turkle, 1995, p. 255). It is, therefore, often hard to be sure whether or not the characters Turkle interviews have retained a notion of an individualized self (which then 'flexibly' transforms) or whether they have genuinely adopted the model of identities 'fluidly' emerging out of patternings of relationship to 'otherness' that Turkle often seems to detect in their words. However, we also cannot assume that the 'common sense' of these subjects involves the ontological presuppositions about substances that Hoffman and Rosenkrantz describe. As Turkle herself comments: 'The technologies of our everyday lives change the way we see the world' (p. 47). Interfacing with an 'other' via a computer brings direct awareness of the way in which complex identities can emerge out of an always shifting, and decentralized network of codes and signs. If it once was, indeed, 'common' sense to adopt an ontology of substance, continued familiarity with computers makes this an increasingly troublesome assumption to make.

The Transformative Self

In the opening chapter of this book I raised the question of what would happen if we disturbed 'common' sense in ways that take the female subject as norm. Perhaps surprisingly, it has turned out that such a question was not first raised by a feminist philosopher, but by Søren Kierkegaard, who needed to rethink the self from the perspective of one whose 'I' was fractured into discontinuities – and who needed to reconcile temporal persistence with the 'others within'. Thus, in Kierkegaard's early 'aesthetic' writings, we find an ontology that can deal with the five features of the female subject-position that I picked out as important. I now want to return to these five features and review Kierkegaard's contribution to these ontologies of becoming.

The first of these features was natality. Although Kierkegaard never explicitly addresses the need to think the normality of the body that can birth, he troubles the notion of identity as a fixed, permanent or pre-given 'thing' or 'substance'. Thus, as we have seen, for Kierkegaard the self is birthed within a multiple play of possibilities. Identity emerges out of movement; change is not simply something extraneous that 'happens' to substances. Nor is relationality extrinsic to the self. Kierkegaardian entities emerge from a dynamic play of relationships that occur over time. Repeated movements configure the self into specificity in a non-teleological fashion, so that what is produced is novelty – not simply the reproduction of 'the same'. 'Becoming' is privileged over 'being'. Each self is a singularity, scored by repeated movements in such a way as to produce its own characteristic individuality: 'the main shoot comes last'.

Kierkegaard's ontology also addressed the second feature of the female subject-position that I highlighted. For the (normalized) woman – as also for Kierkegaard – selves are never just 'equals', not even on an ideal level. Since modern western cultures have regarded the female as the primary carer of children and other dependants within the so-called 'private' sphere, a woman's self cannot be conceptualized without the power-dependencies and inequalities that configure its development. Kierkegaard's strategy of examining the self through privileging the seducer/seduced relationship – as opposed to Hegel's account of the master/slave relationship – is particularly relevant for thinking the predicament of 'woman'. Kierkegaard exploits the ambiguous positioning of the seduced woman (or child), caught between the full subjectivity of an Enlightenment 'person' who freely 'chooses' her fate and a docile object, raped or duped into compliance by the seducer.

Furthermore, instead of presenting this double positioning in negative terms, Kierkegaard exploits it to develop a model of the 'singular' subject in which autonomy, choice and self-determination are neither necessary nor sufficient conditions for remaining a self. As in the case of the abused child who has internalized her (or his) abuser's valuations of a self that has primarily sexual worth, registering psychic 'others' that inhabit the 'I' does not entail regarding the self as entirely moulded by these 'others within'. Since the 'I' is scored by a variety of relationships with 'otherness', it is not a simple product of one originary experience. Like the consumer whose very desires and 'needs' are moulded by advertising media, this 'self' is not entirely free; but neither is it without a specificity that can develop into a form of resistance to modes of domination that do not fit with its own singularity. As in the case of a plant, 'the main shoot comes last'; and, as in the case of a plant (that feeds off water and food and that chemically interacts with air), this shoot comes only after taking 'otherness' into the self.

Thus, the Kierkegaardian ontology also fits with the third feature of the female subject-position discussed in chapter 1. This was that for the (normalized) female, the not-self (the other) emerges from within her own embodied self. For Kierkegaard there is no sharp 'cut' between 'self' and 'other', but this does not imply that 'self' dissolves into 'not-self'. A 'self' (like other 'things') simply is a complex grouping of singularities, so that 'otherness' is within – as well as without. However, since that grouping is not 'just' artificial – not 'just' imposed by the mind – it can function as a unity for some purposes. Like a body that functions as a whole on account of a healthy immune system, there is a kind of (temporary) stability which emerges out of movement, but which can also disperse.

Gradually, over a period of time, goals and modes of directionality develop within the self as habitual patterns of movement pattern potentiality into actuality. From the point of view of a feminist analysis, this Kierkegaardian move is particularly interesting in that it allows us to explain how female selves can be scored into specificity by differential patterns of work experience and other features of acculturation. In effect, this Kierkegaardian move allows us to explain differences *amongst* women, whilst also registering that many of these differences stem from an underlying sameness with regard to their positioning *vis-à-vis* the founding metaphysical categories of 'identity', 'self', 'substance' and 'personhood'.

The fourth feature of the female subject-position that I outlined was linked to the fact that in our culture 'femaleness' is linked to 'fleshiness'. Here, Kierkegaard has the least to say, in that he hardly addressed embodiment at all. And yet, here again, Kierkegaard's ontology of becoming is relevant. Thus, Kierkegaard refuses the notion of a free or autonomous and individualized 'soul' or 'mind' that merely inhabits the flesh, as well as the notion of a 'me' that is constructed (in Kantian fashion) by a 'synthesis' of temporal moments performed by the 'I'. Instead, Kierkegaard offers a model of identity that is non-hylomorphic: identity is configured by patterns of becoming, and is not a form imposed on matter by the mind in a top-down way.

Such an ontology also offers some interesting openings for theorizing a sexually differential relationship with embodiment – and in ways that are not straightforwardly 'biologistic'. Thus, Kierkegaard's account of the internalization of 'otherness' through patterns of repeated movement can be usefully put together with Marcel Mauss's (1934) account of the way the 'techniques of the body' change differentially from society to society, and also vary markedly over quite short periods of time. These different bodily 'comportments' that Mauss lists include postures for sleeping: going to bed/sleeping on the 'floor'; using a pillow; a neck-rest; lying 'flat'. His list goes on: techniques for walking; squatting; holding the arms; for swimming; for making a fist; for giving birth (standing, lying, 'on all fours'); for weaning; for carrying the child. All these 'comportments' that we take to be 'natural' – or sometimes 'unnatural' – are culturally and historically specific. Furthermore, even though particular cultures (or groups of cultures) also differ markedly one from the other, it is not just the techniques of birthing and weaning that serve as sex-differential markers within a particular society.

Within feminist theory we are more used to seeing these bodily variations described in terms of Michel Foucault's ontology, which also
(like that of Kierkegaard) theorizes the way that 'otherness' is inscribed
on the self; but which analyses this process through an account of the
disciplinary practices and the 'microphysics' of power that render bodies and 'souls' docile. (See Foucault, 1975, for example.) We are also
used to the kind of phenomenological analysis of sexually differentiated
comportment that Iris Marion Young offers in her *Throwing Like a Girl*
(1990), and which was discussed in chapter 3 of this book. However,
without denying the need to analyse the power structures that score
'selves' into socially tractable 'subjects' (in Foucauldian fashion) – and
also without denying the need for an analysis of the 'meaning' of bodily
behaviours (in our culture) in the manner of Young – a Kierkegaardian
account of the way bodies are patterned into specificity by repeated
patterns of movement that set up a *habitus* also has a place. In particular, it helps us register the cultural (and historical) specificity of women
in particular cultures and social groupings, whilst also registering how
'women' might also be granted a specificity that emerges through patterns of activity and bodily training.

We can see this more clearly if we put Kierkegaard's account of the
emergence of singularities together with some research on 'The Construction of Perception' by Leif H. Finkel (1992), who worked in con-
junction with the neurobiologist Gerald Edelman. Although these theories
are framed in terms of a Darwinian 'universalism' about the development of the 'human' species, their data would also seem useful in understanding cultural and historical differences. Their theories help explain
the fact that in most cultures women and men seem to attach differential significances to flesh, to age and to skin, as well as to the body's
reproductive capacities. Thus, Finkel (1992) has argued that the ways
in which we map the body through sensations received into the brain
do not simply involve a 'copy' of the body that is assembled in one
single area of the brain. Instead, our experience of our bodies is coded
at a variety of levels via dynamic processes of interpretation drawn from
various body areas. (See also Edelman, 1992.) Like Kierkegaard, the
neurobiologists chart the emergence of patterns of being from modes
of becoming – and in ways that allow a kind of internal 'resonance' a
formative role in shaping the actual from a multiplicity of possibilities.

Although other neurobiologists have compared the self to a photo-
graphic 'negative' in which everything is pre-given, and which is await-
ing 'development', Finkel and Edelman's analyses complicate such a
hypotheses. They argue that when the body is mapped on the cortex,
it is traced in ways that have depth as well as surface, and this depth

is a kind of echo produced through repeated patternings that are set up by memory. Skin has a privileged role in the mapping of the body. However, the way that skin is mapped depends not only on what areas of the body are stimulated, but also on past experience of skin. If an area of skin is not stimulated it becomes lost to the map, just as if an area of skin is frequently stimulated it can also be added to the map. These brain and body 'maps' change radically over time, so that the difference in one animal over a period of months can be as extreme as the difference between two animals. Mapping proceeds dynamically, in that what is perceived is dependent on relationality – not on properties in objects. The 'brain-maps' can be thought of as ways of ordering an underlying fluidity 'and diversity of sensations.

If we try to think sexual difference on such a model, we find ways of thinking 'male' and 'female' that fit broadly with the Kierkegaardian account of actuality emerging from multiple potentialities. 'Male' and 'female' involve (norms of) bodily differentiation, with different skin-organizations and sensory organs providing potential for building up sexually differential mappings. Even where the 'male' and 'female' bodies do not fit the sexual norm, differential ways of treating males and females would establish different patternings of skin (and also of muscle) stimulation which would, in their turn, be dynamically mapped into the brain in terms of past experiences of bodily sensations and also in terms of cultural expectations, norms and behaviours. 'Male' and 'female' can be viewed as different patterns of potentiality. However, differences between women are to be anticipated, and even the individual woman will undergo profound transformations during the course of her life.

Such a model does, then, allow us to theorize the identification and reidentification of an embodied self, whilst also recognizing an underlying fluidity to that self – a fluidity shaped by past experience and by language, society, culture, history. The process of bodily mapping is dynamic, dependent on repetition and multi-layered echoes. This means that we can think 'difference' in sameness. We can also think difference as coded bodily (in terms of difference in bodily morphology), without homogenizing 'woman'. Furthermore, since interpretation is also involved in these dynamic processes of mapping the body, we can also allow a linguistic component in the mappings that develop – without, however, reducing the body to a linguistic construct. Instead, what sets up the specificity of an individual – or of an individualized self – on such a model is repetition, memory, echo and time. Feedback-loops set up patterns of repetition that dynamically establish links between different layers of the cortex and also different areas of the bodily map.

Thus, the self emerges as involving a relational dynamism between past, present and future – not just surface or without depth in a Baudrillardian way. Furthermore, different experiences and different histories would produce different selves, with different potentialities and different futures.

The fifth feature of the female subject-position that I mentioned in my attempt to think identity in ways that take the female subject as norm was linked to the experiential. This again relates to 'gaps' in 'common sense' models for theorizing the relationship between 'self' and 'not-self'. I indicated that the historical link between the female and the fleshy brings with it discordant potentialities and a mode of singularity that is 'monstrous' in terms of those modes of 'common sense' that regard the self as a substance that persists unaltered through change. Even if we no longer believe with Kant that it is 'common sense' to treat persons as autonomous, free and rational, we still all-too-frequently position all relationality as extrinsic to the self. Indeed, when we treat individuals as ideally independent and equal, we continue to take the (idealized) male subject as norm. Here again Kierkegaard's extended analysis of the concept of 'woman' is relevant. Developing an ontology that is appropriate both for 'woman' and for the sexually abused child, he uses a variety of different perspectives and voices in ways that present the monstrous, the inconsistent and the anomalous not simply as negatives, but in a productive manner. For Kierkegaard 'otherness' is not simply a negativity that inhabits 'sameness', in good Derridean and Hegelian fashion. Nor are we dealing here with the 'Other of the Same' (to adopt Irigaray's terminology). Instead, Kierkegaard offers a way of reconceptualizing 'sameness', so that an other kind of 'otherness' can develop out of the 'monsters within'.

'The Terrible *Fluidity* of Self-revelation'

There are ethical and political consequences that could be drawn from the model of identity that is developed in this book, since it does not fit comfortably with ideals of sisterhood, egality, fraternity or self-determining freedoms. For many feminists my ontology that normalizes the self that is positioned always in webs of dependence will produce unease and even hostility. On my account, an emphasis on unequal relationships of power and vertical (mother/child) relationships is made more central to the feminist project than the (horizontal) relationships of equals privileged in early 1970s feminisms. Indeed, for some feminists it will be shocking when I assert that I see no possibility of personal relationships in which power plays no part. Sisters or friends, lovers or colleagues might find a temporary equilibrium as unequal forces or powers balance out. But neither friendship nor love demands equality, or selves abstracted from the force-fields of power.

In broad terms I accept Foucault's model of power: power is always there, and is always inescapable. Power is not bad in itself; but it is, nevertheless, always dangerous.[1] Delineating a self that is neither totally free, nor totally determined, the Foucauldian self is not formed via its confrontation with 'otherness'. Instead it emerges together with its 'others' from intersecting force-fields of power. Foucault is thus useful for thinking the monstrous 'female' – fleshy – self that gains its specificity as it remains in a continuous dynamic play of power with other bodies and other forces. Foucault shares with Deleuze an ontology that is radically at odds with the dominant traditions of western modernity. He develops an account of identity that is (almost) adequate to deal with the complexities and singularity of monstrous, female, birthing flesh.

Like Deleuze, however, Foucault never considers natality. Despite his account of the emergence of self in the force-fields of power, he ignores issues of care, birth or community. It is thus no accident that Foucault is unable to develop a satisfactory ethics when he turns to address this subject towards the end of his life. (See, for example, Foucault, 1983, 1984a.) A (relational) account of 'care for the self' is placed centre stage, consigning relationships with others to a secondary role. As a consequence, Foucault famously fails to develop a satisfactory distinction between abusive and non-abusive relationships of power. Thus, for example, he deals with issues of paedophilia and the sexual abuse of women in a naïve way, claiming that rape should be decriminalized, and that a relationship with a child who begins to seduce the adult should also be outside the law, 'once the child does not say no' (Macey, 1994, p. 376, and see pp. 374ff, 528–9).

But Foucault's failings do not mean that a relational ontology that also focuses on power cannot be developed into a satisfactory ethics. Nor should we conclude that a more satisfactory account of the self-in-relation would lead us back towards Carol Gilligan's 'feminine' ethics that ties the values of empathy, sympathy or 'care' to 'feminine' psychology.[2] Carol Gilligan is locked in an argument with Lawrence Kohlberg, who is Kantian with regard to 'persons', but seems not to know or be interested in the more ontological aspects of Kantianism.[3] Whereas my own concern in this book has been with the 'transcendental' self that persists over time, Lawrence Kohlberg's concern was with the development of what Kant termed 'personhood'. Thus, Kohlberg argued from apparently 'empirical' data (based on the study of boys) that a self matures morally in so far as it recognizes rational principles, universal justice and abstract 'rights'. In other words, Kohlberg privileges a framework that treats selves as 'equals' and as ideally free, responsible and obedient to rationality and the will.

In chapter 4 I suggested that Kant's concept of 'personhood' is so flawed that it cannot be simply reformed, and that Kant's own remarks on women help reveal the weakness of his moral philosophy. Against Kohlberg, Gilligan stresses relationality and an alternative ethics that neither abstracts from difference nor prioritizes notions of universal justice. Whereas Kohlberg argued that most girls are blocked at an early stage of moral development and do not attain the status of (Kantian) persons, Gilligan privileges 'feminine' subjects who are in Kohlberg's terms 'underdeveloped'. She privileges a moral subject who is locked into relationships of care. However, neither Gilligan nor Kohlberg addresses the ontological question of a self that persists through time (Kant's 'transcendental self'), and there remains in Gilligan (as also in Kohlberg) an implicit individualism that accepts selves and others as unproblematized unities. Thus, on Gilligan's account, once the 'self' is established via a gradual process of differentiation from the mother, it is established as a unitary core that is *either* relational ('feminine') *or* isolationist ('masculine'). These differences emerge through sexually differentiated processes of 'weaning' and child-rearing relating to girls and to boys. In either case, the self is (relatively) transparent to itself.

Gilligan's (ontologically conservative) position seems to have 'common sense' appeal – particularly in North America – since it modifies the notion of an autonomous self, without fundamentally disturbing traditional views of the self in modernity. In fact, it comes quite close to the position argued by Arthur Schopenhauer's own anti-Kantian *On the Basis of Morality* (1839, p. xxviii fn. 27). But Schopenhauer combines an ethics of care with a quite stunning misogyny that denies women any transcendental self or any capacity to distinguish 'self' and 'other'. (See Schopenhauer, 1818/44; and Battersby, 1989, ch. 11.) Hence, the concern in this conclusion to contrast the ontological and ethical enterprises.

Gilligan's position is not mine. The self that I am interested in does not emerge as a 'unity' or a 'thing' in a particular slice of linear time that constitutes 'childhood development'. Instead, the self is continually established as self through responses, repetitions and habitual movements over time. It does not know itself through conscious thought, although it does, in Henry James's words, learn about itself through 'The terrible *fluidity* of self-revelation' (James, 1909, p. 11). Of course, during childhood some of the key dispositional responses are established; but the child's relation to the mother is not determining of later responses in the way that Gilligan's model would seem to suggest. A 'feminine' response to a situation is not to be understood via Gilligan's monocausal account, which uses the childhood relation to the mother to explain the 'under'- or 'other'-development of the adult moral subject. Selves ('masculine' and 'feminine') are more diverse and rich than Gilligan's model would suggest.

Gilligan's own methodology and her interpretation of the data yielded by her empirical studies of young women suggest that her 'feminine' subjects do not in general deceive themselves about their motives as they enter into relationships of 'care' for others. I am, by contrast, interested in a self that is by no means transparent to itself, and that has to live with uncertainty – both with respect to its own motives and even with regard to its own past. The 'female' subject-position that I have explored in these pages is neither wholly self-determining (a Kantian 'person'), nor 'fixed' into machine-like passivity, operated by springs that causally determine it via its developmental history or from outside its own self. Instead, I have turned to Kierkegaard's account of ontological relationality in order to better conceptualize the modes of dependence and power inequalities that such an 'interdependent self' requires.

Thus, in *Fear and Trembling*, Kierkegaard's pseudonymous voices opt not for 'feminine' caring, but for a more terrible mothering that births 'self' from otherness, as well as from itself:

> When the child is to be weaned, the mother blackens her breast. It would be hard to have the breast look inviting when the child must not have it. So the child believes that the breast has changed, but the mother – she is still the same, her gaze is as tender and loving as ever. How fortunate the one who did not need more terrible means to wean the child! (Kierkegaard, 1843b, p. 11)

As we saw in chapter 8, Kierkegaard is concerned with even more 'terrible' scenarios than this. For the early Kierkegaard, the self/other relationship is established not via a simple process of weaning, but gradually (and often also violently) over the course of a life. Moreover, for Kierkegaard an Old Testament (anti-)morality of 'justice' completely overshadows a New Testament ethics of 'sympathy', 'love' or 'care'.

I do not intend to endorse Kierkegaard's terrifying move away from morality and towards a religion that can encompass the internalized 'guilt' of the sexually abused child. Indeed, the implications of my position for an ethics are not explored in this book. However, it should also be clear that I have had these issues always in mind as I developed this account of the self-in-relation. For me the key ethical questions would be to develop an adequate distinction between abusive and non-abusive relationships of power, and also between the use and abuse of habit and tradition. Although in my account, personality emerges out of the blur and resonances set up via patterns of relation with otherness (established over time), this does not entail a duty of empathy with those others. Nor does it mean that a female subject has a psychological disposition to adopt a 'feminine' and 'caring' response either towards her dependants or towards those who would dominate, govern or control her behaviour. Instead, the female subject-position is linked not to specific modes of 'feminine' experience, but to ways of thinking identity as emerging out of patterns of becoming. On such a model, 'self' grows out of 'otherness', and 'sameness' is gradually patterned from 'difference'.

If 'sameness' and 'otherness' intertwine, then not only is this notion of identity useful for thinking the identities of individualized women, it is also useful for thinking diasporic identities or identities of collectives (such as 'Europe', the 'west', 'patriarchy', 'Asia', or 'modernity'). A Kierkegaardian analysis of such categories would emphasize repeated patterns of movement, as well as the resonances of remembered tradition; but would not pretend that we have access to a past that is 'given' as 'true' to all parties, and would also not pretend that there are not 'others' within, as well as without. On a Kierkegaardian model, we do not have to think of identities such as 'Europe' as emerging by the policing of its boundaries – or by the abjection of 'aliens' or 'enemies' or 'others' to an 'outside' – although clearly some kinds of political identities function on such a model. Instead, the identity of a collective such as Europe can be theorized along the same lines as that of the collective that counts as 'the self': in terms of a (temporary) patterning or propensity that emerges from an infinity of singularities under certain conditions.

As such, these 'identities' are fluid and might be transformed – or dispersed or metamorphosed into new structures and propensities – as the configurations are subject to further historical change. To speak of 'women', 'Europe', 'modernity' or 'patriarchy' does not imply a homogeneity of particulars embraced by these concepts. Nor does it imply the impossibility of fundamental transformations of change. Even the past – and 'modernity' – takes on different contours as we look back on it from the perspective of the now. Thus, the analyses offered of 'woman' and the 'self' by the characters in Kierkegaard's aesthetic works fit with 'postmodern' scepticism about metanarratives, about historical 'truths', about Enlightenment 'personhood' and about 'difference'. However, Kierkegaard does not simply deconstruct identities. He reconstructs 'self' in relational terms. As such, he remains within an ontological frame – and one that is particularly useful for those feminist theorists who want to make many of the 'postmodern' moves relating to 'difference', whilst also retaining an ability to talk about 'identities'.

Feminism is necessarily linked with a kind of identity politics; but it has been too quickly concluded that any talk of 'essence' or of 'sameness' necessarily excludes difference, and that such a politics cannot register the multiplicity of perspectives and of 'histories' that attention to race, class, ethnicity, sexual preference, age, disablement and other bodily differences also demand. What has emerged for me in writing this book is that these inferences are altogether too quick and are not well founded. Like the most extreme postmodernist I also register a self that is not a unity, but that functions through personae, and I also accept the need to break apart the metaphysics of substance that has been dominant in the west.

However, I see no need to conclude from this that the self, sexual difference or identity itself are 'only' linguistic (and grammatical) fictions, or that we need to renounce a concept of 'being' that emerges from modes of 'becoming'. Nor do I see 'modernity' – or the history of western metaphysics more generally – as being so irredeemably 'phallogocentric' that we cannot find 'others within'. As in the case of Kierkegaard's own complex account of temporality, 'novelty' comes from using resonance and echo productively, and from recollecting forwards. The way on from postmodernism needs to be looped back through the philosophical past.

Notes

Chapter 2 Essentialisms, Feminisms and Metaphysics

1 Naomi Schor (1989) almost provides an exception. Her reading of Irigaray leads her to explore the history of anti-essentialisms more critically, and brings her close to some of the moves through the history of metaphysics developed later in this book.
2 This 1983 essay is reprinted (with few changes) as chapter 1 of Gatens (1996a). However, it belongs to a substantially different stage of her thought than the later chapters (especially chapters 6–9) that develop Spinozist moves. These are extended in Gatens (1996b) in a Deleuzian direction.
3 See n. 2 above.
4 Some modern Aristotelian scholars argue that this is to misread Aristotle on essence. See, for example, Witt (1989). However, what matters here is the traditional understanding of Aristotle and its take-up in the history of the west, rather than exegetical accuracy.

Chapter 3 Her Body/Her Boundaries

1 A version of this chapter was published in A. E. Benjamin (1993), pp. 30–9. It was originally given at the first European Humanities Research Centre Interdisciplinary Seminars on Boundaries, University of Warwick, December 1992.
2 This book contains over two thousand photos of male and female body-posture and gesture. Its historical and causal analysis is badly flawed. However, the majority of the images are from the 1970s, and clearly show a differential use of space by male and female subjects.
3 First translated as 'Volume–Fluidity' in Irigaray's *Speculum of the Other Woman* (1974). A more accurate translation is included in Irigaray (1991), pp. 53–67.
4 One tradition within chaos theory charts the emergence of order out of chaos via dissipative structures; the other examines the hidden order within apparently disordered systems. It is the first of these two traditions, as exemplified

by Prigogine and Stengers (1984), that is relevant to the argument of this chapter. See Hayles (1990), pp. 9–17.

5 See n. 4 above. Irigaray (1985) also references Prigogine and Stengers (1984).

Chapter 4 Kantian Metaphysics and the Sexed Self

1 References to *The Critique of Pure Reason* will be to Kemp Smith's translation of the 1781 (A) edn, except where the passage is only present in the 2nd (B) 1787 edn, as in this case.

2 References to Kant's works in this form provide the volume and page number to *Kants Gesammelte Schriften* (1902–83), prior to the page number in the cited English edition.

Chapter 5 Feminist Postmodernism and the Metaphysics of Absence

1 Kant played an important role in Foucault's thinking from the start. Thus, Foucault's doctoral thesis involved a translation and introduction to Kant's *Anthropology* (1798). This thesis remained unpublished; but key portions were incorporated in later works, particularly *The Order of Things* (1966), p. 385. See also Macey (1994), pp. 89–90. These passages relate to a Nietzschean 'return of masks' as man's face 'explodes in laughter'.

In Foucault this Nietzschean laughter has its origins in a dialogue with Kant. However, as we will see in chapter 6, for Judith Butler it is Hegel who provides the origins of Nietzsche's explosive mockery in ways that also serve to reduce Nietzschean subversion to epistemological moves.

2 See Eribon (1989), pp. 160–86 for Foucault's later views on *The Order of Things*.

3 *Corr.* marks a correction to Fenves' translation, based on a draft of an unpublished translation by A. J. Phelan (German Department, University of Warwick) for which I am extremely grateful.

4 The more philosophical portions of *Speculum* and other texts by Irigaray are often badly translated. *Corr.* marks my revised translation. For Irigaray's strategic use of 'the other of the Other' see especially Whitford (1991), chapter 5.

Chapter 6 Antigones of Gender

1 For the two mentions by name see Hegel (1807), § 437, p. 261 and § 470, p. 284. The theme of Antigone is also taken up elsewhere in Hegel's philosophical corpus. See Steiner (1984), pp. 19–42.

2 See Lacan (1959–60), pp. 240–87. Although this *Seminar* was not published in French until 1986, Irigaray's position as a Lacanian psychoanalyst would have given her access to Lacan's views in oral or note form.

3 Butler's commentary on this passage in *Gender Trouble* (1990), p. 157 fn. 54 puts the reader on the wrong track by emphasizing debates over the relationship between female pleasure and sexual penetration.

4 Puzzlingly, Luisa Muraro (who translated *Speculum* into Italian, and who therefore should know it well) argues that conjoint themes of female genealogies and 'body to body' relationships with the mother first arise in Irigaray's

oeuvre in 1980. Making a sharp division between the series of oral deliveries that were later turned into collections of essays and the earlier, more systematic, written texts, Muraro denies these themes any place in Irigaray's early written works such as *Speculum*. (See Muraro, 1994, pp. 319–20.)

Since Muraro's 1994 essay is one of the main treatments of Irigaray's handling of the Antigone myth, this is unfortunate – particularly because her comments on Irigaray's use of Antigone in *Speculum* are both superficial and misleading (p. 328), and spoil this otherwise extremely useful piece.

5 Works such as Irigaray (1987), (1989), (1990) grew out of oral presentation or interviews, as noted above.

6 See Muraro (1985) and Campari et al. (1985); also Holub (1994), who makes useful links between *affidamento*, Irigaray's influence and a specifically Italian, liberatory tradition of reading Hegel's *Phenomenology*. Muraro is one of the primary advocates of *affidamento* as a feminist practice. As such, her puzzling comments discussed in n. 4 above are perhaps motivated by the concern to annex Irigaray's comments on female genealogies (and Antigone) for a symbolic revolution that privileges lived relationships and the oral interchange between women above written texts.

7 See chapter 5, n. 1 above.

8 Lacan's use of the sublime is only discussed indirectly: through Butler's extended engagement (1993, pp. 187–222) with Žižek's *The Sublime Object of Ideology* (1989).

Chapter 7 Flesh with Trimmings: Adorno and Difference

1 Dews (1989, p. 11) makes a similar point in reference to Adorno based on this passage, but adopts a more 'poststructuralist' interpretation of Nietzsche's strategy than I consider warranted.

Chapter 8 Kierkegaard, Woman and the Workshop of Possibilities

1 The words are Gilroy's, but he is summarizing and expanding C. L. R. James's (1969) comments.

2 In the English version. The much longer French version is without an index.

3 See especially Derrida's *Spurs* (1978). For Kierkegaard's (very different) use of the metaphors of 'spurs', the 'femininity' of appearances and the philosophical 'knight', see the opening to *The Concept of Irony* (1841) discussed below.

4 References to the *Journals* are to the entry number, and not the page number.

5 See n. 4 above.

6 Kierkegaard's use of the German term prefigures the extensive discussion of the *'unheimlich'* in Freud, Heidegger, Lacan, and in deconstructionist and psychoanalytic feminist criticism. *'Unheimlich'* means that which is no longer secret (*'heimlich'*), and therefore that which is revealed. However, it also (more literally) means 'unhomelike', from *'Heim'* for home, and that which is psychically disturbing. For Freud the uncanny was, above all, associated with the female body that has 'lost' its penis: that is 'castrated' and monstrous, and that needs to be covered over or veiled. Kierkegaard also privileges an

unfolding that appears from and disappears into the dark; but, as we will see, it seems to be his father, not his mother, who keeps appearing and then disappearing in his texts in an 'uncanny' fashion.

7 For Lacan's references to Kierkegaard see, for example, Lacan (1972–3, pp. 147–8). Lacan (1964) includes numerous references to Plato and to Plato's use of Aristophanes' myth in *Symposium*.

8 The link between Antigone and the Solomon and David story is established in Kierkegaard (1829–48, 5669).

9 To understand what Kierkegaard might have meant by the reference to Leibniz, see Deleuze (1988). Although Deleuze does not reference Kierkegaard in this study, there are clear similarities between Kierkegaard and Deleuze's responses to Leibniz. The comparison between Kierkegaard and Deleuze will be pursued further in the next chapter.

10 Draft of *Johannes Climacus* from 1842–3 in *Journals and Papers*, quoted in Supplement to *Repetition* (1843c, p. 275).

11 Ibid. p. 274.

Chapter 9 Scoring the Subject of Feminist Theory: Kierkegaard and Deleuze

1 Sacks (1985), p. 37. The comments are in 'The Lost Mariner' (pp. 22–41), which is also an account of a case study which features musical continuities. The comments on philosophy need to be understood in terms of Sacks's narrative in *A Leg to Stand On* (1984) of his 'discovery' of Kant whilst himself disabled with a broken leg (pp. 164–8). This 'discovery' is linked by Sacks to Bergson on 'inner time' and music. In the 1991 Appendix to this work, however, Sack will 'repent, and retract' the turn to Kantian 'mysticism', substituting the neurobiological theories of Gerald Edelman for Bergsonian insights into the temporalities of music (p. 178). I hope my own (brief) comments on Edelman in this chapter and the next indicate that these two frameworks are not as incompatible as Sacks himself seems to suppose.

2 See Deleuze and Guattari (1980), p. 281; quoting Kierkegaard (1843b), p. 38 (in a slightly different translation).

3 Grosz seems to want to make this point; but phrases it misleadingly, by claiming that rhizomatics 'is based on multiplicity' (1993, p. 199), whereas she has just quoted Deleuze and Guattari (1980, p. 21) as claiming that 'The rhizome is reducible neither to the One nor the multiple.'

Chapter 10 Coda

1 See Foucault (1983), and all texts by Foucault after *Discipline and Punish* (1975).

2 The discussion relates to Gilligan (1982) and subsequent writings. See Hekman (1995) for an interesting analysis of Gilligan's developing positions on the self, as well as some comparison with Foucault. Hekman does, however, make Gilligan's position more philosophically sophisticated than is warranted by Gilligan's own empirical methodology.

3 Kohlberg is at some pains to distance himself from Kant, preferring to compare himself (quite implausibly) to Plato or to John Dewey. (See Kohlberg, 1981, chs 2–4.)

Bibliography

The dates enclosed in parentheses and also used as in-text references are to the date of first publication in the original language, wherever possible. In the case of influential lectures, notebook or other posthumously published material I have preferred the approximate date of delivery or composition. The date of the edition or translation consulted is given at the end of the reference.

Adorno, Theodor W. (1931). 'Die Aktualität der Philosophie'. In *Gesammelte Schriften*, ed. Rolf Tiedemann. Suhrkamp Verlag, 1973, vol. 1, 325–44.
—— (1933/62). *Kierkegaard: Construction of the Aesthetic*, trans. Robert Hullot-Kentor. University of Minnesota Press, 1989.
—— (1955). *Prisms*, trans. Samuel Weber and Shierry Weber. Neville Spearman, 1967.
—— (1956). *Against Epistemology*, trans. Willis Domingo. Blackwell, 1982.
—— (1966). *Negative Dialectics*, trans. E. B. Ashton. Routledge and Kegan Paul, 1973.
—— (1970). *Aesthetic Theory*, eds Gretel Adorno and Rolf Tiedemann, trans. C. Lenhardt. Routledge and Kegan Paul, 1984.
Adorno, Theodor W. and Max Horkheimer (1944). *Dialectic of Enlightenment*, trans. John Cumming. Verso, 2nd edn, 1992.
Antliff, Mark (1993). *Inventing Bergson*. Princeton University Press.
Bartky, Sandra Lee (1990). *Femininity and Domination: Studies in the Phenomenology of Oppression*. Routledge.
Battersby, Christine (1989). *Gender and Genius: Towards a Feminist Aesthetics*. Women's Press; Indiana University Press, 1990.
—— (1994). 'Unblocking the Oedipal: Karoline von Günderode and the Female Sublime'. In Sally Ledger, Josephine McDonagh and Jane Spencer (eds), *Political Gender*. Harvester Wheatsheaf, 129–43.
—— (1995). 'Stages on Kant's Way: Aesthetics, Morality and the Gendered Sublime'. In Peggy Z. Brand and Carolyn Korsmeyer (eds), *Feminism and Tradition in Aesthetics*. Pennsylvania University Press, 88–114.
—— (1996). 'Her Blood and His Mirror: Mary Coleridge, Luce Irigaray and the Female Self'. In Richard Eldridge (ed.), *Beyond Representation: Philosophy and Poetic Imagination*. Cambridge University Press, 249–72.

Baudrillard, Jean (1979). *Seduction,* trans. Brian Singer. Macmillan, 1990.
Beauvoir, Simone de (1947). *The Ethics of Ambiguity,* trans. Bernard Frechtman. Citadel, 1948.
—— (1949). *The Second Sex,* trans. H. M. Parshley. Penguin, 1972.
Bell, Rudolph M. (1985). *Holy Anorexia.* University of Chicago Press.
Benjamin, A. E. (ed.) (1993). *The Body: Journal of Philosophy and the Visual Arts,* no. 4. Academy Editions; Ernst and Sohn.
Bergson, Henri (1896). *Matter and Memory,* trans. Nancy Margaret Paul and W. Scott Palmer. Based on French 1908 edn. Zone Books, 1994.
—— (1907). *Creative Evolution,* trans. A. Mitchell. Holt, *c.*1911.
Bertens, Hans (1995). *The Idea of the Postmodern: A History.* Routledge.
Bordo, Susan (1995). *Unbearable Weight: Feminism, Western Culture, and the Body.* University of California Press.
Bradley, F. H. (1893). *Appearance and Reality.* Allen and Unwin, 1897.
Braidotti, Rosi (1994). *Nomadic Subjects: Embodiment and Sexual Difference in Contemporary Feminist Theory.* Columbia University Press.
Brennan, Teresa (1993). *History after Lacan.* Routledge.
Bruch, Hilde (1978). *The Golden Cage.* Open Books.
Buck-Morss, Susan (1977). *The Origin of Negative Dialectics.* Harvester Press.
Butler, Judith (1987). *Subjects of Desire: Hegelian Reflections in Twentieth-Century France.* Columbia University Press.
—— (1990). *Gender Trouble: Feminism and the Subversion of Identity.* Routledge.
—— (1993). *Bodies that Matter: On the Discursive Limits of 'Sex'.* Routledge.
—— (1994). 'Gender as Performance'. Interview with Peter Osborne and Lynne Segal. *Radical Philosophy* 67, 32–9.
Campari, M. Grazia, Rosaria Canzano, Lia Cigarini, Sciana Loaldi, Laura Roseo and Claudia Shanmah (1985). 'Entrustment Enters the Palace'. In Paola Bono and Sandra Kemp (eds), *Italian Feminist Thought: A Reader.* Blackwell, 1991, 126–9.
Chanter, Tina (1993). 'Kristeva's Politics of Change: Tracking Essentialism with the Help of a Sex/Gender Map'. In Kelly Oliver (ed.), *Ethics, Politics, and Difference in Julia Kristeva's Writings.* Routledge, 179–95.
Copi, Irving M. (1954). 'Essence and Accident'. In Michael J. Loux (ed.), *Universals and Particulars.* University of Notre Dame Press, 1976, 331–46.
Cortazar, Julio (1963). *Hopscotch,* trans. Gregory Rabassa. Collins and Harvill Press, 1967.
de Lauretis, Teresa (1989). 'The Essence of the Triangle or, Taking the Risk of Essentialism Seriously'. In Naomi Schor and Elizabeth Weed (eds), *The Essential Difference.* Indiana University Press, 1994, 1–39.
Deleuze, Gilles (1988). *The Fold: Leibniz and the Baroque,* trans. Tom Conley. Athlone Press, 1993.
—— (1993). 'He Stuttered', trans. Constantin V. Boundas. In Constantin V. Boundas and Dorothea Olkowski (eds), *Gilles Deleuze and the Theater of Philosophy.* Routledge, 1994, 23–9.
Deleuze, Gilles and Félix Guattari (1972). *Anti-Oedipus: Capitalism and Schizophrenia, Volume 1,* trans. Robert Hurley, Mark Seem and Helen R. Lane. Athlone Press, 1984.
—— (1980). *A Thousand Plateaus: Capitalism and Schizophrenia, Volume 2,* trans. Brian Massumi. Athlone Press, 1992.
—— (1991). *What is Philosophy?,* trans. Graham Burchell and Hugh Tomlinson. Verso, 1994.

Derrida, Jacques (1966). 'Structure, Sign, and Play in the Discourse of the Human Sciences'. In *Writing and Difference*, trans. Alan Bass. Routledge, 1978, 278–93.

—— (1967). *Of Grammatology*, trans. Gayatri Chakravorty Spivak. Johns Hopkins University Press, pb edn, 1977.

—— (1968) '*Différance*'. In *A Derrida Reader: Between the Blinds*, ed. Peggy Kamuf. Harvester Wheatsheaf, 1991, 61–79.

—— (1973). 'The Question of Style'. In David B. Allison (ed.), *The New Nietzsche* (1977). MIT Press, 1985, 176–89.

—— (1978). *Spurs/Éperons: Nietzsche's Styles*, trans. Barbara Harlow. University of Chicago Press, 1979.

—— (1981/3). 'On a Newly Arisen Apocalyptic Tone in Philosophy'. In Peter Fenves (ed.), *Raising the Tone of Philosophy: Late Essays by Immanuel Kant, Transformative Critique by Jacques Derrida*. Johns Hopkins University Press, 1993, 117–71.

—— (1991). *A Derrida Reader: Between the Blinds*, ed. Peggy Kamuf. Harvester Wheatsheaf.

Dews, Peter (1987). *Logics of Disintegration*. Verso, 1988.

—— (1989). 'Adorno, Poststructuralism and the Critique of Identity'. In A. E. Benjamin (ed.), *The Problems of Modernity: Adorno and Benjamin*. Routledge, 1–22.

Dupré, John (1986). 'Sex, Gender, and Essence', *Midwest Studies in Philosophy* 11, *Studies in Essentialism* special issue, 441–57.

Edelman, Gerald M. (1992). *Bright Air, Brilliant Fire: On the Matter of the Mind*. Penguin, 1994.

Eribon, Didier (1989). *Michel Foucault*, trans. Betsy Wing. Faber and Faber, pb edn, 1993.

Erikson, Erik H. (1964). 'Inner and Outer Space: Reflections on Womanhood'. In Patrick C. Lee and R. S. Stewart (eds), *Sex Differences*. Urizen, 1976, 104–32.

Finkel, Leif H. (1992). 'The Construction of Perception'. In Jonathan Crary and Sanford Kwinter (eds), *Incorporations: Zone 6*. Zone, 393–405.

Flax, Jane (1990). *Thinking Fragments: Psychoanalysis, Feminism, and Postmodernism in the Contemporary West*. University of California Press.

—— (1993). *Disputed Subjects: Essays on Psychoanalysis, Politics and Philosophy*. Routledge.

Foucault, Michel (1966). *The Order of Things*. Tavistock, pb edn, 1974.

—— (1975). *Discipline and Punish*, trans. Alan Sheridan. Penguin, 1979.

—— (1980). English Introduction to *Herculine Barbin: Being the Recently Discovered Memoirs of a Nineteenth-Century French Hermaphrodite*, trans. Richard McDougall. Harvester Press, vii–xvii.

—— (1983). 'On the Genealogy of Ethics: An Overview of Work in Progress'. In *The Foucault Reader*, ed. Paul Rabinow. Penguin, 1986, 340–72.

—— (1984a). *The Care of the Self*, trans. Robert Hurley. *The History of Sexuality, Volume 3*. Penguin, 1990.

—— (1984b). 'What is Enlightenment?'. In *The Foucault Reader*, ed. Paul Rabinow. Penguin, 1986, 32–50.

Fraser, Sylvia (1987). *My Father's House: A Memoir of Incest and of Healing*. Virago, 1989.

Fuss, Diana (1989a). *Essentially Speaking: Feminism, Nature and Difference*. Routledge.

—— (1989b). 'Reading Like a Feminist'. In Naomi Schor and Elizabeth Weed (eds), *The Essential Difference*. Indiana University Press, 1994, 98–115.

Gatens, Moira (1991). *Feminism and Philosophy*. Polity Press.

—— (1996a). *Imaginary Bodies: Ethics, Power and Corporeality*. Routledge.

—— (1996b). 'Through a Spinozist Lens: Ethology, Difference, Power'. In Paul Patton (ed.), *Deleuze: A Critical Reader*. Blackwell, 162–87.

Gilligan, Carol (1982). *In a Different Voice: Psychological Theory and Women's Development*. Harvard University Press.

Gilroy, Paul (1993). *The Black Atlantic: Modernity and Double Consciousness*. Verso.

Grosz, Elizabeth (1993). 'A Thousand Tiny Sexes: Feminism and Rhizomatics'. In Constantin V. Boundas and Dorothea Olkowski (eds), *Gilles Deleuze and the Theater of Philosophy*. Routledge, 1994, 187–210.

—— (1994). *Volatile Bodies: Toward a Corporeal Feminism*. Indiana University Press.

Haar, Michel (1971). 'Nietzsche and Metaphysical Language'. In David B. Allison (ed.), *The New Nietzsche* (1977). MIT Press, 1985, 5–36.

Haraway, Donna (1984). 'A Cyborg Manifesto'. In *Simians, Cyborgs and Women: The Reinvention of Nature*. Free Association Books, 1991, 149–83.

—— (1988). 'The Biopolitics of Postmodern Bodies'. In *Simians, Cyborgs and Women: The Reinvention of Nature*. Free Association Books, 1991, 203–30.

Harvey, David (1990). *The Condition of Postmodernity*. Blackwell.

Hastrup, Kirsten (1993). 'The Semantics of Biology: Virginity'. In Shirley Ardener (ed.), *Defining Females*. Berg, 2nd edn, 34–50.

Hayles, N. Katherine (1990). *Chaos Bound: Orderly Disorder in Contemporary Literature and Science*. Cornell University Press.

Hegel, G. W. F. (1807). *Phenomenology of Spirit*, trans. A. V. Miller. Oxford University Press, 1977.

Heidegger, Martin (1925). *History of the Concept of Time*, trans. Theodore Kisiel. Indiana University Press, 1992.

—— (1927). *Being and Time*, trans. John Macquarrie and Edward Robinson. Blackwell, 1993.

Hekman, Susan J. (1990). *Gender and Knowledge: Elements of a Postmodern Feminism*. Polity Press.

—— (1995). *Moral Voices, Moral Selves: Carol Gilligan and Moral Theory*. Polity Press.

Hobbes, Thomas. (1655). *Elements of Philosophy (De Corpore)*. In *The English Works of Thomas Hobbes*, ed. W. Molesworth. John Bohn, vol. 1, 1839.

Hoffman, Joshua and Gary S. Rosenkrantz (1994). *Substance Among Other Categories*. Cambridge University Press.

Holub, Renate (1994). 'Between the United States and Italy'. In Giovanna M. Jeffries (ed.), *Feminine Feminists*. University of Minnesota Press, 1994, 233–60.

Husserl, Edmund (1893–1917). *On the Phenomenology of the Consciousness of Internal Time*, trans. John Barnett Brough. Kluwer Academic Publishers, 1991.

—— (1900–1). *Logical Investigations*, trans. J. N. Findlay. Routledge and Kegan Paul, 2 vols, 1970.

Irigaray, Luce (1974). *Speculum of the Other Woman*, trans. Gillian C. Gill. Cornell University Press, 1985.

—— (1977). *This Sex which is Not One*, trans. Catherine Porter and Carolyn Burke. Cornell University Press, 1985.

—— (1985). 'Is the Subject of Science Sexed?' In Nancy Tuana (ed.), *Feminism and Science*. Indiana University Press, 1989, 58–68.

—— (1987). *Sexes and Genealogies*, trans. Gillian C. Gill. Columbia University Press, 1993.

—— (1989). *Thinking the Difference for a Peaceful Revolution*, trans. Karin Montin. Athlone Press, 1994.

—— (1990). *Je, Tu, Nous*, trans. Alison Martin. Routledge, 1993.

—— (1991). *The Irigaray Reader*, ed. Margaret Whitford. Blackwell.

—— (1994). 'A Natal Lacuna', trans. Margaret Whitford. *Women's Art Magazine* 58, 11–13.

James, C. L. R. (1969). 'Black Studies and the Contemporary Student'. In Anna Grimshaw (ed.), *The C. L. R. James Reader*. Blackwell, 1992, 390–404.

James, Henry (1909). Preface to *The Ambassadors*, ed. S. P. Rosenbaum. W. W. Norton, 1964.

Johnson, Mark (1987). *The Body in the Mind*. University of Chicago Press.

Kant, Immanuel (1764). *Observations on the Feeling of the Beautiful and Sublime*, trans. John T. Goldthwait. University of California Press, 1960.

—— (1781/7). *Critique of Pure Reason*, trans. Norman Kemp Smith. Macmillan, 1st (A) 1781 edn and 2nd (B) 1787 edn, 1963.

—— (1784). 'What is Enlightenment?', trans. Lewis White Beck. In *Kant on History*, ed. Lewis White Beck. Bobbs-Merrill, 1963, 3–10.

—— (1785a). 'Bestimmung des Begriffs einer Menschenrace'. In *Kants Gesammelte Schriften*, ed. Preussische Akademie der Wissenschaften zu Berlin. Walter Gruyter, 1902–83, vol. 8, 89–106.

—— (1785b). 'Recensionen von J. G. Herder's Ideen zur Philosophie der Geschichte der Menschheit' Pts I and II. In *Kants Gesammelte Schriften*, ed. Preussische Akademie der Wissenschaften zu Berlin. Walter Gruyter, 1902– 83, vol. 8, 43–66.

—— (1786). *Metaphysical Foundations of Natural Science*, trans. James Ellington. Bobbs-Merrill, 1970.

—— (c.1788–1801). *Opus Postumum*, ed. Eckart Förster, trans. Eckart Förster and Michael Rosen. Cambridge University Press, 1993.

—— (1790). *Critique of Judgment*, trans. Werner S. Pluhar. Hackett, 1987.

—— (1793). *Religion Within the Limits Reason Alone*, trans. Theodore M. Greene and Hoyt H. Hudson. Harper Torchbooks, 1960.

—— (1796). 'On a Newly Arisen Superior Tone in Philosophy'. In Peter Fenves (ed.), *Raising the Tone of Philosophy: Late Essays by Immanuel Kant, Transformative Critique by Jacques Derrida*. Johns Hopkins University Press, 1993, 51–81.

—— (1797). *The Metaphysics of Morals*, ed. and trans. Mary Gregor. Cambridge University Press, 1996.

—— (1798). *Anthropology from a Pragmatic Point of View*, trans. Mary J. Gregor. Martinus Nijhoff, 1974.

—— (1902–83). *Kants Gesammelte Schriften*, ed. Preussische Akademie der Wissenschaften zu Berlin. Walter Gruyter, 29 vols.

Kerouac, Jack (1957). *On the Road*. André Deutsch, 1959.

Kierkegaard, Søren (1829–48). *Journals and Papers, vol. 5, Autobiographical, Part 1*, ed. and trans. Howard V. Hong and Edna H. Hong. Indiana University Press, 1978.

—— (1841). *The Concept of Irony*, ed. and trans. Howard V. Hong and Edna H. Hong. *Kierkegaard's Writings, Volume 2*. Princeton University Press, 1989.

—— (1843a). *Either/Or*, Part 1 (*Either*), ed. and trans. Howard V. Hong and Edna H. Hong. *Kierkegaard's Writings, Volume 3*. Princeton University Press, 1987.

—— (1843b). *Fear and Trembling*, ed. and trans. Howard V. Hong and Edna H. Hong. *Kierkegaard's Writings, Volume 6*. Princeton University Press, 1983.

—— (1843c) *Repetition*, ed. and trans. Howard V. Hong and Edna H. Hong. Bound with *Fear and Trembling* in *Kierkegaard's Writings, Volume 6*.

—— (1845). *Stages on Life's Way*, ed. and trans. Howard V. Hong and Edna H. Hong. *Kierkegaard's Writings, Volume 11*. Princeton University Press, 1988.

—— (1848–55). *Journals and Papers, vol. 6, Autobiographical, Part 2*, ed. and trans. Howard V. Hong and Edna H. Hong. Indiana University Press, 1978.

Kohlberg, Lawrence (1981). *The Philosophy of Moral Development*. Harper and Row.

Krauss, Rosalind E. (1993). *The Optical Unconscious*. October Books; MIT Press.

Kripke, Saul (1970). *Naming and Necessity*. Blackwell, with revisions, 1980.

Kristeva, Julia (1980a). *Desire in Language*, ed. Leon S. Roudiez. Blackwell, 1981.

—— (1980b). *Powers of Horror: An Essay on Abjection*, trans. Leon S. Roudiez. Columbia University Press, 1982.

Kwinter, Sanford (1992) ' "*Quelli che Partono*" as a General Theory of Models'. In A. E. Benjamin (ed.), *Architecture, Space, Painting: Journal of Philosophy and the Visual Arts*, no. 3. Academy Editions; St Martin's Press, 1992, 36–44.

Lacan, Jacques (1949 revised/1936). 'The Mirror Stage as Formative of the Function of the I as revealed in Psychoanalytic Experience'. In *Écrits*, trans. Alan Sheridan. Tavistock, pb edn, 1985, 1–7.

—— (1959–60). *The Ethics of Psychoanalysis*, ed. Jacques-Alain Miller, trans. Dennis Porter. *The Seminar of Jacques Lacan, Book 7*, 1st pub. in French 1986. Routledge, 1992.

—— (1964). *The Four Fundamental Concepts of Psycho-analysis*, ed. Jacques-Alain Miller, trans. Alan Sheridan. *The Seminar of Jacques Lacan, Book 11*, 1st pub. in French 1973. Penguin, 1986.

—— (1972–3). Selections from *The Seminar of Jacques Lacan, Book 20*, 1st pub. in French 1975. In Juliet Mitchell and Jacqueline Rose (eds), *Feminine Sexuality: Jacques Lacan and the École Freudienne*, trans. Jacqueline Rose. Macmillan, 1982, 137–61.

Lakoff, George (1987). *Women, Fire, and Dangerous Things*. University of Chicago Press.

Lakoff, George and Mark Johnson (1980). *Metaphors We Live By*. University of Chicago Press.

Laqueur, Thomas (1990). *Making Sex: Body and Gender from the Greeks to Freud*. Harvard University Press, pb edn, 1992.

Lennon, Kathleen and Margaret Whitford (eds) (1994). *Knowing the Difference: Feminist Perspectives on Epistemology*. Routledge.

Lingis, Alphonso (1994). 'The Society of Dismembered Body Parts'. In Constantin V. Boundas and Dorothea Olkowski (eds), *Gilles Deleuze and the Theater of Philosophy*. Routledge, 289–303.

Locke, John (1690). *An Essay concerning Human Understanding*, ed. Peter H. Nidditch. Clarendon Press, 1975.

Lombroso, Cesare (1863). *The Man of Genius*, trans. from revised edn. Walter Scott Publishing Co, 1910; Garland, 1984.

Lyotard, Jean-François (1982). 'Answering the Question: What is Postmodernism?' Appendix to *The Postmodern Condition*, trans. Geoff Bennington and Brian Massumi. Manchester University Press, 1986, 71–82.

McClary, Susan (1991). *Feminine Endings: Music, Gender, and Sexuality*. University of Minnesota Press.

Macey, David (1994). *The Lives of Michel Foucault*. Vintage.

Maconie, Robin (1990). *The Concept of Music*. Oxford University Press, pb edn, 1993.

Martin, Biddy (1991). *Woman and Modernity: The (Life)Styles of Lou Andreas-Salomé*. Cornell University Press.

Martin, Emily (1987). *The Woman in the Body*. Open University Press, 1989.

—— (1994). *Flexible Bodies*. Beacon Press.

Mauss, Marcel (1934). 'Techniques of the Body'. In Jonathan Crary and Sanford Kwinter (eds), *Incorporations: Zone 6*. Zone, 1992, 455–77.

Muraro, Luisa (1985). 'Bonding and Freedom'. In Paola Bono and Sandra Kemp (eds), *Italian Feminist Thought: A Reader*. Blackwell, 1991, 123–6.

—— (1994). 'Female Genealogies'. In Carolyn Burke, Naomi Schor and Margaret Whitford (eds), *Engaging With Irigaray*. Columbia University Press, 1994, 317–33.

Naragon, Steve (1990). 'Kant on Descartes and the Brutes', *Kant Studien* 81, 1–23.

Neihardt, John G. (Flaming Rainbow) (1932). *Black Elk Speaks: Being the Life Story of a Holy Man of the Oglala Sioux*. Abacus, 1974.

Nietzsche, Friedrich (1873). 'On the Truth and Lies in a Nonmoral Sense'. In *Philosophy and Truth: Selections from Nietzsche's Notebooks of the Early 1870's*, ed. and trans. Daniel Breazeale. Humanities Press International, 1994, 77–97.

—— (1874). *The Use and Abuse of History*, trans. Adrian Collins. Bobbs-Merrill, 1957.

—— (1883/5). *Thus Spoke Zarathustra*. In *The Portable Nietzsche*, ed. Walter Kaufmann. Viking, 1968.

—— (1886). *Beyond Good and Evil*, trans. Walter Kaufmann. Vintage, 1966.

Nye, Andrea (1988). *Feminist Theory and the Philosophies of Man*. Routledge, 1989.

Ortiz, Alfonso (1969). *The Tewa World: Space, Time, Being and Becoming in a Pueblo Society*. University of Chicago Press, 1972.

Osborne, Peter (1989). 'Adorno and the Metaphysics of Modernism'. In A. E. Benjamin (ed.), *The Problems of Modernity: Adorno and Benjamin*. Routledge, 23–48.

Plato (*c*.385 BC). *The Symposium*, trans. Walter Hamilton. Penguin, 1975.

—— (*c*.375 BC). *The Republic*, trans. Desmond Lee. Penguin, 1987.

—— (*c*.370 BC). *Phaedrus*, trans. Reginald Hackforth. Cambridge University Press, 1972.

—— (*c*.350 BC). *Timaeus*, trans. Desmond Lee. Penguin, 1977.

Plotinus (254–70). *The Enneads*, trans. Stephen MacKenna. Penguin, abridged edn, 1991.

Prigogine, Ilya and Isabelle Stengers (1984). *Order out of Chaos*. Flamingo, 1985.

Ryle, Gilbert (1965). 'Dialectic in the Academy'. In Renford Bambrough (ed.), *New Essays on Plato and Aristotle*. Routledge and Kegan Paul, 1965, 39–68.

Sacks, Oliver (1984). *A Leg to Stand On*. Picador, revised edn, 1991.
—— (1985). *The Man Who Mistook His Wife for a Hat*. Duckworth, 1986.
—— (1995). *An Anthropologist on Mars*. Picador.
Scholes, Robert (1994). '*Éperon* Strings'. In Naomi Schor and Elizabeth Weed (eds), *The Essential Difference*. Indiana University Press, 116–29.
Schopenhauer, Arthur (1818, with supplements and revisions 1844). *The World as Will and Idea*, trans. R. B. Haldane and J. Kemp. Routledge and Kegan Paul, 3 vols, 1883.
—— (1839). *On the Basis of Morality*, trans. E. F. J. Payne, introd. David E. Cartwright. Berghahn Books, 1995.
Schor, Naomi (1989). 'This Essentialism Which Is Not One'. In Naomi Schor and Elizabeth Weed (eds), *The Essential Difference*. Indiana University Press, 1994, 40–62.
Sloterdijk, Peter (1983). *Critique of Cynical Reason*, trans. Michael Eldred, foreword Andreas Huyssen. Verso, 1988.
Smith, Paul (1988). '*Vas*'. In Robyn R. Warhol and D. P. Herndl (eds), *Feminisms*. Rutgers University Press, 1991, 1011–29.
Spivak, Gayatri Chakravorty (1984). 'Criticism, Feminism and the Institution'. Interview with Elizabeth Grosz. In Sarah Harasym (ed.), *The Post-colonial Critic*. Routledge, 1990, 1–16.
—— (1989). 'In a Word'. Interview with Ellen Rooney. In Gayatri Chakravorty Spivak, *Outside in the Teaching Machine*. Routledge, 1993, 1–23.
Steiner, George (1984). *Antigones: The Antigone Myth in Western Literature, Art and Thought*. Oxford University Press, pb edn, 1989.
Strawson, P. F. (1959). *Individuals: An Essay in Descriptive Metaphysics*. Methuen, pb edn, 1965.
Thomä, Helmut (1977). 'On the Psychotherapy of Patients with Anorexia Nervosa', *Bulletin of the Menninger Clinic* 41, 437–52.
Turkle, Sherry (1995). *Life on the Screen: Identity in the Age of the Internet*. Weidenfeld and Nicolson, 1996.
Wex, Marianne (1979). *Let's Take Back Our Space*, trans. Johanna Albert and Susan Schultz. Frauenliteraturverlag Hermine Fees.
Whitford, Margaret (1991). *Luce Irigaray: Philosophy in the Feminine*. Routledge.
Witt, Charlotte (1989). *Substance and Essence in Aristotle*. Cornell University Press, 1989.
Wittgenstein, Ludwig (1953). *Philosophical Investigations*, trans. G. E. M. Anscombe. Blackwell, 3rd English edn, 1972.
Wood, David (1989). *The Deconstruction of Time*. Humanities Press International, pb edn, 1991.
Young, Iris Marion (1990). *Throwing Like a Girl*. Indiana University Press.
Zammito, John H. (1992). *The Genesis of Kant's Critique of Judgment*. University of Chicago Press.
Žižek, Slavoj (1989). *The Sublime Object of Ideology*. Verso.

Index